Structural Evolution of Indian Economy

Early Phase

Structural Evolution of Indian Economy

Early Phase

Arun Majumder

MANOHAR
1992

ISBN 81-85425-71-X

Published by
Ajay Kumar Jain
Manohar Book Service
2/6 Ansari Road
Darya Ganj
New Delhi - 110 002

Laser Composing by
Ankit Computers Inc.
81 Darya Ganj
New Delhi - 110 002

Printed at
Rajkamal Electric Press
G. T. Road
Delhi

In the loving memory of

my youngest brother Ashu

Preface

The present work starts with that stage of development in the surplus-producing social economy of India which had brought into being, as its consequence, a growth of secondary state formations - formations that had universally paved the way for a *functional* separation between the state and civil society. It ends with that stage of development in Indian economy that inexorably engendered the growth of autonomous mercantile capital as a consequence of, as well as a rival to the surplus-appropriating capacity of eighteenth century state powers in India and gave impetus to easy usurpation of political power by alien mercantile groups.

The projected next section starts with the analysis of socio-economic distortions executed by the colonial land revenue settlements in nineteenth century India and ends with investigation into the dynamics of colonial capitalism in India that was set in motion by the earlier half of the twentieth century.

There is a conspicuous absence of a conceptual-analytical work on India's economic history that tries to capture - in its own terms - each stage of the structural evolution of the Indian economy during its pre-modern and modern phases. Such evolution needs to be explained as the outcome of a series of interactions between the changing processes of surplus appropriation and widely-acclaimed historicity of stagnation in the Indian process of surplus generation. Further, while there have been several scholarly works on the various stages of developments in Indian society and economy based on primary sources, by and large these works are micro-empirical in nature. Nay, such research has rarely been integrated within a conceptual-analytical framework so as to focus on the basic dynamics of a totality of the historical movement in a particular epoch. The present enterprise aims at capturing the basic dynamics of the totality of historical movements in the premodern and modern phases of Indian economic history. However, it cannot claim to have appropriated either as wide an empirical research base (as it is based on widely-celebrated and pioneering secondary material on Indian history) or as profound theoretical insights as are the characteristics of any memorable contribution on stages of development in

European economy, society and state power. Indeed this work can hardly avoid the constraints - qualitative and/or multidisciplinarian - of historical researches on Indian society and economy of a particular epoch.* Nevertheless, we fondly hope that this effort may indeed be a point of departure for more competent analysis of India's economic history by other scholars.

The very nature of our project has obviously demanded a time-consuming study on our part, of secondary source materials on Indian historiography. But the questions posed and the answers sought in this kind of project pertain more to the disciplines of sociology and economics than to historiography.

This work had to bear with a long gestation period not merely because not being a historian we lacked the skill of a historiographer while attempting to raise question (too naive or difficult) on history from the standpoint of our own academic discipline. More time was indeed spent on framing appropriate questions and devising a conceptual method by which one could glean answers to them from the seminal works on Indian historiography. The vastness of the period and region covered has also added an additional hindrance to the early preparation of a draft. Indeed the work itself had to go through innumerable number of drafts and comments; so much so that it has become virtually impossible to remember the names of all the scholars who kindly assisted us over a long period in the process of preparation, rejection and/or modification of drafts. We, however, remain grateful to each one of them even though all names may not be mentioned.

It is to be stressed here that the major findings are to be provisional. The work would be academically worthwhile, only if it can provoke further examination of the issues raised here and initiate investigations into those aspects of Indian social economy in history, which though considered important, remain largely unexplored.

I would like to express my debt to the Indian Council of Social Science Research for awarding me a Senior Fellowship in 1975. The present project had its genesis from somewhat different project on Indian economy that we worked upon under the Senior Fellowship programme.

* For instance, the concept of precolonial self-sustaining village economy supposedly having no jural private right on land, has not been subjected to a thorough historico-empirical or sociological investigation.

In the final phase of the work, I have immensely benefitted from the extraordinary kindness and ageless intellectual ability of A.K. Das gupta who, in spite of his age and other preoccupations, has kindly gone through many drafts and made countless suggestions including the title of the book. Without his help this work could not have reached its present form. I feel extremely sad to note that Prof. A.K. Das Gupta lives no more to see the book in printed form.

A.K. Bagchi and Mihir Rakshit - two old friends - were always available for discussions on many theoretical issues raised in this volume. A.K. Bagchi has kindly gone through a longish draft of the prospective second part, still under preparation. Mihir Rakshit has helped me to streamline my notions on the colonial transfer mechanism between India and Britain in the late nineteenth country. I take this opportunity to express my debt to them here as I have no plan at present to write another preface to the second volume of the project that deals with the colonial period.

Two other friends who helped mainly by controverting my reasonings are Ratan Khasnobis and Kumaresh Chakraborty. Without their help. I could not possibly reason my case. I am thankful to them.

There are many more who have helped me in various ways. In this connection I am thankful to Shyamal Sarkar, Asin Dasgupta, Ranjan Gupta, Ranjan Sen, Arun Ghosh, Barun De, Tapan Raychaudhury, Arun Banerjee, Amalendu Guha, D.D. Narula and many others. However, I bear the sole responsibility for all the lapses, mistakes and inadequacies that may vitiate my work.

Sadhana and Manasi had cheerfully put up with all the troubles that were caused owing to my long preoccupation with this work.

This volume is dedicated to my youngest brother, Ashu, who insisted that people engaged in teaching economic science are to undertake study on Indian economic history. Ashu, however, sacrificed his life for a noble conviction of his own and this work has its share of inspiration from his memory.

Santiniketan
14 Feburary 1992 **Arun Majumder**

[illegible] memory.

[illegible]
[illegible] [illegible]

Contents

Introduction

Theoretical conceptualisation of genesis and reproduction of a social economy is necessary for analytical identification of crucial variables that cause its stasis and change. In the case of pre-British Indian socio-economic formations in general, any attempt towards theorisation is replete with conceptual as well as historio-empirical difficulties. Since in most cases the hitherto available generic concepts and formulations have sprung from West European experiences, striking dissimilarities between socio-economic reproduction processes in pre-British India and those in pre-modern West Europe can hardly allow indiscriminate use of the same generic concepts and formulations for the discernment of the dynamics of Indian economic evolution. There is another difficulty. The state of historical research on ancient or medieval society and economy in India is not comparable with European achievements. What little information we have on early socio-economic formations in India can hardly be used for answering relevant questions that are to be raised in the course of a study of pre-British Indian economic formations.

However, from a simplistic theoretical point of view, one can hardly conceive of an economy (surplus producing or not) where productive and consumptive activities are not reproduced by an ongoing social mechanism. For an economy that does not produce surplus we are not required to probe into history for understanding its dynamics, because at that stage the mechanism of production itself defines how consumption goods are distributed. In fact, the non-surplus producing states of nomadic pastoralism can be conceived of as those where fruit gathering, animal hunting, irregular cultivation of crops, etc., constituted the major functions of human beings. The modern anthropological findings on lingering primitive social formations in some isolated pockets have justified such backward theoretical projection into the earliest stages of economy. A more developed basis of socio-economic formation at the early stage of human society started with the transition of a nomadic pastoral economy to the stage of settled cultivation.

The transition of a nomadic collectivity of human beings bound within a primitive social group (e.g., clan or kinship group) to a stage of society based on settled agriculture was crucial for two reasons: first, settled agriculture could assure a rhythmic cycle of production; second, it could lay bare a wider scope for privatisation of the fruits of labour and the labour activities by members of a communal collectivity, although in some aspects of interaction between labour and nature, the communality of labour activities had to be retained. A communal chieftainship and later, the institution of kingship and statehood, appeared in history as different categories of communality of a group of human beings. Since a settled agricultural society starts producing surplus in a regular fashion, the question that arises is whether privatisation of labour activities in such a society was necessarily instrumental in the rise of private property to the level of a civil society or the rise of a higher communality in the form of a state power.

I

Marx and Engels both try to answer this question, Marx's answer is theoretical, Engels's is historico-anthropological, although both are supposed to supplement each other.

Marx begins by saying that man appeared as a "generic being" in a primitive nomadic community who confronted nature as the material *prerequisite* or means of his labour. Since the condition of labour in such a community was the primitive mode of appropriating nature, the private labour activities of the members could not be *estranged* objectively from their material prerequisites. Only in settled agriculture man as generic being became objectively as much the *proprietor* of such prerequisites of his condition of labour as any other individual of the community was. Man in this new stage of cultivation began to perceive an objective existence of his own, independent of his labour, and accordingly it appeared to him that an appropriation of the material as well as the means of labour available in nature could allow him to subsist and satisfy his well-being without invoking his own labour power. Thus the concept of private property arose when (*a*) an individual could appropriate the material condition of labour of another member of his community and/or his neighbourhood; (*b*) the average productivity of one's labour activity exceeded his subsistence requirement. Condition (*b*) could be attained by labouring individuals in settled agriculture rather in the nomadic pastoral stage of production. But this condition (*b*) was not by itself a *necessary* condition for the rise of private property. The necessary condition was usurpation by an individual of the material condition of labour of others, as under condition (*a*). This condition arose, as Marx points out in *Economic and Philosophical Manuscripts* of 1844, from a subjectively perceived estrangement between the labour activity of man as generic being at the primitive stage and the produce of his labour that regulated his subsistence. This estrangement, arising in a nomadic pastoral community of human beings, could secure its objective scope only when the art of labour activity was improved in a community of settled cultivators. Thus "man" who "appears originally as a generic being, a tribal being. . ." became an individual by means of a historical process.

Such theoretical conceptualisation of a conjoint rise of the "individual" and of private property in history (the "individual" negotiating its transition from the earlier stage of his entity merely as a "generic being" or "herd animal" to the stage of the individual, and private property being conceived by Marx as a *materialised relation* between non-labouring individuals who could usurp others'_material condition of labour and labouring individuals who could not retain their own material conditions of labour), becomes with Marx, a powerful analytical tool to trace the evolution of West European societies from the stage of nomadic pastoralism to that of class society based on settled agriculture. Till 1845-46, i.e., up to the time *The German Ideology* was published, or till 1853, when articles on India were published, Marx had no qualm over his conceptualisation as outlined above. A closer study of East Europe and premodern Asiatic societies and economies made him doubt his earlier conceptualisation of historical stages of development of an evolving human society.[1]

The question that must have tormented him most during the post - 1853 period was why under the so-called "Oriental" social formations, a surplus-producing settled agricultural society based on private appropriation of surplus by the despot and private labour activities by members of "a self-sustaining village community" inhibit the unambiguous rise of the individual and private property either in a *de facto* or in a *de jure* form. It seems that Marx is convinced of the distinct identity of "Oriental" economic formation as a non-European pre-class stage of societal development. One may refer to Marx's highly critical notes on the Russian scholar Kovalevsky's conceptual innovation of Mughal Indian economic institutions as being similar to those under

European feudalism.[2] However, he is uncertain about formulating a general analytical corpus of historical materialism which would enable him to posit a set of common dialectics of genesis and decay of both occidental and oriental social formations.

Engels, on the other hand, tries to trace the historical genesis as well as movement of various stages of evolution of private property in Western Europe in his *Origin of the Family, Private Property and the State* on the basis of what later Marxists stigmatise as "dubious evolutionary anthropology" of L.H. Morgan. Modern anthropological researches almost unanimously reject the view propounded by Engles that there existed a necessary interconnection between the rise of the family as primitive kinship unit of labour exploitation of wife and children by the family's male patriarch and the historical emergence of private property. Whatever perceptive remarks Engels makes on the contrast between the Ancient or Germanic formations and those found in Asiatic or Slav societies, in his *Anti-Duhring* or *The Mark*, by themselves such remarks do not give a comprehensive framework of Oriental social formation to be conceived in terms of historical materialism.

In fact the cardinal basis on which Oriental social formation or "oriental despotism" has been conceived by West European scholars, from Montesquieu to Marx and Engels, is persistently elusive. The countries, societies or state powers included under the epithet, "oriental" had no uniform characteristics that could contrast with those found in pre-capitalist West Europe. However, one can discern a commonness among West European thinkers who contrast "Oriental" and "Occidental" social formations, and that is a kind of inexplicable European orthodoxy about the supposedly common attributes of an oriental state power.

This orthodox trend is discernible even in the writing of Aristotle.[3] In the modern period, Montesquieu was the earliest thinker who, in the early 18th century, propounded the theory of "oriental despotism" so as to contrast the differential traits of all governments and societies of non-European *origin* with politico-legal and anti-despotic qualities of state governance and societies of Europe.

Before Montesquieu, Machiavelli, Chabod and Bodin highlight the qualitative difference between the system of governance of European states and those of the Ottoman Empire. In Charles Bernier's writings we discover for the first time a similarity between the system of governance of the Ottoman state and that of India, China, Persia, etc.

But it was left to Montesquieu to theorise the qualitative dichotomy between European and Asian state systems or societies respectively in terms of occidental and oriental attributes.

It cannot be denied that the empirical postulates of Montesquieu's theory of oriental despotism, namely, the absence of stable private property and a hereditary nobility, religion operating as a functional substitute of law, the unchanging character of societies, abject fear of a subject people, state as the sole proprietor of all land in its domain etc., were liberally drawn from Bernier's account of what is supposed to have existed in Turkey, China, India and Persia. Those postulates are different from those available in feudal absolutism in West Europe. Western European societies, once besieged by barbaric invasions and religious reformation movements, could now temper their conditional property rights of feudalism with a resurrected Roman legal system so as to occasion the growth of a hereditary landed nobility exercising absolute property rights in land.

West European states could embark upon a road to enlightened political and economic individualism of *laissez faire* capitalism from the stage of absolute private property in land and a hereditary landed nobility in society. If the phenomenon of parcellised sovereignty of the earlier feudalism of dark ages had succumbed, as Perry Andreson argues, to the absolutist sovereignty of a monarchical state power, it was only to heighten the politico-legal articulation of private property rights and corresponding labour obligations in early modern Europe.

Montesquieu, however, theorised the genetical cause of the contrasting empirical postulates between non-European (mainly Asian) and European states (Ottoman Europe being an exception) in terms of the initial geophysical differences between them.[4] Although notable contemporary critics, like Voltaire and Anquetil-Duperron challenged many of Montesquieu's empirical postulates the basic thrust of the latter on a sort of qualitative difference that must be there, between Europe and Asia, seems to have driven 19th century European scholars to search the various aspects of such differences. For instance, Adam Smith differentiates the manufacturing bias of the European system of production from the Asian bias towards agricultural production. Hegel and Richard Jones, however, carry forward more closely the tradition of European orthodoxy on Asiatic states charted out by Montesquieu and Bernier, though the former pointed out the differences among the oriental states themselves.

Smith, however, was an exception in noting the good quality of

Asian state system. He characterised the Asian state powers - in China, Indostan and Egypt in particular - as *benevolent* to the subject people engaged solely in agricultural activities, while governments in Europe neglect agriculture, and consequently people choose the second best occupation, namely, manufacturing activity. Smith reckoned that the benevolence of Asian states arose from their dependence on land tax as the only source of public revenue and that was why they maintain public hydraulic works for irrigational purpose and for navigation canals. Smith laments the absence of a similar awareness among European governments about the necessary infrastructure for agricultural production. Although Smith's account does not depict Asian governments as "despotic" ones, the way he differentiates European economy from that of Asia, nevertheless reflects an orthodox faith that Asian economies must necessarily suffer from the absence of manufacturing skill owing to their "virtuous" specialisation in agriculture.[5] Such exercises in building up a qualitative paradigm of continental attributes appear as monsters to a rational analysis. Certainly Smith's thought was trapped under such exercises, that started in modern times from Bernier's contrasting account of European and Asian governments.

Richard Jones, retaining the state's proprietary right on soil as the central variable of the Asian state system, ascribes the common genesis of the despotic character of Asian state systems to "their common conquest by the Tartar tribes of Central Asia"[6] The Smithian account visualises an extent of mutuality between a subject peasantry in Asia paying taxes out of its produce and the benevolence of an Asian government supplying infrastructural inputs to peasant farms. In Jone's account emphasis on mutuality is absent, and unlike Montesquieu, Jones traces the origin of despotic appropriation of surplus not in geophysical attributes of the regions, but in "the racial trait of a nomadic tribe of Tartars that brought China, Persia, India and Asiatic Turkey' under their hegemonistic rule. Jones, however, discerns a difference among the degree of despotic usurpation in accordance to the extent of control Tartar invaders exercised.

Hegel alone among modern West European thinkers dealing with oriental despotism or with the difference between Europe and Asia, propounds the thesis that oriental despotism in contrast to occidental reason might have a social root apart from its political origin.[7] Hegel's account is as follows: While in the case of China, social equality reigned supreme in the relations among people themselves, the Emperor had to be despotic and to transplant and institutionalise inequality among people in its own interest. In India on the other hand, Hegel discovers dual origins of despotism. It originates at the social level with caste system within an autarkic village community, and at the political level, in the relations between village communities and the state power, the latter for its reproduction was to be despotic in response to the autarkical character of the former. Thus in China, though there was social equality, state despotism robbed such equality of its political prerequisite, i.e., freedom. Between India and China, Hegel deprecates the inbuilt social inequality steered by the caste system in India, as he appreciates Chinese social trend towards equality disrupted only by a despotic imperial power. Hegel does not examine as closely the genesis of despotism in other Asiatic states, namely, Persia, Egypt and Turkey, although he subscribes to the received orthodoxy by asserting that "Asia generally is the scene of despotism, and in a bad sense, tyranny'.[8]

II

While many modern West European thinkers before Marx and Engles start with the premise that there did exist a qualitative difference between the state or social systems in Asia and Europe[9] no one apart from Montesquieu advances a meaningful reason which can be called an explanatory variable of such a difference between the two continental societies and state systems. But Montesquieu's reasoning in terms of geophysical difference between the Europe and Asia is ill-informed and that is why perhaps it did not carry conviction to those after him who try to search out an altogether different basis of a supposed difference between Europe and Asia. Montesquieu's stigmatisation of Asian governments as "despotic" finds its echo in Hegel and Jones and among others (except Smith). However, they differ from each other in locating the exact historical reason which supposedly made such despotism an inalienable feature of Asian state systems.

If we carefully examine the evidences on Marx's conceptualisation of the system of production in Asian societies as reflected in his articles on India in 1853 and in *Grundrisse* and his writings thereafter (e.g., his comments on Kovalevsky's formulation on Mughal Indian society or his correspondence with Zasulich in 1881), we find that there was no fundamental change in his conceptualisation of the so called oriental social formation. His successive attempts towards conceptualisation of the Asiatic mode of production (apparently exposing his discreet shift of emphasis from one to the other aspect of that social formation) betray an intellectual battle in him between a received orthodoxy and a constant endeavour towards scientific clarification of his concept on Asiatic social formations. However, it is not evident that Marx has won his battle against orthodoxy, particularly in this regard.

Both Marx and Engels pick up the absence of private property in land and centralised hydraulic works as key empirical postulates of "Oriental" or Asiatic social formations. While the absence of private property in land made them *assume* state or communal property as the *possible* alternative, the reported existence of centralised hydraulic (or public) works under a Asiatic system of state formation made them assign a role to the state in matters of reproducing "the *real possessors*" of land, the material conditions of production.

Marx concedes to a Smithian mutuality between the "smaller communities:" (i.e., village republics) and the "higher community" as represented by the state. He posits that the unit of smaller communities, namely, a 'self-sustaining village community' *possesses* only one component of the conditions of labour, i.e., land, the other components – water and navigational canals – are reproduced by public works of a despotic power in the state – the higher community is 'higher unity' as called by Marx. Thus the smaller communities can supposedly reproduce their subsistence only by realising a higher unity with the despotic state. The cost of subsistence to be incurred by smaller communities is the surplus payable to the state, the higher community or unity.

Since the historico-empirical validity of an universal existence of centralised hydraulic works among Asiatic states is found to be precarious, Marx's entire conceptual model of relations between smaller unities as represented by village communities and the supposed higher unity - the state - falls through. In fact Marx's concept of the 'self-sustaining village community ' goes more with Hegelian concept of autarkic village community in Asian states and can hardly put up with the Smithian notion of the centralised public works as being the deliverer of one of the conditions of labour in agriculture.

Marx's use of the term 'despot' to specify the quality of a Asiatic king or executive head with its power to appropriate surplus goes along more with the received orthodoxy. However, it is not exactly synonymous with the Smithian model of assigning to it a positive role of supplying one of the conditions of labour in village production. There are other problems as well. In fact, Smith is more impressed by the centralised public works in China and Egypt, but he does not cite a similar instance from Mughal India. In fact, except China (and perhaps to an extent Egypt) in no other Asiatic state did a centralised hydraulic work play a decisive role in the major segment of productive activities in agriculture.[10] It seems that the logical contradictions in Marx's conceptualisation of Asiatic mode of production have originated from his unsuccessful attempts towards synthesising Smithian and Hegelian postulates of Asiatic societies and economies with Bernier's qualitative remarks on Asian states.

Engels was more forthright in his orthodoxy than Marx in emphasising the role of the state in matters of land-ownership and 'collective maintenance of irrigation throughout the river villages' under oriental 'despotisms'.[11] That a king or emperor, by virtue of his superior power flowing from armed strength, could distribute or redistribute land among officials and favoured clients did not prove state-ownership. Such distribution or redistribution of land was undertaken not for materialising productive activities but for promoting the ability of the beneficiaries to appropriate surplus either on the king/emperor's behalf or for their own enjoyment. In no way does an arbitrariness of power enjoyed by the state in matters of plundering or redistributing wealth or land possessed by citizens show the existence of state proprietorship of wealth or land.

The European habit of visualising proprietorship of land to be vested either with an individual, or the state or a community in a surplus-producing economy rests not on the notion of property *as a relation of appropriation of the material conditions of labour* but on a notion of property as merely a physical object that fetches surplus to the owner. It is true that in certain circumstances or regions, the two notions may not be contradictory. However, in certain specific social situations where the customary *possession* right of labourers on the physical object of labour is independent of the right of appropriation of a *customarily determined portion* of surplus yielded by labour, there is bound to surface a contradiction between the two notions of property as stated above. In the Asiatic mode of production, the possessing right of a member of the village community on land remained undisturbed. A king or emperor with no productive labour power of his own but with all the armed might at his disposal could hardly afford to usurp this right. What he could do was to impose his claim on a portion of surplus produced by the community members. If he did usurp this possessing right, he would thereby negate by such an act the basis of material reproduction of the institution he presided upon. This was why property as a relation of appropriation of the material condition of labour could not arise in the Asiatic states in general (except such regions in Asia where supply of labour was elastic and available land was not in abundance as was the case in Japan or T'ang China).

From where does a village community of so-called oriental variant sustain its autarkical unity and strength so as to be indifferent to the rise or fall of the empire? Marx answers in terms of a self-sustaining unity of agriculture with manufacture within an 'idyllic village republic' of Asia that 'contains all conditions of production and surplus production'. But the dawn of village society in tribal communal Europe also witnessed a similar unity in village agriculture and manufactures.[12] Then why did the rise of private property and class-society, particularly in West Europe, disrupt this tribal-communal unity between agriculture and manufacture? The answer must be found in a trend towards labour ensalvement and the eventual trend towards enserfment of labour. In a tribal-communal setup, labour as the proprietor of its natural material conditions of subsistence could divide its activity between agricultural and manufacturing spheres according to their necessities. The general usurpation of the material condition of labour by private property-holders replaced this *natural* autonomy by division of labour as required by private property through coercive subjugation of labour time and allocating it so as to maximise its effect on the enrichment of the property itself.

Under feudalism such division of labour caused social differentiation between agricultural and manufacturing labour activities. It drove out manufacturing labour from the countryside where extra-economic appropriation of the material condition of labour in agriculture left no scope for an agricultural slave or serf to retain his labour time to pursue his earlier non-agricultural vocations. Although this process started earlier, town economy as the centre of manufacture and trade could not disentangle itself from the dead weight of its dependence on surplus from slave-worked agriculture till the advent of feudalism. It was only under feudalism that there began a social division between agricultural and non-agricultural labour activity and between the extra-economic mode of appropriation of the material conditions of labour both in the countryside and towns. Thus during the feudal period towns in Europe, for the first time, gained *economic autonomy* from the enserfed countryside.

In the village community of the so-called 'orient', a similar development did not take place by virtue of an absence of private property in agriculture. But this does not explain why the surplus-producing 'communal' economy at the level of a village community within the Asiatic mode with privatised labour activities and privatised appropriation of surplus (the two apparently propitious conditions for the rise of private property in western Europe) did not lead to the rise of private property in the Orient. This question escaped Marx or Marx escaped the question by an assumption, borrowed from earlier European thinkers like Montesquieu or Bernier, that the Oriental despot devoured the *entire* surplus yielded by a village community, or that the village community could not retain a portion of surplus generated by it either for itself or for the mini-despots or the caste-lords (as was the case in India). The problem arises when one accepts that within a village community of the so-called orient there is privatised surplus appropriation. The problematic is as follows : if there did exist the phenomenon of private surplus appropriation in an Asian village community, what prevented it from being transformed into an appropriation of the material conditions of labour within it.

The answer can be traced only in the specificity of *initial differential conditions*, namely, in the state of natural *material conditions of labour*. If the initial conditions represent too little labour compared to relatively vast prerequisites of labour, certainly *privatised surplus appropriation may not require its transformation into a private appropriation of the material prerequisites of labour*. Because under such initial conditions, an eventuality of appropriation of the material condition of labour by a powerful member of the community would beget alienation of labour from him and drive labour to a new area where no such appropriation could inhibit free use by labour of the natural material conditions. From this point of view, Montesquieu is correct only by default. In other words, the Oriental despot could arise not because the initial geophysical conditions of Europe were better than that in the Orient, but just the reverse. Thus, compared to the Occident, the Orient contained a more favourable geophysical environment with too small amount of labour available to use it as material prerequisites.[13] This can be confirmed by scientific investigation in the initial conditions of social formations on settled agriculture in ancient Europe and Asia.

These geophysical as well as geographical differences impelled the human communities in European history towards moving in a way different from that persued by their Asian counterparts so as to preserve their respective modes of obtaining unity between conditions of reproduction of human collectivities and condition of labour for production. While in one case the initial conditions necessitated the rise of private property in labour or land (labour or land being the material conditions of production in a human commune either through slavery or feudalism), in the other case the initial conditions did not ordain a similar necessity for disruption of natural community as the condition of labour. The free natural prerequisite labour (rather than its transformation into private property as the instrument of production) would continue undisturbed. In the latter case, privatisation of labour activity could however be mediated only through the membership of the natural community rather than through that of the community that found its articulation only by the relation of private property. In the Orient the privatisation of appropriation of surplus was actuated not by any objective but subjective parameters of that community.

III

So far the received theories of economic evolution of a society have been framed in the light of historical experiences of European societies where private property was the basic datum. However, there can be no doubt that such a theory cannot explain the economic evolution of a surplus-producing society where private property as relation of appropriation of the material condition of labour never appeared in its premodern phase of history. Again, one can discern- that in those surplus-producing societies where private property did not emerge though, there had emerged privatisation of labour activities and privatisation of surplus appropriation within a community. The only ubiquitous feature of such privatisations is that the community itself acted as mediator of the conditions of such privatisations (as non-labouring surplus appropriators, and labourers could gain access to surplus or land only by virtue of being a member of the community) and notwithstanding a functional separation between labourers who generated surplus and those non-labourers who appropriated the same within that community, the material reproduction of the community itself was not mediated by such privatisation.

What are the subjective/objective reasons that forced a community to retain such functional separation between labouring and non-labouring members? What is the objective reason that prevented a non-labouring member of the community from transferring its communally acknowledged surplus entitlement into private appropriation of the material conditions of labour? Why is it that the power was vested with the community in matters of adjudicating decisions on land allotment and the distribution of surplus from land itself possessed by the community?

What was the cardinal basis of communality among households (labouring as well as non-labouriń one) within such a community? These are questions we would like to answer in our work by tracing the structural evolution of Indian society and economy during its early phase. To do this, we have resorted to using two analytical constructs – one is related to private property and the other is related to community.

The first construct that deals with private property as a *private* relation of appropriation (as against the communal relation of appropriation)by a non-labouring individual or class of the material conditions of labour, has been derived from Marx's investigation (in *Grundrisse*) into logical genesis of such relation in course of evolution of societies in the Occident. The other construct, namely, the construct of a community of so-called Oriental type[14] that possesses both the objective condition of labour as well as the subjective condition of surplus appropriation by the non-labouring members, has been developed on the basis of actually operating caste-ridden village community of an autarkic character in ancient India that is indeed a variable in the Hegelian model of Oriental despotism in India.

While it is easy to comprehend the first construct, the second one may not be that easy. As it is in Hegel, our community is located in the village, and unlike Marx, we do not conceive the state as a higher communal entity. Our concept of community, i.e., the village community, is as the *possessor not proprietor* (as presumed by Marx) of a definite quantum of available land and member households. The village community so conceived can grow in a situation of elastic supply of the material conditions of labour (in this case, land and unhindered objective scopes for community formation) and inelastic supply of labourers. The landholding as possessed by our village community does not necessarily imply communalisation of labour use, although that is not totally ruled out for the sake of use of labour for a communal purpose. However it is predominantly a holding by cultivating from which the member households (labouring as well as non-labouring) procure their individual means of livelihood.

There exist only two categories of households in our village community – the labouring and the non-labouring ones. The labouring members secure their means of livelihood only by virtue of their actual labour services. The non-labouring ones are, however, able to appropriate a portion of surplus produce of labouring households *not* owing to any control they individually or collectively exercise on land or labour of the community but due to an acknowledged social superiority over the other subcommunal group, i.e., the group of labouring households (how it was brought about has no objective implication on the conditions of production in the community).

The village community thus represents a socio-economic corporate unity between the two *socially* differentiated groups, i.e., between those who are *socially obliged* to procure livelihood only by rendering individual labour services and those who by virtue of their acknowledged *social superiority* enjoy the *social* custom of living off others' labour. Both the groups, though mutually antagonistic in socio-economic terms, are forced to retain a semblance of a *social* unity in a static context. While the non-labouring group favours communal unity for its own communal reproduction, for otherwise in the event of its decommunalisation, it looses the advantage of appropriating surplus from labourers working within the community. The labouring groups of the community, despite surplus appropriation by the non-labouring group, favour a subjective unity with the latter for an undisturbed enjoyment of its communal condition against actual or potential extraneous interference.

From what has been stated above we come to the most important dynamic components of our analytical construct:

(1) The socio-economic corporate unity in a village community is not *absolute* but *relative*.

(2) This social unity to the extent,it is dependent on the requirement of livelihood of the non-labouring group, can be compromised as and when the group can completely identify its interest with that of an extra-communal surplus-appropriating power or agency or institution. If that happens a new community tends to arise either by replacing or in addition to the older one.

(3) On the other hand the static social unity of a village community required on the part of the labouring group rests only on a presupposition of actual or potential extra-communal power, agency or institution that tends to or is supposed to disturb its mode of reproduction. In a dynamic context, i.e., when an existence of the exogenous power acting as the cause of social unity within a village community, tends to be weak or non-existent, the intra-communal unity among labouring and non-labouring groups tends to replace itself by mutual antagonism between the two. Thus, while communal unity is *relative*, the mutual

antagonism is *absolute*. Though the latter surfaces only in the event of near absence of any external power.

(4) The *economic self-sustenance* of a village communal unity is therefore conditional on (i) the social power of labourers of the community to appropriate a *just* entitlement to their productive activity and subsistence living, and (ii) an unity between agriculture and manufacture.
In the event of the violation of (i), labourers of a community tend to realise the condition (i) by migrating to a new area for new community formation. On the other hand, if any extra-communal authority or power or intra-communal non-labouring group precipitates the violation of (i), it runs the risk of loosing the surplus which acts as its material condition of reproduction. The violation of (ii) can arise in the event of specialisation of community labour in a particular agricultural or non-agricultural pursuit. Then, the self-sustaining unity of a village communal economy is compromised by its abject dependence on exports to and imports from outside in order to materialise condition (ii) as well as (i), Therefore, the economic self-sustenance of a village communal economy can hold good only when both (i) as well as (ii) are satisfied.

(5) While our village communal economy in a static context possesses no *endogenous* compulsion for economic growth, some *exogeneously* determined factors, e.g., population growth, specialisation of labour in a particular pursuit or such other developments, may bring about a change in the productive configurations of its communal economic set-up, but by themselves such changes cannot cause distortion, dislocation or decay of the material condition of labour or production.

(6) Although the village communal unity in a static context abandons the actual/potential possibility of supra-village affiliation of a labouring or a non-labouring group with a kindred group existing outside the community, in a dynamic context such supra-village affiliations are possible either when the autonomous right of the village labouring group to free labour activity and subsistence is at stake by the supra-village affiliation of the non-labouring groups subsisting within or outside the communities or when the amount of surplus appropriated by a village non-labouring group is actually or is deemed insufficient (after satisfying the

just subsistence requirement of the labouring group).

Such an eventuality may occur either as a sequel to excessive external claim (by the state or any external authority) from the village or as the consequence of the poor state of production even in the absence of excessive appropriation by an external authority or agency. But in some of these specific situations, either the village labouring group or the non-labouring group can appropriate the communal condition of labour exclusively in its favour so as to occasion a tribal communal economic equality among members or its opposite, i.e., the rise of private property. But such specific situations can hardly be the result of any supra-village affiliation of either labouring or non-labouring people. Because the material presupposition of any supra-village affiliation is the communality of a group that resorts to such affiliation.[15]

The analytical construct on the village community in the Indian context, can explain why the actual historical growth movements of a village economy in the earlier period tended to relapse into a stagnant spiral and why, as a consequence, there could arise private wealth, but not private property in the early phase of Indian history. In other words, the historical development in the Indian economy of the early period consists *essentially* of more changes in the modes of appropriation of surplus rather than of those in the modes of generation of surplus.

IV

By using both the constructs - one on private property and the other on Indian village community - we are able to delineate the specific features of structural evolution of the surplus-producing communal economy of early Indian history in the following terms.

(1)While a stubborn persistence of corporate communality as one of the basic conditions of labour (or the absence of the rise of private appropriation of material condition of labour), set in motion an overall stagnant spiral within the surplus-producing social economy in premodern India, whatever changes there occurred in the economy of that period were brought about at the instance of varied forms of the non-productive surplus appropriation. This is in sharp contrast to the premodern European history where the historical movements in a social economy had dispensed early with corporate communality (what Marx terms as 'communal-tribal') as the condition of labour and succumbed to an individualised communality, subject to private appropriation on the part of a few non-labouring individuals of the material conditions of labour. European history since ancient times starts not with a natural community but with a community formed at the instance of private property.

(2) The characteristic feature of the structural evolution of the Indian economy withnesses an irreconcilable contradiction between a natural-communal production base and its subjective presupposition, assuming the objective forms of surplus appropriation by anyone who could establish his superiority either by socio-ideological or by coercive means (i.e., either by means of consent or force). Since only the labouring groups belonging to innumerable village communities were capable of material reproduction of the communal production base, the structural feature could register no significant change or shift in the power equations within a village communal economy. The endemic socio-economic contradiction within a village community could however manifest itself in the form of socio-religious movement. This could happen particularly at those historical periods, when the supra-communal authorities were sufficiently weak in matters of claiming surplus from subordinate village communities. Such contradictions or conflicts at the village community level tended to search out an *ad-hoc* resolution in new community formation on the basis of a new socio-religious ideology. But such new village community formations tended to promote the old socio-economic cleavage, between social obligations of the labouring population and the new customary right of surplus appropriation by a few non-labouring elite groups.

This was because of two complementary reasons. First, the community of village production process was characterised more by the need for material reproduction of village-level productive labour power than by the customary pattern of distribution of village surplus among village non-productive labour as well as the non-labouring elites. Second, any village community formation - old or new - based on the pre-supposition of an externality, tended to germinate and consolidate its own communal internality in the creation of its internal non-labouring elites (for the subjective preservation of the community) rather than in an objective uniqueness of its material production base or economic autarky.

The other important aspect of the structural evolution of Indian economy was the state of perpetual conflict and cooperation among all categories of surplus appropriators at the supra-village level. Cooperation needed for the reproduction of a supra-village surplus appropriation mechanism necessarily ended in conflict. For example, cooperation among local potentates of the period of Delhi Sultanates was needed for their survival against the imperial mode of maximising its surplus appropriation, but such cooperation could turn into mutual conflict, in the event of an imperial power being strong enough to withstand or defeat a cooperative endeavour for subsistence among local surplus appropriators (as it was in the Mughal period). No category of supra-village surplus appropriation either executed by *power* (e.g., by secondary zamindar, Iqta-assignee, jagirdar, subadar, mansabdar, etc.) or that by *exchange mechanism* (e.g., by supra-local merchants, port merchants, artisan-traders, etc.) could establish unity or cooperation among themselves on an unassailable material basis. On thc other hand, wealth differentiation was the consequence of inescapable competition and conflict among each and every category of supra-village surplus appropriators.

(3)However, the mutual exclusiveness bordering on a total estrangement between the modes of reproduction of innumerable village communities and those of supra-communal surplus appropriation from below (i.e., from village communities) by power-wielding local oligarchs or the imperial state, could yield premium to mercantile activities that mediated between revenue-paying village communities and the people enjoying supra-village authorities that appropriated surplus by dint of armed or religious or ethnic power.

By their *exchange* operations, merchants on the one hand helped a supra-communal power caucus to consummate its surplus appropriation in real consumable terms and, on the other hand, facilitated the transformation of the amount of village communal surplus into its universalised form, i.e., legal tender money.

To accomplish this, merchants resorted to unequal exchange between them as buyers or sellers of merchandise and a village community as supplier or a supra-communal power caucus as consumer of real merchandise. Since the village communal base of production was more or less inelastic in India, the degree of exchange inequality in mercantile transactions with a village community was low or negligible, compared to the degree of exchange inequality in similar transactions with people belonging to a supra-communal power establishment. In ancient Indian history, the first form of unequal exchange between a merchant and a village community was non-existent because the elasticity of mercantile demand for merchandise from rural areas was much less than the village elasticity of demand for legal tender money.[16] On the other hand, the demand on the part of the non-productive people belonging to an estranged supra-communal power establishment for consumable merchandise was at least as much inelastic as that of the demand of merchants for merchandise to be procured from villages. Therefore, a presupposition of exchange transaction between merchants selling merchandise and the people, belonging to revenue-appropriating power establishment, buying *consumables in kind,* would necessarily involve a high degree of inequality of exchange in favour of the former and against the latter. This was how the dependence of Indian towns or cities on the village economy led to the growing economic power of merchants as a group. The above exchange inequality caused a drainage of a part of appropriated surplus, in money wealth form, from the people belonging to a supra-communal surplus-appropriating power caucus to merchants.

At the stage when mercantile activity was weak, power establishments could prosper not only at the expense of villages but also by supplying credit to the merchants. With the progress of money wealth and differentiation among merchants themselves, there arose a group of big merchants, who wielded greater wealth so as to reverse the earlier trend. The Indian big merchants could thus acquire a portion of village surplus *not by using but by imposing* unequal exchanges not so much on village communities as on the State power as well as on the urban dwellers, belonging to a local or imperial satrap. Therefore, the mercantile appropriation of surplus assuming its money wealth form, became directly proportional to the amount of village surplus that was usurped by a local or imperial power and its establishment. Another important means by which Indian big merchants could augment their money wealth was by exchanging Indian merchandise for precious or less precious metals from foreign merchants anxious to buy Indian goods. Indian development in mercantile wealth accumulation coincided with certain global developments. India as a traditional buyers' market of metals and a sellers' market of commodities or goods, witnessed during the 16th-17th centuries the fall in international prices of metals (particularly of the most popular one: silver) and a rise in internationl prices of consumer goods (including cotton and silk piece goods).

(4)The enormity of mercantile money wealth accumulation of 16th - 17th century by Indian merchants in general, and the big Indian merchants of the 17th century in particular, had two repurcussions. First, in the drainage of surplus in money form from inland state power and its people (i.e., from the people belonging to imperial and local oligarchic establishments that earned income from revenue paid by the village communities). And second, from the relatively greater inflow of gold and silver in exchange of a given quantum of exports of merchandise goods to Europe and the other continents.

The structural evolution of 17th century Indian economy had three aspects: first, the enormous liquidity of money wealth causing devaluation of the inland legal tender money and the consequent price rise within India. Second, a relative decline in the money power of the state, local oligarchs, etc. (i.e., supra-village power establishments) in the context of inelasticity of a village production base and hence of revenue appropriation from village communities. Third, a phenomenal rise in investment hunger of mercantile money wealth in India causing an extended credit network of wealthy merchants more among the revenue-collecting authorities, individuals and their dependents, than among the village communities.

On the other hand, the growth of mercantile money wealth confronting, as it did, a general scarcity of saleable merchandise goods, faced an unprecedented crisis of its investment outlet. The rise in specialisation of labour in the production of various horticultural or handicraft products, the sprouting of artisan villages and of putting-out systems in commerciably ebullient regions, etc, were all mediated by Indian merchant capital. But the entire spectrum of such developments was ultimately circumseribed by the relative inelasticity of the material base of agricultural production steered by village communities. This led to serious imbalances between the aggregate money wealth in circulation and the aggregate supply of urban provisions and drove up the general price level of 17th-18th century India.

The growing disproportion between mercantile wealth accumulation and the growth and diversity of the material production base in the Indian economy of the period was poised to bring about a *change* in the material condition of labour.

While one cannot escape the fact that such a change in the village communal mode of reproducing the material conditions of labour was inevitable, it is also difficult to say what would have been the most probable course of such *antonomous* and *endogenous* change in Indian village economy in that particular juncture in India's history - a change that could not actually take place due to massive intervention of European Commercial prowess more by their arms than by capital or merchandise.

(5) If we assume that the developmental movements of 18th century Indian history were shaped by the movements of world history, then we can observe that the propitious conditions for a possible *endogenous change* in the material conditions of labour in India were perversely distorted by the rise of the predatory political power of European merchants. The extent of such an exogenously-determined change in Indian polity cannot be accounted for given the historical parameters of 18th century India with an absence of a strong centralised state, weak localised state powers, crisis-ridden prosperity of Indian mercantile wealth and the inelasticity of the material production base of Indian village communities.

Whether a similar structural evolution can be traced in the pre-modern history of other so-called oriental societies is the subject matter of comparable historical studies and is beyond the scope of this study.

Notes

1. This is manifested in his incorporation, for the first time, a novel historical system, namely the 'Asiatic' or 'Oriental' system, into the famous Preface to the *Critique of Political Economy*.
2. Arguing against Kovalevsky's view that three of the four main criteria of Germano-Roman feudalism were to be found in India, which therefore ought to be regarded as feudal, Marx points out that "Kovalevsky forgets among other things serfdom, which is not of substantial importance to India. . . . "Nor do we find that 'poetry of the soil' so characteristic of Romano-Germanic feudalism (cf Maurer) in India any more than in Rome. In India the land is nowhere *noble* in such a way as to be, e.g., inalienable to non-members of the noble class". E. Hobsbowm (ed.), K. Marx, *Precapitalist Economic Formations* (Lawrence and Wishart edn., 1964), p.58.
3. For instance, Aristotle asserts in a cannonical passage: 'Barbarians are more servile by nature than Greeks, and Asians are more servile than Europeans; hence they endure despotic rule without protest'. *Politics*, Ch.III, Sec.IX.3 Cf Perry Anderson, *The Lineages of the Absolutist State* (London), 1974), pp. 597-99.
4. '. . . the Asia of which we know has vaster plains than Europe; it is broken up into masses by the surrounding seas; and as it is further south, its springs run easily dry, its mountains are not so covered with snow,

and its rivers are lower and form lesser barriers. Power therefore must be despotic in Asia, for if servitude were not extreme, the continent would suffer a division which the geography of the region forbids. In Europe, the natural dimensions of geography form several states of a modest size, in which the rule of laws is not imcompatible with the survival of the state; on the contrary it is so propitious to it that without laws a state would fall into decay, and become inferior to every other. It is this which has created that spirit of liberty which renders each part of the continent so resistant to subjugation or submission by a foreign power, law or the advantage of commerce' Charles Montesquieu, *De L' Esprit* des Lois, I, pp.291-92, from Perry Anderson, *op. cit.*, p.465.

5. Adam Smith, *Wealth of Nations*, Vol.II (London, 1950), pp.251-53.
6. Cf. Richard Jones, *An Essay on the Distribution of Wealth and the Sources of Taxation* (London, 1831), pp.6-8.
7. The account of Hegel has been constructed from extracts in his *The Philosophy of History* as available in P. Anderson, *op.cit.*, pp.468-69.
8. Extract from *ibid.*, p.469.
9. An Ottoman State in south-eastern Europe is believed to be an Asian intrusion into Europe, the former is treated as non-European.
10. Again in China, during the Tang period, some sort of private property in land emerged. Japan developed a full-fledged feudal ownership of land. Cf. Twitchet, *Land Tenure and the Social Order in T'ang and Sung China* (London, 1962), pp.21-28.
11. Cf. Engels, *Anti-Duhring* (Moscow, 1947), pp.211-18.
12. Perry Anderson however claims that the 'union of crafts and cultivation was common to virtually any pre-industrial rural community in the world, whatever its mode of production, *op.cit.*, p.489, n.11.

It seems, Anderson's observation is valid *not in regard to all crafts or manufactures in general.* It may be valid strictly in the case of such crafts that are required only for agricultural production. In prefeudal Europe, other village craftsmen who might have used agricultural raw materials but turned out consumable manufactures, (e.g., cotton fabrics, oil or vinegars, woollen goods, iron or wooden furnitures and fixtures) for household consumption, began to migrate to towns which began appearing as specialized autonomous centres for manufactures of non-agricultural use and centres of trade and transit. In premodern Asia we do not witness towns as centres of manufactures. Unlike premodern Europe, it was not the town but the village which was the centre of production of manufactures.

13. Marx observed, 'For instance, where [in the initial natural conditions of tribal-communal unity - A.M.] each individual [communal being] is supposed to possess so many acres of land, the *mere* increase in population constitutes an obstacle [to the reproduction of the old situation]. If this is to be overcome, colonisation will develop and this necessitates wars of conquest. This leads to slavery etc., e.g., the enlargement of *ager Publicus* and hence to the rise

of the Patricians, who represent the community, etc.' Marx, *Pre-capitalist Economic Formations* (Hobsbawm ed.) *op.cit.*, pp.92-93.

14. Our use of the term 'Orient' differs from the way it was used by Montesquieu and the European thinkers. The latter used it as a historico-empirical category, while we use it to denote only such regions where natural community, rather than a community based on private property relation, was one of the subjective/ objective condition of labour.

15. In the absence of assumption of power by private property or labour nothing can transform a supra-village affiliation among labouring or non-labouring people descending from various small communities into a larger community. History is full of examples of how religion, ethnicity or any other extra-economic social identity fails to occasion the rise of a bigger community consisting only either of labourers or non-labourers.

16. We should admit that this is an inferential observation in the absence of historical data. The basis of this inference is that absence of availability of legal tender money in a village community never undermined its basis of material reproduction, but non-availability of merchandise made reproduction of mercantile activities extremely precarious

2

Society and State Power

2.1: Some Theoretical Problems of Conventional Formulation on Society and Economy in Ancient India

Human history is like Paleontology. Owing to certain judicial blindness even the best intelligences absolutely fail to see the things which lie in front of their noses.

Marx to Engels, 1868

Our immediate task is to tackle two kinds of problems. The first one consists of the problems of choosing a suitable historical point of departure and that of identifying the areas to be covered by our study. The second category of problems is related to generic formulation of ancient Indian society and economy.

With the regard to the first problem, we feel that the historical point of departure for the early Indian economy and society was when India witnessed the phenomena of secondary state formations.[1] Among secondary state formations we prefer to start from the Mauryan period, since the available historical knowledge about the pre-Mauryan period does not warrant its meaningful use for our purpose. It may be pointed out that even the secondary state formations during the Mauryan period or even later (during the period of the Delhi Sultanates or the Mughals) could never impose its writ throughout the empire with as much force as it could in its core region. Since this is found in the case of all pre-modern secondary state formations in the ancient and medieval world, let us ignore this aspect of the problem of choosing an arbitrary historical point of departure.

The other problem of this category is that of identifying pre-British India in terms of its geographical coverage. The problem stems from the fact that we can hardly identify India as a compact *natural* geographical entity. Again if we could somehow overcome this problem in terms of certain distinctive geophysical attributes, the geography of India, so conceived, would rarely coincide with the geography of social settlements or politically organised territories. For the purpose of our study we will adopt an arbitrary standard of identifying the geographical coverage of pre-British India. If we identify pre-British India to comprise those geographical regions that eventually fell during the 18th-19th centuries under direct as well as indirect governance of colonial administration, that would serve our basic purpose of study on contrasts and continuities between pre-British and British Indian dynamics of socio-economic formations. We do not, however, promise that every region indicated above can be brought under the scope of this study and that we have to be selective because of our limited knowledge and, of course, due to constraints of space. We propose to make a selective choice of those Gangetic and trans-Gangetic sub-regions of India's north, the regions of the east and the west and those of the south Indian peninsula, about which historical studies can claim to have made reasonable progress. Again among the sub-regions we propose to include, we may be allowed to abstract from specific socio-economic attributes of a locality unless the latter is likely to challenge our basic formulations.

The second category of problems are largely theoretical in nature. The problems arise from the general inability of scholars to conceptualise the passage of Indian society from the stage of – what Marx and Engels would call – "primitive communism" to the stage of private surplus entitlement and privatisation of labour use in social production. This is not a peculiar problem of India. In fact, it still vitiates scholarly deliberations on premodern societies of Europe. However the problem, in the context of Europe, is less shadowy. In Europe, private surplus entitlement tended to assume a politico-legal and social form in opposition to an obligation of productive labour activity. Therefore scholars of early social formations in Europe have less difficulty in discerning the theoretical ancestry of private surplus entitlement and labour use in communal landholding and the communalisation of labour process. Such transitions, however, did not take place in the same way among different regional societies of Europe.[2] But neither the private surplus appropriation by a despot or an acknowledged communal elite nor the privatisation of productive labour activity ever assumed either a clear politico-legal or institutional form during the ancient or medieval epochs of Indian history.

We may ask what were the inhibitions that stood on the way of transformation of communally practiced private surplus appropriation and labour use into private property in ancient India, or what were the objective compulsions or dialectics of such development. These questions continue to plague historical enquiries and elude precise answers. Indeed without conceptualising evolving conditions of labour, no conceptualization of the passage of Indian early societies of communal landholding and communal labour process to those of private surplus appropriation and individualisation of labour activity is possible.

Most scholars on ancient India agree that even the early Indian village societies, of the Vedic period of second millennium BC, were surplus-producing societies. Where they differ among themselves is only in the modes of delineating the trajectory of evolutionary processes of interaction between kingship or monarchical institution and the various forms of society.

Most scholars of ancient Indian society invariably exclude investigation into the specificity of the condition of labour under each stage of Indian social evolution. Some, however, try to conceptualise the condition of labour in post-Vedic societies, but that is invariably aimed at discovering European traits of property ownership so as to build up a universally valid model of successive economic stages of social evolution. But even in such models the assumption of landownership does not spell out in clear terms the specific material condition of labour associated with each stage of development of "landownership". In this connection we cite the basic postulates built mainly by three famous neo-Marxian Indologists.

The pioneer was D.D. Kosambi[3] who divides the entire post-Vedic region into districts (*janapada*) each of which had its urban headquarter (*paur-janapada*). During the pre-Mauryan as well as the early Mauryan period, the residents of *paur-janapada* were taxed more than those of the *janapadas*. This led to newer private settlements initiated by urban residents with the help of the rural dwellers. This is similar to the model of developments in ancient Europe. However this development in India eventually strengthened the power of the urban citizens.

This development reared a tendency towards conflict among *paur-janapada* chiefs themselves. To avoid this Ashokan reforms were introduced, which introduced state-sponsored clearance of wastelands and village settlements for their cultivation. Here Kosambi identifies a departure of India from Europe. The *paur-janapadas* now began to be taxed less by the imperial monarch. The urban brahmans, kshatriyas and others were awarded liberal landgrants so as to encourage extension of cultivation and help them to appropriate bigger surplus from the communities so settled. A self-sufficient village community, lorded over by elitist citizens or their agents belonging to urban centres, became a new development during this period.

Together with this development, there was a substantial degree of demilitarisation at all levels as it was a period of peace. This, however, paved the way for the eventual decline of the Mauryan empire. With the decline of Mauryan empire, urban centres as centres of commodity production and exchange lost their viability and independence. As a consequence, there emerged two interrelated developments. The first was the decline of urban centres in the districts, and the second, the beginning of a tendency among urban craftsmen and urban upper caste citizens to move into the rural areas.

Many small kingdoms came up during this phase. These minor kings could assert their surplus appropriating right on the subordinate village communities. Whether the emergence of local kingdoms was the direct outcome of the entry of caste elites into the rural areas, or because of wealth differentiation among villagers themselves is not, however, clear from Kosambi's account. Kosambi, nevertheless, seems to have developed the idea that with the decline of centralised Mauryan empire, the earlier state control on land began to decline and *came to be substituted by private landownership of a local king or his retinue in village*. However, this process reached its climax after the decline of Harshavardhana's empire around the middle of the 7th century A.D. Kosambi depicts this phase as "Feudalism from above" under which "an emperor or powerful king levied tribute from subordinates who still ruled in their own right and did what they liked within their own territories – as long as they paid the paramount ruler". Only at a much later stage after "a class of landowners developed within a village between the state and peasantry" could it wield armed power over the local population.

Kosambi traces in this the genesis of "Feudalism from below".[4]

The synoptic view of Kosambi's model traces how there was evolution of supposedly "landed property", from the stage when it was owned by a state power to the stage when there emerged community ownership of village land exercised only by brahmans as exclusively dominant members.[5] The ownership rights on land held by others became frozen by implication. How did such community ownership impose its writ on peasant producers and why should it, at all, be called feudal, is, however, not evident from his analysis. What his model tries to show is the changing relation between the state power and the village community. The former is forced "to protect and encourage [such] private settlements (of a brahman community) on condition of paying in kind, much lighter taxes than under the Mauryeans".[6]

R.S. Sharma, dwelling, though in a somewhat eclectic fashion, more on detailed historico-empirical findings, seeks to build up a seemingly consistent model. But Sharma never tries to build up the required theoretical postulates of a feudal economy on the basis of which we could test his findings and observations. He stresses more on the construction of an empirical postulate of land-ownership in ancient India, without underscoring its theoretical underpinning. On the other hand, in his projection, imposed social obligation confronted by a sudra labour in a brahmanic society, amounts to feudal serfdom. However, he does not explain how this was feasible in the midst of a mobility prone peasantry and in a land-abundant situation.

In our view, Sharma's analysis is theoretically not an improvement on that of Kosambi. We, therefore, need not detail the empirical parameters of his conclusion. For better or worse, he tries to relate so-called private property in land to the social existence form of labour power without bringing state as a variable in the process. A succinct expression of his view is "land is assigned to the cultivator (*Karsaka*) by the landowner (*Kshetraswami*), the king being entitled only to the fruits of improvement made in the land in absence of owners".[7] But what cannot be grasped from his analysis is the material form in which the social presupposition of private land-ownership exercised by a brahman or Kshatriya elite found its manifestation in ancient India.

Romila Thapar's treatment deserves closer attention. Unlike Kosambi and R.S. Sharma, her analysis does not find in ancient India comparable generic economic systems of pre-modern Europe, such as slavery or feudalism. She outlines the process of evolution of a "lineage mode of production" into a system of private land-ownership during the

Mauryan period, the primary state formation being a necessary axle in the process.

A lineage, as defined by Thapar,[8] is "a corporate group of unilineal Kin with a formalized system of authority". Several unilineal descent groups go to make up a clan which "traces its origin to an actual or mythical founding ancestor". In this sense, clan is a system of extended lineage. Since the basic unit in such a system is the extended family of several generations, the relations between the supposed kin family and descent groups are based on the system of marriage alliances, involving circulation of women and wealth within it. In such a scheme of things, Thapar visualises the emergence of a jural community from "the dominant authentic lineage segments". This jural community exercising control over production and wealth constituted the sub-community of clan elites and claimed obedience, gifts, presentations from others belonging to the non-kin groups. Myths of origin became significant in emphasising the superior status of the elites on whom were dependent a heterogeneous group of commoners for materialising their livelihood and labour service.

A clan dominated by the kin family under the lineage system inexorably developed a stratification, first between senior and junior lineages and then, another between lineage and non-lineage groups. Senior lineages were the brahman, kshatriya and vaisya households, junior lineages, the *Vis*. If lineage status (i.e., senior or junior) was the sole determinant of rights and duties among members of a clan, what forced differentiation within a particular lineage group – senior or junior? Thapar appears to be ambivalent about this.[9]

According to Romila Thapar during the earlier stages, clan land was held by both senior lineages of the *rajanyas* and the junior lineages of *vis*, the former having only landholding right and the latter functioning only as cultivators. Since at that stage *rajanyas* were mainly chariot-driving raiders, collecting crops and cattle from other village – settled clans and *vis* were supposed to take care of rotational cultivation from land where it settled, it seems that Thapar does not suspend the possibility of a common descent of both. Then how does she explain functional differentiation among them? She speculates that a claim to differentiation might have been the consequence of "differentiation between elder sons and younger sons", or "ability of some to lead in cattle-raids, to protect the clan [by physical force] to establish new settlements. . . ." etc.

Rajanyas, so differentiated, claimed obedience and prestations from *vis*. The priests became necessary to ritualise and thus, legitimise the differential propensity and power towards plunder, pillage and clan protection found among members known as *rajanyas* sprouting from the ranks of ordinary clan members. The priests assuming the status of brahmans claimed fees or *dakshina* from *rajanyas* for their service. The occupation of vaisyas became that of receiving and storing cattle from *Yajmanas*. Therefore, the occupation of vaisyas arose not from any acknowledged power of plunder or ritual service which gave occupational status to the *rajanyas* and priests. On the basis of literary evidence from *Rig Veda*, Thapar constructs her speculative model to explain, among other things, how and why stratification within a lineage-based clan society of the early Vedic stage developed.[10]

While one can explain the rise of *rajanyas* on the basis of their unequal physical power, the ritual superiority of priests cannot be explained unless one assumes their unequal capacity to hoodwink not only the *rajanyas* but also others. Even if one accepts this possibility, it is not clear how could such individual attributes as having extraordinary physical prowess or the capacity to deceive be institutionalised in caste terms without any objective material basis.

It is held that the *vis* was the only productive plank of a clan society and that it voluntarily agreed to be the lowest rung of the stratified order. The economic function of *vis* became agricultural cultivation and rearing livestocks on clan land. Its social function was reduced to paying prestations to *rajanyas* and the brahmans and vaishyas. What objective compulsion forced the members belonging to *vis* to accept a position of socio-economic subordination remains unanswered.

During the later Vedic stage, the growing requirement of paying more prestations and gifts forced, Thapar argues, the *vis* to practice and extend sedentary cultivation, and with this germinated the household economy within a *vis*. Groups of clans began to settle in tracts known as *janapada*. Each *janapada* developed its *paur-janapada* or urban headquarters. Those who began to rule *janapadas* came to be known as rajas – selected from among the *rajanyas* or from an assembly of *janapada* rajas. Each raja took a sixth of the total production yielded by a *janapada* and began to rule from his seat in the *paur-janapada*. The emergence of household economy within the lineage system began to proliferate with a shift towards settled cultivation, and the *vis* became the pivot around which the household economy claiming "permanent usage" over land began to develop.

The *rajanyas*, now converted to kshatriyas, were anxious to ensure that prestations continued flowing to them from the *vis*, and this became the main instrument of surplus redistribution among people belonging to senior lineages. The household economy of *vis* came to be lorded over by a patriarchal head, *Grhapati*. A *grhapati* came to acquire family holding over the land it worked. An extended family of *Grhapati* cultivated land with the help of family labour as well as with that of *sudras* and *dasas* who came from outside. During this period there also developed clan households of kshatriyas, brahmans and vaishyas, the former two depending more on presentations and gifts from lower ranks and, the latter, from "cultivation and cattle breeding". The erstwhile functions within a *vis* drove it to be an amorphous social category in Romila Thapar's account.

She postulates the development of the next stage that witnessed further extension of cultivation, when the members of *janapadas* multiplied in number. Each *janapada* chief or raja became more prosperous. This prepared, according to Thapar, the objective preconditions for the rise of primary state formation. Such state formation emerged in order to avoid conflict among rajas and to perpetuate the production mechanism possessed by *janapadas*. The extension of cultivation paved the way for permanent claim of the *grhapati's* family on land it worked.

Growth of trade and commerce between a *janapada* and its urban centre, and among the *janapadas* themselves, brought about territorial delimitation of each *janapada* inhabited by several clan societies. The *grhapati's* family appeared as the unit of production and the *janapada* became a unit of sovereign territory. A raja being the symbol of political authority and a *grhapati* family as a unit of production tended to erode the objective need for a lineage-based clan society. Clan control was replaced by the family control of land exercised by a *grhapati*. The new agrarian economy became essentially a peasant economy where the new private landowners descending from erstwhile *grhapatis* of senior or junior lineages stood in opposition to sudra and *dasa* agricultural labourers.

Romila Thapar's model, as briefly outlined above, focuses our attention on two mutually interacting identifiable processes. First, the process of transition of early and later Vedic Indo-Gangetic societies belonging to the lineage system to the post-Vedic village communities of, by and large, a non-lineage character. Second, the process of mutation and re-articulation undergone by the system of *gana-sangha* chiefships of Vedic period leading to primary state formations during the post-Vedic period.

Romila Thapar seems to postulate (although she does not say so clearly), that widening of settled agriculture and increase in the amount of surplus generation played the key role in the transition of a society, economy and their internal correlation among interest groups from the pre-Vedic to the post-Vedic stage. The institution of the monarch or the raja came into being. The only conspicuous absence in her otherwise elegant model is an analysis of the contours of change in the specific material condition of labour that must have necessarily accompanied the transition of pre-state lineage-based society into non-lineage social formations. The speculative account that she builds to explain the genesis of caste stratification within a clan society characterised by cattle raid and pastoral-type crop raising does not require any objective rationale of collectivity.

A lineage society with open frontiers is unlikely to encourage exploitative status of a few and allow the *rajanyas* to impose their social privileges and rights on a *vis*. At the next stage, when household economy became the general feature of lineage society, it is not clear from her model, what material compulsion forced a household to pay prestations and gifts to members claiming senior lineages, when members of junior lineages retained the option of migrating elsewhere.

Thapar says that with the erosion of lineage society after primary state formation, there began to occur a rise of "private land-ownership" of erstwhile *grhapatis*. It is not clear by what mechanism a *grhapati* appropriated the requisite condition of labour so as to secure his right of land-ownership. In our view, "private land-ownership" even as a *de facto* phenomenon cannot be derived from her model as she does not specify its associated material condition of labour. What can, at best, be derived is, what we may call, private landholding which did not necessarily require appropriation of a specific condition of labour. Thapar deals with a stage *when labourers could migrate and could themselves appropriate fully their own condition of labour.*

Since *property* in any premodern (e.g., slave, handicraft etc.) or modern form (e.g., capital) is in essence a relation between the labour power and the appropriation of its condition (i.e., the means of production), the concept of property must necessarily have two theoretical presuppositions. First, that any property must necessarily appear as appropriation of specific condition of labour; the subsidiary one must be the differential identity-specifics of property from those of non-property. Thereby one can differentiate the concept of property used in the science of political economy from that assuming a mere jural form.

The jural concept of property covers the basic essence of property as appropriation of the condition of labour, but in its naive interpretation it obscures this essence and harps only on its non-essential aspects, namely, the physical transferability of the object or its inheritability, saleability etc. As a consequence, the jural concept of property does not distinguish such legal possession that does not really appropriate condition of labour from that which does. My residential house or even uncultivated farmland is my property as it satisfies the legal criteria of identifying property in jural sense, but in the sense of political economy, it is not property, as by assumption, my residence or farmland is used *only as one of the objects of my consumption not as appropriation of a specific condition of labour*. The subsidiary theoretical presupposition which helps one to distinguish property from non-property is that while property exists and can reproduce itself only as a *relation*, possession of non-property does not. If I give my physical labour to raise more crops from my land than I require for myself, that does not make land, so cultivated by my own labour, as my property in the sense of political economy (not, however, in jural sense), it is only my nonproperty possession.

Now let us have a different hypothetical situation. I cultivate a piece of land by my own labour for my own subsistence. The condition of my labour, i.e., the land (which I cultivate) is freely available. My labour activity gives me a surplus. Now either just to pay obeisance to a military chief or to avoid his possible wrath, I voluntarily or involuntarily agree to part with a portion of surplus to him as gift or tribute. Such payment of tribute does not make the land I cultivate chief's property. My gift or tribute is contingent only on my decision to cultivate the land. Payment of such gift or tribute is essentially a transfer payment. Since property in the sense of political economy is in essence a relation between pure possessor of labour power and pure possessor of the condition of materialising that labour power, all other categories of social surplus entitlement except those arising out of this relation between the owner of material conditions of production and the owner of labour power, cannot be deemed to originate from property in the sense of political economy. In other words, all surplus-producing societies cannot be characterised as those which can be deemed as necessarily based on proprietary rights on land, labour or any other material means of production.

None of the models of Kosambi, Sharma and Thapar use "land ownership" or "landed property" with its proper theoretical underpinnings. What they try to do is to implicitly define land-ownership mainly in terms of characteristics found in early medieval and ancient India, namely, transferability of title and inheritability of land-holding, subsidiarily in terms of unrequited surplus transfer from direct producers to fictive or actual holders of land. Their absence of a theoretical insight into the concept of property and the resultant confusion led them to construct diametrically opposite hypotheses on the genesis of land rights in ancient India. For Kosambi, it is the state formations that precede consummation of ownership rights in land, or feudal basis by upper caste people during the phase, "feudalism from above". For Romila Thapar, "the question of ownership of cultivated land is the crux of the issue *which leads to the necessity of government*". (italics added)

We do not, however, suggest that with our concept of property right it will be convenient for us to identify the stages of development of private surplus appropriating social rights during those periods. For a meaningful attempt towards a theory of economic evolution for any oriental society (conceptualised by many as a society where private property in land, labour or craft as an appropriation of material condition of labour did not develop) it is necessary to make a departure from a theoretically meaningful concept of property right in land or labour.

It is widely admitted that in ancient India various forms of societal use of land were found. Since the land-man ratio was high, there always existed vast stretches of land which were not cultivated. Such wasteland acted as leverage of power for the labouring population in general, and the direct producers, in particular. In the settled agricultural regions, there was land where state-sponsored *sita* cultivation (hence, corresponding village settlement) was predominant. There was also common land which was largely village pastures, and land possessed by peasants.

Historians claim that peasant possessions in land were within the *rastra* category of cultivations, where those who initiated village settlements could claim a reward or prestations from the peasant possessors. There was also land held absolutely by peasant holders or tenants, the latter giving a percentage of produce to the "landholders".

Since all the multiple categories of land use outlined above bore concomitant obligations of paying taxes or tribute out of surplus produce to the immediate superior powers – social and state – two kinds of observations regarding the nature of property have been made by the concerned scholars. The first kind is common among the European historiographers working on pre-British India. It states that land in India was always a state property. The second kind made mostly by Marxist scholars is that a phenomenon of virtual land-ownership is found in all the stages of Indian history of the pre-British period. While the common criteria used by both for identifying the ownership right in land are surplus entitlement and sovereign power of a supposed owner (state or raja or *grhapati*) to redistribute land at his own discretion. Neither questions how labour was controlled for extraction of surplus. Indeed any theory of land-ownership for pre-British India must necessarily delineate its corresponding specific paradigm of appropriation of the condition of labour.

None of the exercises so far available on land-ownership by state or *grahapati*, either explains the dialectics of relationship between such landowners and the direct producers, nor explains why such land-ownership failed to assume even a nominal politico-legal form as late as during the Mughal period in the 17th century. In fact, no theory of Indian precapitalism (if the generic term "pre-capitalism" conveys the pre-British stages of development) is likely to be meaningful unless it is capable of analysing dialectical interconnections at least between modes of surplus production and distribution and the general absence of politico-legal emergence of private property in land in pre-British India.

Instead of making relevant enquiries, some historians have constructed a model of pre-British Indian economy that supposedly shows a subdued manifestation of European stages of precapitalism. The theory of Indian feudalism built so far is the product of this brand of intellectual ventures.

All the three models, we mentioned earlier, seem to have been the outcome, perhaps unwittingly, of this line of venture. Among them, Kosambi and Sharma are more categorical in their generic formulations on ancient Indian economy. Romila Thapar, contrary to her avowed objective, seems to have lent broad support to them by concentrating her effort on the laborious task of delineating the process of evolution of social formations of Ganges valley that ended with the rise of primary state formation and of a class of private landowners by the mid-first millennium BC.

Since we have to depend on secondary sources, we can outline a plausible theory of structural evolution of Indian economy through logical interactions between existing hypotheses and widely acknowledged historical data. We, therefore, delineate our path through analysis of the available secondary sources on pre-British India.

To start with, we choose Kosambi's model of Indian feudalism for critical evaluation. Between Kosambi and Sharma, the former seems to be more careful in constructing a theoretically consistent model and to have more persuasive reasoning and ordering of historical data. Through a brief methodological critique of Kosambi's model on the genesis of Indian feudalism we arrive at positive formulations on the early stages of development in pre-British India.

Notes

1. Ideally, the point of departure should have been the stage when the social economy in India began to witness the emergence of, what Romila Thapar would call, "primary state formation". Because the emergence of primary state formation decisively indicates the stage of society at which it began to produce enough surplus to feed the primary state power. But scholarly investigation into this stage in India is not sufficiently detailed to warrant our attention.

Under primary state formation a number of village societies or communities having ties of mutual kinship constituted a larger society that for either successful reproduction of its constituent units or for any other unitary purpose (for instance, protection against external interference or for organising external venture), assumed the form of a local state power. The secondary state formation on the other hand, imposed its command over the local state powers and collected taxes from subordinate village communities through coercive methods. Its mode of reproduction made it function independent of the village communities. In the pre-modern stage, the secondary state formations in India assumed, in general, the form of imperial rule either having its own militia or commanding obligatory armed support from subordinate local kings or both. Therefore, the basis of power subsumed by a secondary state formation was necessarily alien to the power base constituted by local kings or monarchs represented by the primary state formation.

2. The 10th century European historiography by and large emphasises the difference between the primeval modes of social formations in the eastern and western parts of the European continent. In the modern period, Marc Bloch highlights this difference, "The greater parts of the Slav East in no way belonged to it [the European West]. . . It is impossible to consider their economic conditions and those of their western neighbours together, in the same object of scientific study. Their wholly different social structure and very special path of development forbid each a confusion absolutely. . . " cf. Perry Anderson, *Passages From Antiquity to Feudalism* (London, 1978), pp. 15-17.

3. Kosambi's model starts with extant modes of land administration during

the late Mauryan period. He refers to two categories of state-sponsored cultivation that characterised the relation between secondary state power and civil society. The first is *sita* category of cultivation carried out by peasant societies or communities under direct crown supervision. The second is the *rastra* category of cultivation, manned by peasant societies which had their settlements under the patronage of upper caste brahman or kshatriya elites or individual crown officials having huge land grants from the state. In Kosambi's account there is no reference to a third category of surplus-producing type of cultivation by village societies. It is implied that all villages had their settlements either directly under crown initiative or under the initiative of others who secured land grants from the monarch. Thus, a state, in his account, is the direct initiator or indirect promoter of settled cultivation during the post-Vedic period. Cf. D.D. Kosambi, *An Introduction to the Study of Indian History*, 2nd revised edition (Bombay, 1975), pp. 227-37.

4. *Ibid.*, Ch.IX *Passim*, pp. 295-341.
5. *Ibid.*, p. 329.
6. *Ibid.*, p. 302.
7. Cf. R.S. Sharma, "Stages in Ancient Indian Economy", *Enquiry*, No.4, 1960.
8. Romila Thapar, *From Lineage to State* (Bombay, 1984).
9. It seems that a *vis*, as conceptaulised by Thapar, was a moving clan (based, however, on a common descent or lineage) that survived through rotational cultivation and cattle raid on other clans. In this sense, *vis* was itself a clan society in its primeval form. But under which particular process a *vis* was reduced to be a junior lineage group of a bigger clan dominated by a senior lineage group is not clearly postulated by Thapar. Again what prompted the members of a senior lineage group to divide themselves into those who professed mythical power (i.e., brahmans) and those who practised brute force (i.e., kshatriyas) is not clear from her reckoning.
10. *Ibid.*, pp. 31-32.

2.2: On Theoretical Presuppositions of Kosambi's Model of Feudalism in India

Before we denude the significant empirical findings of Kosambi given in his *Introduction to the Study of Indian History*, we will make a brief review of the implicit theoretical presuppositions that lie behind his otherwise pioneering attempt at studying the dynamics of pre-state as well as post-state situations in ancient India.

His first presupposition is that *a surplus-producing society at its early stage of development may engender class division within itself on the basis of a totemic or religious belief system.* This presupposition is implicit also in Romila Thapar's account. According to it, a material foundation of class society originates from a primitive subjective response of mankind to inexplicably immense power of the physical universe.

Kosambi is of the opinion that every urban civilisation is necessarily based on a particular category of class exploitation. Therefore, the ancient Indian civilisation of Harappa and Mohenjo-daro was based on class exploitation of surplus-producers. Such class exploitation, in his view, was mediated not by property relation but by a set of totemic or religious beliefs pursued by the labouring population.[1]

Even after a supposed Aryan invasion had destroyed Harappa and other cities around 1700 BC and perhaps set in motion new technique of production with iron-nailed plough, such developments did not cause a major departure from the old Indus system of ritual and sacrifice as the dominant modes of surplus distribution. Such modes of surplus distribution persisted both in the old northern Aryan settlements (i.e., Indus basin).and in the eastern areas of new settlement (i.e., Gangetic valley). The fundamental reason of this continuity of the ritualistic modes of surplus distribution is that Aryans, who were themselves a pastoral tribe, possessed no superior belief system that could dispense with pre-Aryan ritualistic practices relating to social production and distribution.

Thus, the destruction of the pre-Aryan cities and the introduction of a new technique of production by invading Aryans, could expand agricultural production and Aryan spheres of influence, but such material developments possessed nothing in themselves to destroy pre-Aryan beliefs in ritual and sacrificial practices. The latter on the other hand, found its justification in the new situation. The consequence was the appearance of caste divisions within the new Aryan society.

To maintain the ritual performers and warriors the new Aryans stipulated surplus payment on the part of husbandmen to those two dominant groups among Aryans in the form of ritual prestations and sacrificial gifts.[2] The only new dimension an erstwhile Aryan tribal society could accomplish in India, was to develop a new group within its control, constituted by *dasas*. The *dasas* were gifts extracted by Aryan warriors from the conquered non-Aryans in India. Kosambi seems to have developed a hypothesis that at the Yajurvedic stage Aryans without giving up their pastoral nature could make early transition to a four caste society[3] by virtue of possessing superior technique of cultivation and appropriating the knowledge of pottery, weaving, carpentry, etc. from the now decimated city culture of Indus civilisation.[4] 'The principal change in the productive relations [at this stage compared to the earlier] was the formation of servile class from the conquered *Dasa* population'. But 'the *dasa* was not a chattel slave, because individual property among the Aryans had not developed sufficiently nor [was developed] extensive commodity and surplus production for trade'.[5]

Kosambi claims to have used 'the method of dialectical materialism' in his analysis. Thus, it was expected that he would unfold the dialectical interactions between the old and new modes of production that brought into being an objective process of surplus distribution. But, in his account, the subjective belief in ritual and sacrifice continued to persist and the objective process of surplus distribution did not undergo change in spite of changes in technique of production. In fact, in Kosambi's analysis, no dialectical reasoning is used to explain why either the rise of ritual and sacrifice among pre-Aryan Indus people occurred or why it persisted among members of post-Aryan societies. In standard Marxian view the primitive myths associated with rituals and sacrifices grew up broadly as subjective human perceptions of the relation between human species and their external being - nature. Since early human perceptions of any such relation is essentially mythical in character, those myths reflected a subjective alienation between a human perception of reality and the actual physical process of nature. In this sense all ritual and sacrificial rites on the perceived modes of sustaining human livelihood (e.g., rites associated with hunting or fishing, taming and rearing useful animals or trees, fertility, or food gathering) were products of the human brain. While myths represent relational alienation between human perception and an objective process of reality that manifests in the cycle of behaviour of physical universe, they cannot be instrumental in determining the objective social nature of relations within a human collectivity.

The basic dynamics of a human society must necessarily have its genesis from within the paradigm of dialectical relations among its members. Though one cannot deny that a dialectical interaction between a primitive mythical perception of nature and the actual process of nature itself may cast a shadow over primitive social formation, such dialectical interaction by itself cannot govern the basic objective dynamics of social formation.

Again if religion not force, ritual and sacrifice not plunder, acted as causative factors in the genesis of class and in shaping class antagonism within the pre-Aryan society of Harappa and Mohenjo-daro, as Kosambi tries to argue, it is necessary to explain how ritual and sacrifice evolved as an objective historical process with which both direct producers and urban surplus appropriators of such society had to forge an essential dialectical unity. But Kosambi's interpretation makes religious belief system, a subjective phenomenon, the point of departure, and he argues that primitive ritual and sacrifice paved the way for the emergence of an objective phenomenon, i.e., the class society. Except in the form of ritual and sacrifice class antagonism had no other manifestation in that society, although Kosambi presupposes its existence without assigning any objective reason.[6] Kosambi fails to remember that a social process of appropriation of surplus by a non-labouring stratum from labourers in a class society - which is by itself an objective process - must have as its determinant only a prior objective precondition. Such precondition must necessarily be an objective requirement for material appropriation by the non-labouring stratum of the material conditions of labour.

Thus the second theoretical presupposition that a surplus producing society can develop class division mainly on its a priori socio-ideological basis follows from his first presupposition. This type of formulation, having its genesis in Hegel is entirely opposed to materialist dialectics as visualised by Marx.

Kosambi argues on the one hand that the objective change in the technique of production as stated above, involved a change in the social relation of production within new Aryan societies without, however, specifying the mechanism of that change. He observes, on the other hand, a continuity that 'the first Brahmins were a result of interaction between the Aryan priesthood and the ritually superior priesthood of Indus culture'.[7] His observation on the genesis of Brahmanism does not bring into focus the role of the supposed change in the relations of production (in post-Aryan societies) as an explanatory variable. He explains the genesis of the brahman caste in terms of a supposed interaction between the pre-Aryan and post-Aryan priesthood. Kosambi's reasoning here sounds somewhat eclectic and certainly does not grow out of known Marxian postulates.

Kosambi's *third theoretical presupposition is that it is only the rise of the institution of kingship (state formation) that ensured the unambiguous growth of settled agrarian societies and private property in land.*

Kosambi does not identify the objective forces that paved the way for the rise of a kingship institution among Aryan societies. He tries to answer only in terms of social dominance of kshatriyas and brahmans over vaisyas – the three early Aryan castes possessing sudra helots from conquered non-Aryan tribes. But why and how chieftainship grew up either among Aryans or non-Aryan tribal societies are not made adequately explicit.

Kosambi mentions that specific group of non-Aryans such as the *Nagas*, who were in perpetual conflict with the Aryans had their own state power. He does not explain how the state power of *Nagas* was developed? Nor does he explain the compulsions that led to the state formations among Aryans. He vaguely suggests that it was Aryan absorption of non-Aryan tribal societies or non-Aryan absorption of Aryan tribes that explains the rise of kingship institutions along with its caste-class syndrome. Without delineating the causes that led to the transition of tribal *janapadas* into kshatriya-brahman dominated *janapadas*, he only highlights the violent forms of the transition. But why violence and war actually took place in course of the transition, and why a post transitional Aryan caste society relapsed into old pre-Aryan religious and ritual practice as the norm of social distribution is not explained. Moreover, what prevented non-Aryan tribal societies (who often possessed their own state) from adopting plough cultivation without entering into the Aryan social fold, is not explained. What one can infer from Kosambi's account is that a dominant group of Aryans, though having superior technique of cultivation, did not possess adequate labour force that could help them in cultivation.

Kosambi visualises Aryan incursion into the areas of non-Aryan pastoral settlement so as to meet its growing requirement of cultivating labour. If force and violence were used by Aryans to capture labouring population from non-Aryan tribal societies, those must have been the necessary traits of an Aryan social formation. But Kosambi insists only on religious ritual and sacrifice and does not categorise force and violence as the basis of surplus distribution within an Aryan social order. While the institution of kingship was based on ritual and sacrificial rites, conflicts among the kings always assumed extremely violent form. Kosambi seems to have failed to account for ritual and sacrifice in a society, the development of which was, in his own account, based on violence and force.

In Kosambi's account, the relationship between an Aryan king and his subordinate *janapada* and *paur janapada* was essentially a relation of domination and servitude that manifested itself in obligatory surplus payments by peasants to the king and the practice of obligatory surplus generation by vaisyas with the help of sudra labour. The *paur janapadas* were merely intermediary institutions that collected on behalf of a king, the *bali* tax from *janapadas*. Before the development of Aryan *janapadas* and the corresponding emergence of a caste-class order, 'a brahmin member of an Aryan tribe had the same *property rights* as all others except its chief'[8] (italics added). This suggests that even an Aryan tribe with its priests had developed the phenomenon of uniform *property* rights.

While Kosambi visualises *extraordinary* 'property right' of a chief in an Aryan tribe, he nowhere explains the nature of this extraordinariness or the 'property right' itself.

What Kosambi reports is that the Aryan tribal groups of Kasi-Kosala-Videha regions could form 'the great Gangetic kingdom'. Such kingdom initiated a social process of coalescence between the priestly function of brahmans and the plundering function of chiefs (later turned into kshatriyas). The supposed alliance between the priests and the chiefs was formed in order to appropriate under 'the garb of ritual and sacrifice' the fruits of labour of the Aryan tribe (later turned into vaisyas).[9] From his account it appears that 'property right' of a chief originated from his social exploitation of husbandmen belonging to an inferior social order. Here Kosambi finds correlation among the four simultaneous developments: (*a*) rise of state formation; (*b*) widening of the practice of settled cultivation; (*c*) unforeseen degree of sophistication of priestly rituals to be performed only by brahmans who became indispensable to kshatriyas; and (*d*) the disappearance of the tribal character of Aryans who had to form their four-caste social order by awarding pure labouring status to sudras.

In this account of the genesis of the four-caste social order of Aryans as explained by Kosambi, it is evident that Aryan mode of ritual practices grew, not from any subjective religious belief system, but as an objective necessity on the part of non-productive caste people to procure their means of subsistence through religious practices (by brahmans) and physical force (by kshatriyas).

In the new Aryan society the *paur janapadas* became the administrative as well as mercantile headquarters of the *janapadas*. From *paur-janapadas*, kshatriyas, brahmans and vaisyas discharged their respective functions, namely administrative, ritualistic, trading as well as supervisory functions. Sudras living in rural areas discharged their labour service in the cultivation of *janapada* land. This, in brief, is Kosambi's model of the caste society of Aryans which in his view, implies a higher level of production [compared to the earlier Aryans' tribal society], regular settlements, the inevitable decay of tribal organisation with the rise of *a new type of property*.[10] But he does not specify what this 'new type of property' is.

It is clear from his account that the kshatriyas and brahmans were the surplus appropriating castes. Since in the new society, the vaisyas rendered various functions, except labour services, they appeared more as surrogates to their upper caste patrons, and not as having a specific functional trait of its own. It is also clear that sudras constituted the labouring population attached to land in a *janapada* territory. Sudras cultivated land under the supervision of vaisya husbandmen, but nowhere does Kosambi show how a specific type of surplus entitlement of an Aryan upper caste grew up from a specific category of appropriation of the material condition of labour or a specific type of property relation. Since any property presupposes a specific mode of appropriation of the material condition of labour and in Kosambi's Aryan society nothing indicates the specificity of such appropriation of the material condition of labour in agriculture, his theory of emergence of a 'new type of property' in an Aryan civil society is entirely untenable.

With above theoretical presuppositions which can hardly claim Marxist methodological lineage, Kosambi develops his model of Indian feudalism.

Notes

1. 'No urban culture without a class division has been known till the 20th century socialist revolutions. It follows that we shall have to reason out the class structure (as well as the productive structural) of the Indus cities directly from the (archaeological) evidence without the aid of [in absence of] historical writings. That there was a sharp class division at Harappa and Mohenjo-daro is clear from the different types of dwellings excavated. . . . The main question is, how was this class structure maintained?. . . The answer seems to lie in religion'.
Cf. D.D. Kosambi, *op.cit.*, Ch.III, Sections 3.2 and 3.3, pp. 56-66.
2. *Ibid.*, Ch. IV, Sec. 4.4.
3. It is, however, not clear from Kosambi's account how the four-caste Aryan society came into being. Kosambi in one place is categorical, 'the first Brahmins were a result of interaction between the Aryan priesthood and the ritually superior priesthood of Indus culture' (p.102). While the above observation suggests a continuity between pre-Aryan and Aryan social orders, he does not explain why and how a pre-Aryan social order based on ritual and sacrifice came into being. On the other hand, he repeatedly underscores the egalitarian social ethos pervading within a non-Aryan tribal order. He again does not answer a pertinent question that may be raised about the possible relation of mutuality between the practicing of ritual and sacrifice and mode of susistence through hunting, irregular food gathering etc. on the part of non-Aryan people. Kosambi makes the following comment about non-Aryans:

'The basic feature of a primitive life in the *Stone Age* was a meagre and irregular supply of food. This means what it had to be shared on terms that involved no other obligation than reciprocal sharing at some future date . . . . It is also important to note that the mechanism of sharing was never a calculated transaction. The love of display, the potlatch for the validation of some transactions, ceremonial feasts without number, and primitive generosity all play their part. . . Similarly, for the exchange between groups. . . . The exchange is of gifts, made voluntarily between partners in some definite relationship. No gift can be refused, but it implies an obligation to return the accepted equivalent in some other form' (p. 25).
4. *Ibid.*, p.96.
5. *Ibid.*, pp. 97-98.
6. In fact Kosambi admits, 'the ideas of ritual and sacrifice develop before (the emergence of) classes - as first efforts on the part of mankind to control a mysterious environment beyond its logical and technical power' (*Ibid.*, p.23). This is absolutely correct for it points out the independence of the social process of development of ritual and sacrifice from that of emergence of class society. But he does not reason

out what could be the social process of growth of the Indian class society at the Harappa stage, if class society had at all existed at that stage.
7. *Ibid.,* Ch.IV., p.102.
8. *Ibid.,* p.106.
9. Kosambi does not think that husbandmen or *vaisyas* accepted the status cheerfully. Kosambi observes : 'The Vaisya (settler, husbandmen) and sudra (helots) [later plundered from non-Aryan tribes along with cattle raid] are to be exploited for the advantage of the ruling warrior castes with the brahmin priest's help. The struggle with the vaisya was earlier, reflected in the Rigvedic strife between the collective Maruts (peasantry or *vis*) and their [the tribal] chief, Indra. We are later told that these Maruts are the peasantry (*vis*): 'Indra eats them up as the king the peasants'. *Ibid.,* p.100.
10.*Ibid.,* p.107.

2.3: Important Empirical Postulates of Kosambi's Model

Kosambi identifies late Mauryan or early Gupta period as that when Indian feudalism began to develop 'from above'. His implicit assumption seems to be that the pre-Mauryan stage of Indian agriculture represented a sort of quasi-tribal mode of production that could yield only tributes to local kings; conflicts and realignment among whom brought into being the powerful centralised state power of Mauryans. With the eclipse of the centralised administration of the Guptas, which is supposed to be the consequence of wider areas of village settlements, a band of semi-independent local *Samantas* having armed retinues developed.

The system of tax collection by *Samantas* from subordinate villages became widespread in various areas. This development set in motion a process which Kosambi calls, 'feudalism from below'. However, Kosambi seems uncertain about the exact period when 'feudalism from below' became operative,[1] although, in his reckoning, 'feudalism from above' began to emerge since 6th century A.D.

Kosambi does not build a theoretical construct for 'feudalism from above' under which the crown could assume the role of a feudal lord forcing sudra labour to settle in crown land in order to yield surplus for the monarch. Neither does he specify the socio-economic compulsions that led to the transition of the Aryan social order from its tribal pastoral phase to its four-caste feudal economic phase. He does not explain how 'feudalism from above' could synchronise itself with a supposedly reverse but incipient process of development, stigmatised by him as 'feudalism from below'. What he suggests is that the local *Samantas* built up a competing process of surplus appropriation. Kosambi explains how and to what extent the empire could procure surplus from crown land and how an intermediary 'class of landowners' came into being with the decline of the centralised state and town economy. But one can hardly discern from his account the dialectics of the development process that on the one hand depressed the centralised state as surplus appropriator and on the other threw up a civilian class of powerful 'landowners'.

While relative change in the power relations of the centralised state and *Samanta* landowners seeks to demarcate feudalism from above from that from below, Kosambi seems to suggest a novel basis on which power apparatus had developed in the ancient society of India. He categorically states that 'social superstition in ritual and sacrifice' not 'social coercion' was instrumental in such a transition. To him such superstition is responsible for the 'non-emergence of chattel slavery' of the Graeco-Roman type. In Kosambi's account it is an inbuilt social psyche of the labouring population that induced it to succumb to sacrificial rites so as to germinate a feudal social order in India. His identification of Indian feudalism, not based on theoretical conceptualization, is entirely dependent on *a few* empirical postulates of general feudal order, as outlined by Marion Gibbs for Western Europe,[2] namely, low level of techniques of production, primitive level of division of labour, production for use rather than for a wider market, *compulsory* labour service on the lord's estate, political decentralisation, conditional holding of land by lords on some kind of service tenure etc.[3]

Kosambi admits that many of Gibb's empirical specifics were not available in India when 'feudalism form above' was set in motion. In his view, the 'feudalism from above' in India failing to develop either 'demesne farming' or 'new techniques' [of production] is 'a basic contrast with medieval European achievement'.[4] The villages, after ruralisation of craft and ruling castes had taken place, produced surplus for the monarch who could impose a politically centralised administration over 'semi-autonomous' *janapadas*. Although, the centralised state of crown at this stage of development appears as 'landowner' or, at least, deliverer of feudalism, he does not explain how the semi-autonomy of a *janapada* can be reconciled to 'feudalism from above'.

Kosambi asserts that sudra labour's service on crown land was quasi-compulsory in the sense that if a sudra cultivator neglected his cultivation, land (his means of livelihood) was to be transferred from him to another. But on the admitted basis of a normative stipulation as laid down in the *Arthasastra*, he arrives at his observation that no labour could desert *sita* land. He does not, however, cite any unassailable evidence from real life situations of sudras to support his argument. He only cites references to archaeological evidences from a wide variety of regions. The only deduction that follows from this is that sudras in crown land formed the bulk of independent agricultural labour that was ready to pay a portion of produce to the crown. Nothing more, nothing less.

He stated that brahmans or merchants were assigned land grants by the centralised state in order to get jungles cleared with the help of sudra labour in order to extend cultivation and to help grantees in appropriating, in return, a sizeable portion of surplus produced by sudra labour. But Kosambi nowhere specifies the nature of property under 'feudalism from above' nor does he identify the contrasting socio-economic specifics of the Indian variant of feudalism that stood in the way of the 'full flowering' of itself in the European manner.

Again in his concept of 'feudalism from below', *samantas* appear as landowners. On what basis *samantas* appropriated surplus from subordinate villages, or the basis by which a *samanta* appropriated land-ownership Kosambi cannot say. While one cannot dispute the empirical postulate that *samantas* were appropriators of village surplus in their respective domains, this fact by itself does not prove their status as 'landowners'.

In fact the practice of exclusive dependence on a set of empirical postulates, without any theoretical construct, made many scholars question the meaningfulness of the concept of feudalism itself. Based on identifiable empirical specifics of European feudal order as outlined by various authors,[5] some Indian scholars argue that in India feudalism did not exist either during the ancient or early medieval period or for that matter at any stage of Indian history.[6]

Indeed many modern European historians question whether the middle ages of western Europe should at all be labelled 'feudal'.[7] But one has to point out that all the controversies, either on Indian or European feudalism, revolve around contrasting differential empirical postulates of society and economy, natures of state power and labour relations, etc. Perhaps to bail out Marx from trouble, some Marxist scholars claim that Marx was not the architect of the concept of 'feudalism' in the sense he was of the concept of 'competitive capitalism'.[8]

It is certainly true that Marx nowhere 'attempted a systematic exploration' of either the philosophical or historical specificity of feudalism as a *universally valid* historical stage of precapitalist economic formation. It is also true that a major bulk of his analysis of precapitalist economic formations is based on his study of the precapitalist epoch of West Europe. But despite limitations of the scope of his study and informations, what is striking in his analysis is *not what he actually observed, but how he arrives at his observations.*

Marx's method of studying history, rather than his actual findings, leads him to develop a theory of a particular precapitalist economic formation that specifies either the absence or presence of private property as an instrument of appropriation of the material condition of labour. In the case of precapitalist class societies, the contrasting instruments of appropriation of the condition of labour lead Marx to differentiate one type of precapitalist economic formation from another or the precapitalist class societies from that under capitalism itself. While the labour activity for livelihood is a universal phenomenon, the difference among human societies and their natural geographical and other physical environments, determines the differential material conditions of labour. Marx's concept of feudalism distinguishes the specific nature of *extra-economic* mode of appropriation by a few of the material condition of labour of others. Therefore, the existence of feudalism in ancient or medieval India, or in medieval West Europe presupposes an enquiry into the specific form of appropriation of the material condition of social labour and the specific form of the extra-economic relation between an appropriator and the subordinate labourers. If Marx, by using his method of identifying dialectical forces as they appear in the course of human social history, constructs a theory of occidental precapitalism (in which feudalism is taken to be the most matured stage), he did it to confirm the correctness of his method of studying modern capitalism of West Europe. In this sense, Marx's study of a precapitalist class society such as feudalism is an integral part of his study of competitive capitalism. Therefore, if one intends to develop a theory of Indian (or 'oriental') precapitalism by using Marxian method of unfolding materialist dialectics, it is not sufficient to observe whether there existed European empirical postulates of feudalism in India or not. It is, however, necessary to identify the dialectical forces in Indian history that decided the course of structural changes in economy from the various stages of pre-British formations to colonial economic formations.

The pertinent question is, what were the dialectics at a particular stage of development in ancient or medieval India? To answer this, one has to identify the specific material condition of labour in that particular historical stage of pre-British India. This particular methodological specificity that characterises Marxian formulation on feudalism (or any other pre-capitalist society) distinguishes it from others' concepts of feudalism or social formation.

It was indeed the legal practitioners of the seventeenth and eighteenth century Europe who, for the first time, used the term 'feudalism' to denote a system in which 'fief' and 'vassalage' were the dominant empirical features. The French term 'feudalite' can, however, be traced to the beginning of the 16th century. Later those nobles who opposed absolutist state power in their own class interest embraced the concept of 'feudalism' in opposition to the doctrine of absolutism. This started a prolonged controversy over the use of the term in which Montesquieu and Voltaire were also participants.

What is necessary to identify feudalism, as conceptualised by Marx, in a country's history, is to find out whether social production is, by and large, regulated by specific form of at least *de facto* private property in land to which labour is extra-economically forced to remain attached and whether surplus product is appropriated as *revenue* or *rent*. At issue here is not the *extra-economic mode of acquiring surplus* as such (in fact, even under tribal primitivism one may acquire surplus off others' labour), but of *appropriating by extra economic means the material condition of labour*.

There are scholars who emphasise a particular type of political or social paradigm so as to identify the specificity of feudal mode of production. For instance, there has been traditional Marxist scholarship which places more emphasis on the phenomena of politico- legal compulsions imposed by those who control land system under a specific type of service tenures (in the form of 'fief' or 'vassalage'). But this does not always require political decentralisation as a *necessary* condition for identifying a feudal mode of production. The political form of the superstructure of a feudal economy is derived from the specific politico-historical requirement for feudal appropriation of the material conditions of labour. Not all feudal consolidations took place in Europe under uniform political system. Political decentralisation that *helped* consolidation of the feudal mode of production was a unique trait of only some of the European variants of feudal development.

In West Europe there appeared diverse forms of private appropriation of the material condition of labour under the slave mode of production or the Germanic modes. By the eighth and ninth centuries AD, a hierarchically structured synthesis between donations of land and bonds of service among the apex level nobility under a politically *centralised* system appeared in Europe. In the specific context of the late Roman empire vassals became benefice-holders of princes who were themselves vassals of their superiors. As a consequence, each vassal had, in his turn, to collect his means of sustenance and power (in kind and labour services) from the subordinate peasantry. The entire development became further institutionalised in course of the 'barbarian invasions' when the latter could successfully impose its *free* warrior peasantry and the system of production by bondsmen (inherited from traditional Germanic society) on Roman *latifundia* and on corroding slave mode of production of Roman imperial tradition.

The material basis of traditional Germanic socio-functional unity between fighting and tilling land, yielded to sedentary cultivation by peasant serfs recruited from among the ranks of bondsmen. War activities became the prerogative of not only old bondsmen, now peasant serfs, but also of the new nobility. The consolidation and extension of agricultural settlements on the one hand and military campaign 'of less frequency and lengthier duration' on the other created a hiatus between the mass of agricultural population and the nobility with a professionalised militia.

The peasantry had to surrender a part of the produce to the royal armies. Thus, there was a growing unity between an agrarian society and the new state structure, and between subordinate agrarian society and supra-ethnic new nobility.

It is evident from our very sketchy account of the West European transition from anterior modes of the feudal mode that two distinctly different forms of appropriation of the condition of labour (one representing Roman slavery and the other representing the condition of labour in production as well as war activity of Germanic bondsmen) were synthesised so as to germinate a new mode of appropriating the material condition of labour, namely, land. Within the new order of a civil society, classes of seigneurial nobility stood in opposition to the enserfed peasant tillers, the condition of labour of the latter being appropriated by the former.

For obvious reasons, the above change in social mode of surplus acquisition developed differently in different agricultural regions of Europe. In West Europe itself there 'was no simple horizontal concentration of two basic classes within a single, homogeneous property form'.[9]

The structural specificities of West European feudalism as pointed out by Anderson, are in brief:

(*a*) heterogeneity among the property forms ('communal village lands and peasant allodes co-existing with the *demesne* had critical implications for the development of feudalism itself')[10];

(*b*) the parcellisation of sovereignties caused the emergence of town economy standing in opposition to the economy of feudal countryside (this specificity of West European feudalism led Sweezy to highlight it more than it was necessary as the decisive dissolvent of feudalism); (*c*) 'An inherent ambiguity or oscillation at the vertex of the whole hierarchy of feudal dependencies'.[11]

While Anderson uses parcellised sovereignty of a state power as an *essential* variable for the emergence of feudalism in West Europe, he does not analyse how an absence of parcellised sovereignty or the pressure of centralised state power could suspend the development of the feudal power of the rural nobility.

European feudalism as a whole provoked heterogeneous responses on the part of systems of government to various regional modes of peasant enserfment. Where state power was weak, the system of extra-economic or politico-legal exploitation by feudal lords of enserfed peasantry was wholesome. But where state power was strong, as it was, in general, in Eastern Europe it was the state power itself that played a decisive role in peasant enserfment in the countryside. The difference in feudal developments between Western and Eastern Europe certainly had implications from the point of view of transition of feudalism to capitalism, but one can not claim that East Europe was less feudal than West Europe in the middle ages.

Therefore there can be no universally applicable set of empirical postulates to identify feudal mode of production. The only necessary condition, which Marx visualised, was the specific extra-economic mode of appropriating the material conditions of labour.

If we follow this conceptualisation of feudalism, we cannot agree to Kosambi's characterisation of Mauryan period or early Gupta period as the stage representing 'feudalism from above' or of the later period as 'feudalism from below'.[12]

Kosambi's narrative account helps us to explore afresh the dialectical working of ancient Indian society, but it does not offer any insight into the dialectical interactions among the evolutionary processes of state formations, specific conditions of labour and social changes. Marx's formulation of Asiatic mode of production only helps us to explore the dialectics of relationship between an 'oriental' state structure and its subordinate rural societies but does not enable us to grasp the unity and opposites within an 'idyllic village republic'.

What is, however, the seminal contribution of Kosambi to the understanding of ancient economic order in India is not his generic formulation but his graphic presentation of crucial empirical features of relations among centralised power of the monarch and the sudra peasant labour in crown villages and of the rise of *samantas* as a veritable group of surplus appropriators with the eclipse of centralised empires. The features he has outlined and the evidence he has supplied about the genesis of Indian village economy in the pre-state and post-state phases of its evolution, may lead to a formulation different from his own.

For instance, from the way Kosambi draws a picture of similarity of developments among cities of European antiquity and *paur janapadas* of the Mauryan period, one can underscore more clearly their essential differences. Compared to Greek city-states that guided and shaped the slave-supporting rural production processes, Mauryan town economy with its royal establishments, trade and manufactures never controlled the surrounding rural production process. While the population of towns and cities of Greece and Rome were *dominated* by slave-owners and armed troopers with pauperised artisans and free peasants acting as craft slaves or screws of the war-machine, the ancient towns of Mauryan India were, as attested to by Kosambi himself, '*crowded*' (not dominated) by 'philosophers' (brahmans), free artisans and retail merchants (vaisyas), fighting men (kshatriyas) and 'assessors-councillors' (kayastha segment of vaisyas) who, pursued respective occupations for their livelihood *on condition of paying taxes to the crown.*[13]

In the city-states of European antiquity slave-owning wealthy magnates constituted the ruling stratum, the task of the supreme city authority was to work out a unstable equilibrium of conflicting interests in a city. But a Mauryan *paur-janapada* (town) had to rear an unflinching loyality to the king or imperial monarch who was neither selected nor elected by the dominant interest groups operating there. It is true that both European city-states and Indian towns had to depend on the rural areas for food and other agricultural consumer goods but there was a basic difference between their nature of appropriation of rural surplus. Greek city-states and later Roman cities, by the very nature of their foundations, could not reproduce them without coercive accumulation of wealth by city-based slave-owning landed magnates. The *paur-janapadas* of ancient India neither owned nor controlled labouring populations of their *janapada* territories, nor exercised any *control* over rural production process. The elite of a *paur janapada* (belonging mostly to twice-born upper castes) had to subsist on stipulated professional income from various royal assignments, gifts, mercantile profits etc. This meant that the functional disjunction between royal towns and countryside in ancient India was only a superficial feature that obfuscated unilateral dependence of the former on the latter.

If there was a town in every *janapada*, both during the pre-Mauryan and Mauryan period, it was because such towns were local instruments of appropriating voluntary prestation or gifts from *janapadas* or of collecting compulsory taxes or earning profit from the countryside. In contrast to the cities and towns in classical antiquity that spearheaded agricultural cultivation in rural areas, the ancient towns and cities of India had no positive role either in extending cultivation or augmenting agricultural production. Therefore town elites in ancient India could not foster the possible emergence of a class of landed magnates that could subsequently build up objective preconditions for the rise of a feudal gentry from amongst them.

In ancient Europe, towns came into being not merely because of administrative reasons. The basic reason that promoted their rise was a primal division of social labour between agriculture on the one hand and industry as well as trade on the other. That was why European towns were not merely appropriators of surplus from countryside, they became primal centres of manufacture and trade from their very inception.

It may be argued that during the Gupta period in India innumerable land grants to brahmans and others (assignees could hold land during their lifetime),[14] might have paved the way for feudalism installed from above. But unless the social process of generating the essential condition (i.e., specific form of appropriation of the condition of labour) for the rise of feudalism was developed, no landgrant by itself could germinate feudal landholding. Landgrants by a state to extend its revenue catchment area began in West Europe much before the advent of the feudal mode of production. In fact, even in Europe landgrants made by the monarch either to officials or nobles did not instantaneously germinate the preconditions of feudalism.

Landgrants only helped the rise of *latifundia* organisation in West Europe where slaves purchased by *latifundia* owners were used for cultivation. In fact, when the Roman Republic faced a political crisis, landgrants to ex-army men, and loyal non-Roman nobles became a common feature. The trends continued before, during and after the barbaric invasions.[15] The Roman land grantees extended the political power of the emperor, to whom such grants at least in the initial stage, fetched more political and military dividends than purely economic one.

The landgrants to brahmans, royal officials and others during the Gupta period and thereafter had little religious or political basis. The dominant objective behind such landgrants in ancient India was to extend cultivation. Since brahmans supposedly possessed the art of inducing or inducting an autochthonous population clearing jungles through ritual persuasions (rather than violence), they (rather than the Buddhist monks) acquired the major share of landgrants made even by a Buddhist emperor. The ostensible purpose was to extend revenue catchment areas in the long run, and in the short run the grantees were allowed complete or partial tax relief.

There is no doubt that the *social existence form* of sudra peasant labour in ancient Indian agriculture was servile. But whether such social servility was instrumental in *enforcing* labour activities of sudra artisans or bonded sudra peasants is nowhere explicit. In Kosambi's view, the social prescription in matters of surplus entitlement of a brahman or kshatriya was determined by the *social* caste-differentiation among people belonging to a *gana* (in contrast to tribal *jana* of late Mauryan or early Gupta period). The service obligations of the people belonging to menial castes were determined not by any extra economic compulsion but by socio-economic values and customs prevailing at that time. In Kosambi's view, the ancient social values and customs had their genesis not in violence or coercion, but in ritualistic and sacrificial rites practised in a caste-society. Kosambi is not required to explain why there was no conflict of interest between the imperial tax and the ritualistic levy of upper castes on vaisya or sudra households settled in villages. What Kosambi repeats is that a village society or community, though socially differentiated within itself, *could nevertheless form a closely knit entity with its own productive and distributive processes and having a kind of functional disjunction with the process of reproduction of the state power*. Kosambi in this connection highlights the self-sustaining autonomy of village communal economy.

During the phase of Kosambi's 'feudalism from below', the more a caste society replaced the tribal one, the more powerful the supra-tribal chief became, by now assuming the role of a local king. On the other hand, the growth of Brahmanism or Buddhism tended to efface inter-tribal socio-economic (disputes and/or) distinctions and promoted a sort of socio-religious and socio-institutional homogeneity among village communities. A non-stratified tribal society yielded place to the homogenously stratified non-tribal village community. Previously, 'the wealth accumulated by officials, satraps, princes, tribal chiefs always provoked raids for loots which were highly profitable'. But 'to hold the country steadily under a large empire, as the Guptas managed to do for about two centuries, implies something more than a raid, namely, an expansion of the productive basis. This meant new village settlement in hitherto uncleared territory, with initial profits of lucrative trade in new areas'.[16]

Kosambi's inference is that the Gupta empire must have depended on a class of feudal lords in the form of powerful and wealthy brahmans or kshatriyas which had to pay revenue and military service to the Gupta emperor. Unfortunately, he does not give substantial prima facie evidence to substantiate this inference. Where he deals with the theory of 'feudalism from below', he does not cite a single instance of how a north Indian brahman or kshatriya organised feudatory structure of surplus appropriation by imposing a specific form of appropriation of the condition of labour upon sudra peasants. The epigraphic evidence he gives refers to the Satavahana empire, but even those are not hard evidence in favour of his inference.

A self-sufficient village, of which rural crafts was an integral part, flourished under the 'feudal governance' of ruralised ruling castes. But what specific material change was set in motion as a consequence of such 'feudal governance', or in the case of a change, why it is to be characterised as 'feudal', are not clearly argued or evidenced by Kosambi. What we do get is a kind of hypothetical reasoning so as to explain the empirical features of a village community. He asserts that village people were ideologically indoctrinated by the brahmans. To him a brahman was an essential adjunct of the imperial state in reducing the mechanism of violence. By preaching submission he reduced the total administrative costs. At the same time he was a pioneer into wild territory, a main instrument of change.[17] Even if we accept, following Kosambi, that brahmans were the most sagacious people, it is necessary to delineate the objective social process by which their sagacity could help them to appropriate the extant material condition of labour. Elsewhere Kosambi observes, 'any merchant or village headman who accumulated a little surplus by trade could arm a few retainers of any caste, command a following and lord it over its locality. He would collect taxes without passing them on to the state'. In some other regions, 'land grants to persons other than Brahmins, with feudal tenure involving revenue paid [payable] to the state, became commoner thus resulting in the growth of a new class, feudal landholding barons of a new type'.[18]

It seems, anybody who could appropriate surplus was, in Kosambi's reasoning, a 'feudal landholding baron'. If a socio-ideological opportunity of a non-labouring person for appropriating a portion of surplus becomes the criterion of defining his feudal power, then the entire non-labouring population of a village community can be designated as feudal barons. More absurd is his theory of alliance between brahmans and state power. He cites no evidence to show that the brahmans were the products of a scheme of state-craft, or that they served as paid officials having obligation to champion a state cause, or that they were ready to perform any preassigned duty allotted to them by the state power. If an emperor in ancient India had any brahmanic kinship ties (which he did not always have) one would have been able to visualise such brahmanic mission of preaching non-violence among sudra peasants. Even if brahmanic hegemony was a historical fact, it cannot be construed as feudalism which necessarily involves coercion by those who control the means of production in a natural economy. However, one plausible hypothesis that may follow from Kosambi's account, is that in the event of contradictions between the state and the brahmanic village society, a civilian brahman may have acted as the mediator so as to cover his parasitic role vis-a-vis the labouring population of his village. The state power, in its turn, might have taken advantage of this mediatory role.

The brahmans in ancient and medieval India remained only as a social entity that could hardly help them to appropriate feudal power. What brahmans in Indian village economy of the post-vedic period could enjoy was only their *socio-ritualistic entitlement* to a part of the village surplus, but such entitlement can hardly be treated as a necessary instrument of appropriating the feudal condition of labour.

Again Kosambi does not explain how non-brahmans, 'Kshatriya chieftain or a merchant or village headman' underwent transformation 'into a feudal landholding baron'. Why these people are at all called 'feudal landholding barons' is again not obvious. Like brahmans, kshatriya chieftain or merchant or village headman could claim a portion of village surplus without rendering productive labour service. It may be accepted that this type of social distribution of surplus was the necessary outcome of the brahmanic ideological indoctrination of sudra peasant labourers. But it is not obvious why this allocation of surplus to non-labouring populations should be construed as 'feudal', when the former rarely resorted to coercion or violence, or could not reduce their landholding, if any, to an inescapable condition of labour. In fact, Kosambi in a different context speaks of the absence of an use of force by the state power or by a brahmanic elite in the course of expounding his thesis on the process of 'feudal consolidation from below' in India.

What is more significant is that contrary to what happened during first to tenth centuries AD in Europe, state, warfare, military invasions, etc., hardly played a *decisive* role in the transition from tribal to caste societies or from the pastoral stage of cultivation to the stage of settled agriculture in India. Kosambi, however, testifies to devastating wars launched by an emperor against belligerent petty kingdoms or against rival empires. In most of these cases plunder was the dominant motive. No war was fought to subjugate sudra labourers by a kshatriya or brahmanic kingdom. The latter fought among themselves either to extend their territories or to resist encroachment.

Pre-feudal history of Europe was characterised by similar types of wars. But the purpose of these wars was different. They were not just for plundering wealth, but were conducted either for procuring slaves (i.e., means of production) or for planting a specific form of labour exploitation, the eventual consequence of which was the rise of feudal mode of appropriating the material condition of labour.

Before the rise of feudalism in Europe, the centralised state power of Carolingians had to build up a class of trustworthy landed nobles for collecting revenue from the rural areas. In ancient India a similar process, initiated and organised by a state power, was conspicuously absent.

Then how is one to explain the rise of a category of supra-village or supra-local chiefs of different nomenclatures during and after Harshawardhana's period. Such a development was a likely consequence of the underlying contradiction between the interest of a state power and that of a self-sustaining settled agrarian community. Here the syndrome of despot-village community contradiction postulated by Marx is analytically more relevant provided a despot is identified as any supra village surplus appropriator, Marx, however, only vaguely suggests that the rise of a oriental despot was feasible because of the social preconditions existing in an idyllic village community possessing no property relations within it.

While Marx locates contradiction outside the village community, Kosambi locates it within the village community. Though Kosambi is perhaps more correct in locating the sphere of contradiction, he is unable to exactly identify the nature and dynamics of such a contradiction. Since all kshatriyas or brahmans were not equally powerful so as to command loyalty either from other fellow caste members or from the community as a whole, one must presuppose the existence of an ongoing social process of rearing up *individual inequality* among members of a caste category.

Caste-specific *inequality* cannot be the sole explanatory variable in an analysis of inequality in wealth accumulations and power distributions among households in a settled as well as self-sustaining village community. It must have been this social process of germinating *individual inequality* among upper caste households that caused the rise of a supra-local chief, a *Samanta* or a 'despot'. The same is true in the case of a village community consisting only of sudras where a few among them could rise to the status enjoyed by a wealthy brahman or kshatriya or eventually that of a local king.

Therefore, the local or supra-local 'despot' necessarily came into conflict with the most powerful imperial despot who also claimed a share of village surplus. The village community on its part needed a despot for its own external defence and hence for its material upkeep. But the unity between a supra-village despotic system and a village community could not be eternal because the interest of the village was in opposition to the interest of a despot.

While the interest of a local or imperial despot prompted him to build a protective wall around loyal (*but those existing independent of him*) villages and to promote the extension of settled cultivation, the immediate interest of a village community itself might have induced it to pay various portions of its surplus to the supra-village despot.

Notes

1. Kosambi, *op.cit.*Ch. vi-x
2. Marion Gibbs, *Feudal Order* ('A Study of the Origins and Development of English Feudal Society'), Past and Present Series No.8, 1947, p.403, cited by Kosambi.
3. *Ibid.*, pp. 353-56.
4. Kosambi, *op.cit.*, p.355.
5. Rushton Coulburn, *Feudalism in History*, Princeton, 1956, pp. 2-4. Marc Bloch, *Feudal Society*, Eng. trans. by L.A. Manyon (London, 1965).
6. This is the contention, among others, of Harbans Mukhia, D.N. Jha, D.C. Sarkar, etc. Cf. Harbans Mukhia, "Was there Feudalism in Indian History?" Presidential address Section II, Indian History Congress, 1979. D.N. Jha, "Early Indian Feudalism: A Historiographical Critique", Presidential address, Section I, same as above.
7. Friedrich Cheyette treats feudalism as 'concept-theory' - a theory of historical causation or ideal-typical construct to help empirical research. He does not feel the need for any uniform empirical postulates for such a concept-

theory. Although he apparently accepts Coulburn's definition of feudalism as mainly a system of government, it seems that he does not entirely agree with the semi-economic derivatives of that system of government as expounded by Coulburn.

Elizabeth A.R. Brown however directly assaults the concept of feudalism itself. She deplores 'contradictory' and 'countless' definitions of feudalism and contends that from the eighteenth century the employment of the concept of feudalism has been obstructing historians' understanding of medieval Europe. Indeed, she feels 'the tyrant feudalism must be declared once and for all deposed, and its influence over students of the middle ages finally ended'. Cf. Friedrich Cheyette (ed.), *Lordship and Community in Medieval Europe* (New York, 1968).

Elizabeth A.R. Brown, 'The Tyranny of a Construct: Feudalism and Historians of Medieval Europe', *The American Historical Review*, Vol.79, No.4, 1974, pp. 1087-88.

8. Ashok Rudra, 'Against Feudalism', *Economic and Political Weekly*, Vol.XVI, No.52, 26 Dec. 1981. John Pryor, 'The Historical Foundation of a Feudal Mode of Production', Edmund Leach et al., *Feudalism, Comparative Studies* (Sydney, 1985), pp.69-85.

Although Rudra's main attack is directed against the theory of Indian feudalism, the philosophical foundation of the attack is essentially based on a critique of the concept of feudalism itself. Pryor, in contrast, tries to show that shorn of inarticulations involved in descriptive-analytical mode of conceptualisation, feudalism is an important analytical tool for understanding the European medieval society and economy.

9. Perry Anderson, *Passages from Antiquity to Feudalism* (London, 1978; reprint, 1981), p.149.

10.*Ibid.*, p.151.

11.*Ibid.*, p.151.

12.It appears that Kosambi explains the emergence of state power in ancient India as the consequence of extension of social production base. But he does not differentiate between the stage of development when innumerable kings could grow up and the stage at which Mauryan state power arose. Since Kosambi's 'Feudalism from Above' has its genesis from the delegation of surplus appropriating power of an Imperial monarch to his subordinate petty kings, he was to explain how such delegation of power brought about a change in the earlier mode of production and surplus distribution. But he is unable to do this. As a consequence his 'Feudalism from Above' can hardly be distinguished from the process that supposedly caused the rise of 'Feudalism from Below'.

The mechanism of the 'Feudalism from Below' is explained by him as follows: 'State felt fiscal need, hence appointed local warrior kings, chieftains, as revenue collectors from villages. But the extension of agricultural settlement, and a consequent need for far and wide revenue administration germinated

in the process autonomous local barons, thus setting in motion a rise of feudalism from below'. From the above account of 'feudalism from below', Kosambi fails to clarify the dual origin of Indian feudalism.
Cf. D.D. Kosambi, *op.cit.*, Ch. VI, pp. 144-83.

13. Kosambi's comparison, however, largely depends on Megasthenes' account of Indian rural-urban polity, *op.cit.*, pp. 189-219.
14. Kosambi, *ibid.*, Ch.IX, *passim.*
15. Perry Anderson, *op.cit.*, pp. 70-141, *passim.*
16. D.D. Kosambi, *op.cit.*, p.301.
17. Cf. *ibid.*, Ch. IX, see 9.14.
18. *Ibid.*, pp. 358-65.

3

Medieval Land Administration and Changing Economic Formations in India

3.1: Elements of a Village Economy Deduced from the Empirical Postulates of Kosambi's Thesis

From our critique of Kosambi's thesis on Indian feudalism following deductions seem plausible.

(1) During the ancient period an imperial monarch or even a supra-local potentate / chief was, functionally and otherwise, external to civil community in rural areas. Because of this, at least at the initial stages of secondary state formation, two categories of administration of cultivation developed : the *sita* category organised by the centralised state power, and *rastra* category organised by land grantees belonging to brahman or kshatriya castes or senior officialdom of a state.

If Kosambi's hypothesis on the genesis of self-sustaining village communal settlement is acceptable, then it is probable that in some areas, brahmanic ideological indoctrination and sagacious manoeuvres led to the formation of brahman *dominated* village communities. Brahmans acted as local chiefs of these communities. With the rise of Buddhism kshatriyas became local chiefs in regions where the new religion had its sway. Apart from brahman and kshatriya *dominated* villages, where low caste or tribal people were direct producers, there existed lineage-based villages (where most of the village land was controlled by extended family members of a lineage chief who by our assumption was not necessarily a brahman or kshatriya). The low caste members of some of these villages had no possession right on village land and they had to function merely as crop-sharing productive labourers. In others, the direct producers within the community must have enjoyed the possession right on land. A lineage chief, whatever its basis, by virtue of being the supposed initiator of village settlement in an area, received a portion of output from village economy not as a matter of *right* but as an expression of *loyalty* or as a *protection fee*.

In course of time such loyalty might have turned out to be customary obligation under the *rastra* category of cultivation. Furthermore, the dichotomy in modes of cultivation management between *sita* and *rastra* during the post-Mauryan period was perhaps a transitional phenomenon as there is no further reference of such differential modes of cultivation in literature. This indicates the growth and diversification of the politico-economic power of local chiefs (including brahmans and kshatriyas) over contiguous villages in a setting of growing non-viability of a centralised state power. The collapse of centralised state power and the eventual rise of regional chiefs in Bengal, the Northwest and West Deccan after Harshavardhana's death must have been the logical consequence of such developments.

(2)After the process of ruralisation of caste and crafts became complete, the village communities became, as Kosambi points out, functionally autonomous. This is the opposite of what happened in ancient Europe, where the peasant slaves of urban citizens or free peasants lived in villages. Towns inhabited by slave owners sought to patronise urban craft production.

Rise of towns in ancient Europe set in motion a trend towards migration of village crafts to towns. To the extent, the condition of labour in agriculture could be appropriated more fully by owners of means of production (e.g., owners of slave, land, capital etc.), more specialisation in divisions of social labour between a town and country could be accomplished in Europe. Thus towns in Europe could acquire a productive identity of their own.

The politico-economic power of local chiefs in the early medieval period of India was not based on a particular form of appropriation of the material condition of labour in villages. Nonetheless, such power could be retained as long as it could appropriate a part of the village surplus paid out to it by a supposedly subordinate community. While the power of a local chief must have arisen from the complex of unequal wealth relations among members of non-labouring caste groups, its perpetuation could be marshalled only by chief's ability to promote or defend these relations. Thus within a village community higher accumulation of wealth by a few households was due to their ability to avoid labouring, but such accumulation had no feedback effect on village production base. Accumulation of wealth tended to transform into accumulation of social leisure. A particular chief of a village could establish his hegemony over the chiefs of other villages depending on his extent of accumulation and armed manoeuvre over others. In this sense an ability to engage in conflict formed the rationale of the existence of a local king.

The conflicts among local kings sometimes led to the elevation of a particular local king or chief to the status of a regional king. A regional chief had to devise his own process of acquiring tribute from subordinate local chiefs. This must have been the mode of subsumption of political power at various levels of supra-village political hierarchy without requiring any direct political involvement of village communities in any kind of supra-village power-struggle.

(3)Under such situations there could arise no objective need on the part of either the supra-village or intra-village institution of power to execute a *proprietary control* over village land or labour. The intra-village control mechanism by which village society's land and surplus output were distributed among cultivators and non-labouring households respectively was decided by the specific norms and requirements of the village society. Whatever the specificity of such norms, no caste-stratified village community could avoid private surplus appropriation by a set of non-labouring members. The basis of foundation of such a village community could be outright violence against an autochthonous tribe or brahmanic indoctrination. But with its internal caste order it paved the way for inequality and such inequality could be bred only under *private* surplus entitlements and labour obligation.

Two village categories benefited from surplus consumption. The first belonged to the people of non-productive service castes. And the second consisted of village elites who by virtue of being socially superior and members of the initial group of settlers or land grantees, became landholders without requiring performance of any manual service. The elites were entitled to surplus raised from their holdings, but *they could not gain right to occupy them.* The peasant producers within a community were necessarily the actual possessors of all village land.

A village community had to acquiesce in such private right to *hold* surplus entitlement from land by a household which might not engage its members in actual cultivation.[1] But the concerned surplus-yielding-holding must be in actual *possession* of those members of a community who cultivated it and the amount of obligations of cultivator-possessor of land to the non-labouring formal landholder was to be communally approved. *So long as the actual possessor of a holding cultivated it himself, village community or a formal holder of surplus entitlement or even the crown could not dislodge him from his land. Thus, a land grantee or any village elite having claim over surplus from his holding possessed no power to appropriate the material condition of labour.*

In pure economic terms the labourers were free agents in the sense that they were not required to be coerced into producing for any individual non-labouring holder of surplus entitlement from his land-holding. Why coercion was not necessary can only be explained by the extant form of material conditions in which productive labourers subsisted. Brahmanic social order cannot explain it.

One specific material condition of labour was the abundance of cultivable waste, and the other was chronic shortage of labourers. Because of the latter peasant labourers were required to be *persuaded*, perhaps by various ideological means, to give labour rather than being coerced by village-based communal elites. Had there been no such persuasion, the existing reproduction of non-labouring village-stratum or caste order would be at stake. The entire order of caste differentiation, the built-in ideology of rituals and sacrifices were various modes of such *persuasion* which sprang up as superstructure on the base of stated material conditions of labour.

The relative economic autonomy of peasant labourers in a village communal economy was the plank on which the functional autonomy of a village-based community was based. The relative autonomy of a peasant right was circumscribed only by his communal obligation to pay tribute to a non-labouring member within a village community. Again the relative autonomy of a community in matters of its reproduction could only be challenged in the event of an actual or potential possibility of intervention from outside.

(4)While the ancient and early medieval period witnessed payment of peasant surplus either to an intra-communal village elite or to a chief, or to an extra-communal raja, or a regional/centralised state power, the amount of surplus payable in all cases had no necessary correlation to the size of land that the village peasantry or community possessed and cultivated. The supra-village movement of an amount of peasant surplus bore relation only to the actual amount of disposable surplus output lying with a village community as a unit. In this sense, land 'ownership' of a state or an individual as postulated by Kautilya, was nothing more than a tributary entitlement from produce yielded by labour of a village community from 'owned land', it was not ground rent *per se*.

Since in our reckoning, the main dynamics of village-level production were (*a*) the consumption requirement of those who rendered productive or non-productive labour services, and (*b*) along with it the need for communal reproduction of extant intra-social distribution of surplus consumption goods within a given community, the extant mode of production comparablc to a tribal one possessed nothing in itself that could supply incentive for economic expansion or growth.

For a long time imperial land grants were made in order to extend cultivation. The resultant increase in cultivation might have pushed up the absolute level of economic powers of an emperor or a local chief. Apart from landgrants, royal expenditure on digging canals and dams was directed towards extension and improvement of cultivation in many areas. But such measures were merely incentives, none constituted a material condition of labour or an essential dynamic of village-level cultivation. These measures reflect the dependence of Indian polity on the surplus of crops and crafts yielded by village communities.

From above deductions one can surmise that there was economic inequality among landholding members (labouring and non-labouring) owing to unequal social status. But such inequality could not act as one of the dynamics of social production within the community. Moreover, the peasant-producers probably gave a share of the produce to the 'owner' of the holding he cultivated. Such shares were decided not by the individual non-labouring landholders but by the existing communal custom governed by socio-ideological traits located in a region. The most important aspect of such intra-communal surplus distribution was that the private surplus entitlement of a non-labouring household did not germinate private appropriation on its part of the material condition of peasant-labour.

Nevertheless, the surplus entitlement by the caste elites laid down the basis for a major socio-economic contradiction between the labouring population and its non-labouring counterpart within the community throughout the pre-British period. This contradiction must have nourished a trend towards materialisation of private property in land in a village community.

Historically inequality in landholding and wealth relations among members of a surplus-producing village community was the precursor of coercion that occasioned usurpation of the material condition of labour in the form of private property in land in West Europe. In India it did not happen owing to a different nature of dialectical interconnection between the process of material reproduction and a village community and its geophysical and other conditions.

Notes

1. We here distinguish right to hold land from the right of its occupation. When somebody was granted land, granted land was not his possession. The grantee enjoyed only the surplus (or a portion thereof) generated from that land actually occupied and cultivated by peasant labour.

3.2: Dialectical Interconnections Within a Self-sustaining Village Communal Economy of India

Kosambi's account of the relations between crown or *samantas* and a self-sustaining village economy does not prove the existence of a class-society either in ancient or even in medieval India under the Sultanates or the Mughals. However, it shows that there existed in India during that period, a self-sustaining village communal economy that generated sufficient surplus within itself so as to meet the requirements of upper caste brahmans and kshatriyas, the external revenue requirements of the imperial crown and local kings, *Samantas* and others.

Kosambi stresses the *possession right* of labour on the land it cultivates. However he cannot meaningfully explain how a tribal-pastoral economy of Aryans or non-Aryans, made the transition to settled agricultural communities where 'individualisation'[1] became the redeeming feature. Even if one ignores this serious analytical gap in his account and takes the structural parameters of the self-sustaining village communal economy of his description as a point of departure, it is necessary to explain why at a certain stage of extension of settled agricultural communities in India, the centralised state powers decayed and were succeeded by regional political powers. The question is important because centralised state powers including that of the last one, Harshavardhana, resorted to extending its revenue-catchment areas by liberal landgrants. If we go by Kosambi's account Harsha's period witnessed the most spectacular rise in the area of agricultural cultivation. Then what led to the decline of Harsha, or more precisely why was there a prolonged absence of any centralised political power following the decline of the last imperial power?

The answer to this question must be found in terms of the endogenous process of development itself, as there was no exogenous factor like external aggression or a political rebellion. The cause can be traced to the unprecedented extension of cultivation. While an extension of cultivation increased the revenue-catchment areas of the emperor, it fuelled the wealth of the local potentates. The latter were essential adjuncts both in imperial effort towards patronising extension of cultivation by clearing or retaining hitherto unused lands as well as in the imperial process of revenue collection from the various old and new regions.

This suggests that even before the decline of Harsha's empire parallel rural power centres began to develop which functioned *independently* of the centralised power.

The other aspect of development belonged to the social arena of the rural communities. As pointed by Kosambi, the town economies began to decline even before the final collapse of Harsha's empire. As a consequence, the urban plebians of elite castes were forced to migrate to the rural areas for their own survival, and intrude into village communities which were earlier predominantly peasant-based. This led to an intensification of social contradictions in the rural areas between the low caste tillers and the old or new non-labouring people who sought to appropriate a part of the village surplus by virtue of their socio-ideological superiority. This development consummated only after several centuries. It is possible that as the centralised political powers were replaced by the rural politico-economic power of local potentates, a perpetual state of conflict among the latter occasioned the rise of various regional power centres such as either *Palas* of Bengal or *Pratiharas* of the northwest India. On the other hand, the actual or latent social antagonisms within the brahmanic order occasioned the rise of *Puranic* stipulation so as to tame such antagonism.

The objective phenomenon that had its manifestation in the recorded history of medieval India was the recurrence of social conflicts between caste-superiors in a village and low caste toiling masses. However, no less objective was the fact that these intra-communal contradictions could not basically change the material process of reproduction of a village community. The customary right of a non-productive landholder to enjoy a portion of village surplus coexisted with the customary entitlement of the low-caste tiller. The question is what were the material dialectics that could paper an unity in the process of reproduction in spite of its internal socio-economic antagonism between surplus appropriators and surplus generators? It was certainly an actual or supposed contradiction between an external power that usurped a portion of village communal surplus and the village community as a corporate body that generated surplus.

The long period between the eclipse of the ancient empires and the rise of the Mughals in the 16th century was by and large a period of social disequilibria at the level of village communities. This period can be divided into two unequal parts : the first, longer part witnessed an absence of any centralised political power, and the second, began with the rise of a new centralised imperial power of the Delhi Sultanates.

The first part, according to H.C. Ray,[2] represented 'a rather drab history of endemic warfare' among three super-village regional king ships or dynasties, the Palas of Bengal, the Pratiharas of the northwest and the Rastrakutas of the western Deccan. During this first part, Ray discovers an emergence of 'power structures based on landholding' both in the arena of a village community and dynastic politics.

Kosambi designates this development as one of 'steady consolidation' of 'feudalism from below' initiated by *samantas* as 'feudal nobles' who by the time of Firuz Tughluq (1351-86), could eventually consummate a well organised control system over subordinate villages.[3] Kosambi traces the genesis of feudalism from below from the state of imperial political vaccum. He does not specify either the caste-nature of the *samantas* nor does he specify the social process by which a caste-stratified village community could beget a class of supra-village lordship of *samantas*. Moreover, he is completely silent on the nature of relation that a *samanta* had with the Delhi Sultanate or its agents.

Irfan Habib also discerns the appearance of *rajas* and *ranas* in the pre-Sultanate period[4] and cites Barani's reference to the existence of a floating class of intermediaries between the central administration of the Delhi Sultans and village communities.[5] But neither Ray, Kosambi nor Habib marshalls any evidence to show or explain how a landholding group came into being either from within a village community or without it and could enforce whatever type of right it had on village land or produce. If a primal wealth inequality among village caste elites or initial landholders is visualised as the causal factor in the rise of *samantas* or *raja* as supra-village local lords, it is necessary to work out, at least in theoretical terms, the possible dialectical configuration of relations between intra-communal process of surplus appropriation and the process of gaining power within a village community or outside. In other words, if the hunger for power was fed by the greed for wealth, it is necessary to specify the mode and nature of exercising such power that could help wealth accumulation.

Available historical data show that the power of these local lords manifested itself only when they were in conflict among themselves or against the Delhi Sultanate. It is debatable whether the latter as alien usurpers and therefore having no direct access to a village community had to enforce coercive command over these local lords. But there is no evidence or logical reason for the land-ownership-hypothesis that required a local supra-village landowner lord to invoke *force* so as to extract surplus from his supposedly subordinate villages. Irfan Habib[6] observes: 'the *khots* and *muquddams* [supposed village chiefs, not exactly local supra-village lords] were [themselves] peasants, but peasants standing on the borderland of the rural aristocracy. When prosperous they could imitate the ways of a knight; when hard-pressed, they would sink to the level of ordinary cultivators and even wage earners'.[7]

How could these *khots* and *muquddams* assume so much wealth power within a village that helped them to imitate the ways of a knight? Were such powers qualitatively different from those of *rajas* or *ranas* or regional *samantas* or lords? No clear answer is available. Habib, however, treats *khots* and *muquddams* as mere 'village chiefs'. Sultan Alauddin Khalji calls them 'mischievous people' allegedly 'shifting their tax obligations on *balaharas* [sharecropping peasants].'[8]

From all empirical accounts available so far it appears that between a village community and the emperor or even a regional lord, more than one category of intermediaries existed. But to call any such intermediary a landlord (feudal or not) amounts to an assumption that they could appropriate the material condition of labour in villages. Almost all historians emphasize that although the village peasants had an obligation to pay surplus to the state, the community elites and the local political lord, none could disturb their possession right on village land as long as they were ready to render individual labour service. It is also emphasised that it is the village community as a corporate body that paid surplus to an external institution and no peasant individually had to meet such external obligations. But such an assertion about a peasant's communal identity goes against the essential conceptual requirement of a land-ownership-hypothesis.

Alternative formulation, namely that *samantas* could forcefully impose their extra-economic right on village land or labour, requires hard empirical evidence on the nature of relations between village peasant producers and any such supra-village or intra-village surplus appropriating right. No historian has yet tried to specify the socio-economic relations among the diverse categories of intermediaries themselves, or that between a *khot* or *muquddam* on the one hand, and the labouring members on the other.

With the present state of knowledge we can gather that there existed different levels of intermediary activity between a centralised power at Delhi and village communities. A hierarchical structure of tributary obligations was imposed on the village communities. In spite of this, at least in the initial stages, a Sultanate with all its armed might could rarely mop up adequate surplus from the countryside. Because of this two additional modes of acquiring surplus were invoked by the most powerful Delhi Sultans. One was state sponsored *khalisa* cultivation around the Doab regions with the help of slave labourers.[9] The entire surplus from such *khalisa* cultivation went to the royal treasury.[10] The other was the systematic war-expeditions undertaken by a sultan so as to secure booty from regions outside his territory. Both these modes of extra-revenue surplus acquisition by a sultanate indicate that every Delhi Sultan including the most powerful ones like Alauddin Khalji, failed to introduce stable intermediary control structure by which a regular system of revenue receipts by the royal treasury could be accomplished.

We know that the *iqta* assignment by a Delhi sultanate was supposed to ensure flow of revenue to the royal treasury. But the *iqta* assignees, though engaged by the Sultan for revenue collection, were constantly transferred from one locality to the other. The temporary nature of his tenure made an assignee more interested in short term gains. Since no detailed system of revenue assessment emerged during the period, the extent of revenue collection left a wide scope for individual dishonesty on the part of *iqta* assignees. Moreover, till the end of the period the economic relation between the imperial state and village-based communities was as uncertain as the relation between the Sultan and his revenue officials.

One implication of this confusion was that in the midst of on-going estrangements and conflicts between the Sultanate and its revenue officials, the village communities did not remain at the receiving end. It is more likely that the village communities could enjoy a considerable extent of freedom in their internal functioning as well as in their external relations to town-traders, local potentates and/or state officials. But to the extent an external intervention on the process of production and distribution failed to be systematised, the corporate identity of a village community was exposed to disequilibrium. A village community in such a situation tended to relapse into social disequilibrium between the intra-communal social rights and obligations.

All available historical evidence shows that between 11th to 15th century AD, Indian village communities and even the upper caste groups were not free from fierce internal conflicts and contradictions. There is enough evidence to show that the village communities during the 14th-15th centuries were repeatedly rocked by socio-religious movements against the brahmanic culture system.

It can be observed that the long period between the decline of Harsha's empire and the ascendancy of Mughal centralised power was a period characterised by fierce intra-communal conflict and contradiction and their ad hoc resolutions in various forms (e.g., migration of labouring populations to different parts where oppressive brahmanic social order was less rigorous, growth of new non-brahmanic religious groups, replacement of brahmans by kshatriyas or other elite caste-groups as village chiefs, migration of tribal or quasi-tribal societies to less fertile or mountainous regions, etc.).[11] It is at the same time interesting to note that this early phase of intracommunal conflicts within a medieval Indian polity (consisting predominantly of innumerable village communities) rarely witnessed conflicts between a centralised state power and peasantry. The virtual absence of rigorous external intervention prompted the weakening of unitary bondage within a village community and led to fierce socio-religious conflicts on social rights and obligations within the brahmanic polity of northern India till the 15th century.[12]

At the initial stage of the Sultanate period, the Sultanates had to draw important battle lines between themselves and the various categories of supra-village intermediaries, but never between them and village communities. Sultanates sought to survive at that stage more at the expense of civilian intermediaries like *rajas, ranas*, etc. (either by conquering them or dislodging them from their position) rather than by enforcing tributes directly from villages. But the later sultanates made selective alliance with them so as to acquire revenue from villages. In spite of the fact that the later Sultanates on occasion tried to help the village peasants so as to augment revenue potential of the villages, the entire sultanate period was characterised by the chronic incapacity to rule the countryside or to ensure steady acquisition of surplus from villages.

As to why the socio-religious movement against upper caste elites rather than against the imperial Sultanates or their *iqta* holders became the dominant feature of the time, can be answered in terms of perception of the nature of the major contradictions prevailing at that stage of Indian polity. Our perception is that the peasantry and artisans of a village community directed their wrath against the upper caste village social oligarchs (from which there must have arisen *samantas, rajas, ranas*, etc.) rather than against the imperial power of Sultanates.

However a basic historical weakness of such socio-religious movements was the lack of specific articulation of their positive demand within the perceived framework of a village community. The private entitlement to surplus was based on socially acknowledged claims. On the other hand, in the absence of a systematised usurpation of surplus by the royal power that could harden corporate unity of a village community, the intra-communal elitist imposition of surplus claim on low-caste peasantry or artisans must have seemed unbearable. This might have forced the latter to rise in revolt or to migrate to virgin land for new habitation and cultivation.[13] This in effect could cause marginal extension of village settlements and social production.

But none of the socio-religious movements of the peasantry or the artisans could destroy the innate tendency of a village community towards labour-non-labour stratifications. Almost every socio-religious movement in India ended in the formation of a new society based on egalitarianism, but it tended eventually to resurrect the old stratification within the new social order. Thus intra-communal tension and conflict tended only to multiply sectoral or subsectoral divisions of the brahmanic social order without destroying its inherent tendency towards breeding new set of stratification in the image of the old. This was because socio-religious movements of that time did not contain anything that could radically break down caste barriers and change the economic anchor that went with it.

In Europe, the religious reform movements, helped to unleash the economically oppressed segments of society. The Ana Baptist movement is an illustration of this trend. No similar type of religious movement in India could by itself lead to formation of sharply dichotomised village communities on the basis of non-labouring or labouring castes. Unlike Europe, religious movement in India did not bring into sharp focus the emancipation of a class-society from the mystification of an antequated socio-religious order. In Europe much before the rise of the Papal empire, West European civil society could acquire the genesis of private property and class formation within it, but civil society in India acquired none. This explains why no new anti-brahmanic religious movement stirring up a village community in India could retain its egalitarian stance.

The difference between India failing to occasion the rise of private property in land and Europe succeeding in this respect, can be best grasped if we refer to a perceptive observation of Plekhenov : 'The development of productive forces, which in the final analysis, determines the development of [the nature] of all social relations, is determined by properties of the geographic environment. But as soon as they have arisen, the [nature of] social relations themselves [itself] exercise a marked influence on the [degree of] development of the productive forces'.[14]

If in spite of a phenomenon like individualisation of labour activity and non-productive surplus entitlements, neither labour enslavement nor enserfment of labour could assume a conspicuously clear form in India, this was certainly due to her geophysical environment. It is this geophysical environment that could make a village community's surplus-yielding material reproduction feasible independent of private property.

The geophysical factor prevented the rise of individualisation in India from acting as an economic agent of social production. In Indian village communities a non-productive private entitlement to surplus could be materialised only in terms of socio-ritual obligations. Any coercive appropriation of material presupposition of labour (i.e., condition of labour) in such a situation was bound to appear as a fetter to the material reproduction of a village community itself. It was not feasible to use extra-economic coercion as the mode of appropriating the conditions of Indian labour and this acted against the historical transformation of a private non-productive surplus appropriation (though by *non-economic* means) into the private property right in land.[15] The freedom to acquire objective material presupposition of labour by labourers themselves acted against compulsive change in the Indian system of production.[16] In the absence of scarcity of objects of productive labour in medieval India, the intra-communal dialectical relation between labouring and non-labouring members within a village settlement could neither find its resolution in terms of socio-economic equality among members, nor could attain such ferocity that would germinate a clear class society within the womb of a caste stratified village community.

Notes

1. By the term 'individualisation' we mean the existence and reproduction of individual mode of functioning of community-members. Such individualisation is found even in a tribal society. But it is not independent of communal division of social produce and stock of labour. Since a community making departure from primitive communalisation of labour must necessarily germinate privatization of labour activity by a member and/or group, it necessarily causes the emergence of another member and/or group within the community that tries to live off others' labour. Both, however, must work out a *modus vivendi* so as to ensure a temporary equilibrium. At any post-transitional stage, a society reflects 'this equilibrium' or *modus vivendi* in the relation between groups having mutually antagonistic interests. But this unity underscores its opposites.

2. Cf. H.C. Ray, *Dynastic History of Northern India, Early Medieval Period*, 2 Vols, 2nd ed. (Delhi, 1973).

3. D.D. Kosambi, *op. cit.*, Ch. X, p. 374.

4. Cf. Irfan Habib, 'Social Distribution of Pre-British Landed Property (referred to as 'Pre-British Landed property') in R.S. Sharma (ed.), *Indian Society : Historical Probings, op. cit.*

5. *Ibid.*

6. Cf. Irfan Habib, 'Agrarian Economy from c. 1200-1500', *The Cambridge Economic History of India*, Indian edn., Delhi, 1984) Vol.I, Part I, Sec.2

7. *Ibid.*, p. 55.

8. *Ibid.*, p. 59.

9. Although Kosambi denies the existence of 'chattel slavery' of the Graeco-Roman type in ancient India, he says that Aryans acquired sudras as slaves from vanquished non-Aryan tribes. But in course of extension of cultivation and formation of caste stratified village community, sudras were integrated within the Brahmanic four caste social order.

Irfan Habib, however, contends that with the advent of the Delhi Sultanate, there was a resurgence of slavery in India. But again this was not of the type found in Europe. The slaves in India were both male and female and sold or bought in specified markets. The use of slave labour ranged from that for household work to that of acting as helpers in urban craft production or *khalisa* cultivation. Cf. Habib, 'Economic History of Delhi Sultanate - An Essay in Interpretation', *The Indian Historical Review*, Vol. IV, No. 2, 1978, pp. 287-303.

10. Cf. Habib 'Pre-British Landed Property', *op. cit.*

11. Cf. Ray, *op. cit.*, Vol. II. Irfan Habib seems to have explained the existence of 'semi-autochthonous tribes' in less fertile and mountainous regions of northwest as a consequence of the oppressive nature of Brahmanic order of society in the Gangetic plains. See his 'Pre-British Landed Property', *op. cit.*

12. However, in exceptional cases, the policy of an individual Sultan may have adversely affected the reproduction process of a village economy (as it was in the case of Mohammed Tughlaq in the early years of his rule). But such policy could be successfully thwarted by the mass-scale migration of peasants.

13. Babar had observed this agility of the Indian peasants:

> 'In Hndusthan hamlets and villages - even town - are depopulated and set up in a moment. If a people of a large town [or village] who have lived there for years flee from it, they do it in such a way that not a sign or trace of them remain . . . . On the other hand, if they fix their eyes on a place in which to settle, they need not dig water-courses or construct dam, because all their crops are rain grown.' Quoted in Irfan Habib, 'The Systems of Agricultural Production in Mughal India', *Cambridge Economic History of India*, Vol.I, *op. cit.*, p.215.

14. Plekhanov, *Fundamental Problems of Marxism.* (Moscow, 1974), p.42.

15. In such situations, private appropriation of surplus by a brahman or kshatriya chief and private labour service of a low caste peasant had to depend on mutual subjective and objective forms of communal bondage of one with the other.

16. This was because the extent of social production was delimited by the subsistence requirement and apriori surplus obligations of the direct producers.

3.3: Nature of Change in Agrarian Societies under Delhi Sultanates

By the time the Sultanate grew into an imperial power, the structure of civil society in India was undergoing a process of internal destabilisation, mutation and reconstitution that had actually started centuries earlier.[1] There are reasons to infer that during this period, social formations in India were in such a state of flux that no village collectivity of households could arrive at its own decisive norms of intra-social surplus distribution. This instability is indicated by the rise of many written norms for brahmanic social governance during that period. But rural society, despite its lack of internal cohesion, had to necessarily charter an ad hoc path of internal unity in opposition to any external interference. The emergence of *khots* and *muqaddams*, *rajas* or *rewats* was the result of this ad hoc unity of village societies.

By the 13th century, new towns appeared and some older ones were resuscitated. The towns during this period appeared as embodiment of Sultanate politico-economic power and acted as trade centres for encashment of the surplus usurped from rural areas for the imperial exchequer. Although Mohammed Habib[2] is apparently correct in pointing out the contradiction between an imperial town and country in medieval India, this contradiction is not comparable to that in early West European feudalism.[3]

During the period of the Delhi Sultanates Alauddin's taxation measures were for the first time aimed at curbing the economic power of *khots* and *muqaddums* so as to facilitate acquisition of rural surplus. That Alauddin during his short tenure of 20 years (1296-1316) could not succeed in implementing this measure is evident from the following: a remedial measure had to be adopted by Ghiasuddin Tughluq (1320-25) in the form of concessions to *khots* and *muqaddams*. Firuz Tughluq had to end the erratic policy pursued earlier by Mohammed Tughluq (1325-50).

While Allauddin's measures were essentially of an aggressive nature, the successive royal tax policies with similar objectives were largely free from aggression. Mohammed Tughluq had begun aggressively but the rebellious response he received from the countryside under the leadership of *khots* and *muqaddams* compelled him to change his policy and come to the aid of the peasantry through widespread sanctioning of loans.[4] The other thing they did was to encourage *khalisa* cultivation in the districts around Doab. Since the time of Allauddin, *khalisa* land was cultivated by war captives and slaves procured by a Sultan in course of his war campaigns. The surplus crops raised from *khalisa* land were solely appropriated by the Sultan's central treasury. The institution of *khalisa* system of cultivation helped the Sultanate cushion against uncertain food supply from the remote countryside.

Agricultural land was not allowed to operate free of levy. It came under *iqta* assignment, and the assignees, known as *muqtis*, were usually members of the imperial establishment. The assignees were transferred repeatedly. Their main job was to collect crop taxes, commute them into cash, maintain themselves as well as their armed troops and to despatch surplus troop and cash to the royal centres of power.

That *iqta* holders, mostly living in the towns, were often dishonest, is evident from the institution of the *khwaja* (accountant) to watch *iqta* holders since Sultan Balban's period. Allauddin harboured no illusion about the extent of royal income from *iqta* holdings as there existed scopes for multi-level leakages within the system. During the entire period of Delhi Sultanates, no system of measurement of assessable crop yield per unit of land was developed. Therefore, a village or its chief had the advantage or disadvantage of not submitting an accurate account of the crops it raised. The advantage lay in paying less tax, but the disadvantage was in the arbitrarily extortionate rate of taxation as was the case in the early period of Mohammed Tughluq's reign. The *iqta* assignees themselves submitted distorted accounts of taxes collected and their subordinates, the *muqtis* tended to understate the surplus payable to a Sultan.[5] The difficulties related to revenue collection led Mohammed Tughluq to separate payment to troopers from *iqta-holders'* personal expenses (to be met out of only *iqta* income).[6] Under the Lodhis, this system did not undergo any change.

Thus, the policy of taxation was not so comprehensively designed that it could force a village community to adopt a sharply antagonistic attitude to the state power. At the same time, during the Sultanate period one notices intra-social contradictions arising out of socio-economic differentiation within a village society. Though contradictions developed between the state and the village society, these were on a subdued scale. The major contradictions in society were between the structure of dominance and that of servitude. As a consequence, independent patterns of mutually exclusive developments took place as much in the art of state craft as in the internal ordering of village societies during the period.

If the Sultanate period is treated as one of social transition and turmoil, at the village level, it can be compared broadly with early medieval western Europe. Before the advent of Christianity, the rural society was already ruptured by massive inter-regional migrations prompted by the slave requirement of *Latifundia* and by onslaughts from successive republican state powers. As a consequence the rural society had to develop an antagonism against the extant state power and its dominant class of *Latifundia* owners.The state power dominated by the class of Roman *Latifundia* owners sought to subvert the pre-existing fabric of tribal social order and to implant a new set of socio-hierarchical surplus entitlement over its ruins. The barbaric invasions from the East and West further reinforced this trend.[7] The resultant chaos and confusion bred a fecund soil for the spread of Christianity which appeared as a solace to the oppressed and exploited. An European state power adopting Christianity as state religion provided a Christian ecclesiastical establishment in its territory with large land grant for its independent maintenance. A church establishment on its part began to procure its source of earning by exploiting slave labour working on its land and began to vest its bishops with the power of supervising cultivation by slave labour. *However in ancient and medieval India there was a clear functional disjunction among state, religious order and material reproduction process.* The Sultanates as external despots were interested only in surplus to be acquired from local or supra-local chiefs of village communities. Socio-religious order was concerned with defining only intra-social entitlements to prestations or gifts to the non-labouring strata within a village.

The differences between western Europe and India are more pronounced in the case of resultant internal orders within their respective village societies, that were to surrender a portion of village surplus to the state authority or monarch. While in medieval West Europe particularly after tenth century AD, the nobility and church officials were more powerful than the crown in matters of surplus appropriation, in medieval India the imperial state power had little direct access to village social surplus, and had to extract village surplus through intermediaries. In mediaeval Europe there was sharp antagonism between extant state authority dominated by a class of civilian surplus appropriators and the direct producers. In medieval Indian society there was neither a powerful class of civilian surplus appropriators nor a powerful imperial lord who could force a village community to produce for state.

The consequence was that in Europe social relations within a village society in the rural areas could be restructured according to the requirement of a supra-village nobility, in India a village community's texture of social relations could retain its extant autonomy. This does not mean that the Indian village community was static. On the contrary, it shows the peculiar propensity towards unity in case it was confronted by an external power. And in times of peace there was a contradiction between the labouring and non-labouring groups within a village community.

The Sultanate period contributed, however unwittingly, to a strengthening of elements of instability within an religio-social milieu of a village community. Due to historical reasons, the installation of the alien Delhi Sultanates paved the way for reinforcement of conflict between extant brahmanic social norms and the norms of the labouring people in the context of the imported social norms of Islamic societies.

The absorption of indigenous Hindu elites into the royal administrative structure during this period 'opened the doors' of such privileged assignments to plebian elements. As Al Barani points out that since the Khalji coup of 1290, 'the ruling class of the Sultanates had been marked by an acute instability in [its] composition'.[8] While this may explain induction of Hindu elites within the royal administrative structure, it does not explain the readiness among such indigenous elites to be absorbed as holders of royal privilege.

In our reckoning, the instability within a village community was intensified by two factors: the principal one was the reinforcement of contradiction at a village community level; the subsidiary one was a slow and steady rise of the Muslim civil society on the basis of more pronounced socio-religious equality that subjectively challenged the stratified brahmanic social order.

From the writings of Mohammed Habib we can construct the proposition that the process of civilian social formation among Muslims began to develop from the days of the Delhi Sultanate. He puts forward a thesis that the main prop behind the formation of a stratified Muslim civil society was supplied by a mass-scale conversion of low caste Hindu artisans into civilian Muslims.[9]

M. Yasin also claims that there is not a single reason for the rise of Muslim civil society in India. According to him, there grew up three strata among Muslims in India according to their places of birth and nature of parentage. The most aristocratic stratum was constituted by immigrant Muslims of pure Persian or Afgan origin. It is widely supposed that a considerable extent of immigrations was the direct consequence of repeated Turkish invasions of Persia and Central Asia since the 10th century.[10] The second stratum in socio-hierarchical order among Muslims consisted of those who were fathered by immigrant Muslim nobles, soldiers etc, but whose mothers were indigenous women. In India, each Muslim immigrant retained a number of concubines of diverse ethnic origin. Yasin reports that this stratum of Muslims mostly living in town was known as 'nau-Muslims', and that it constituted the real progenitor of Muslim social community of urban India during the last days of the Sultanate.[11] The lowest stratum among Muslims grew up from the rank of Sultanate slaves, constituting in the process a Muslim peasantry and artisans in the countryside around Delhi and who later spread to the outlying regions of the Mughal empire, such as Gujarat, and Bihar. This third stratum of rural Muslims were none other than the converted low caste Hindu artisan slaves who with the decline of a Sultanate migrated from towns to the countryside.

The genesis of this third stratum can be constructed on the basis of the account of Sultanate slavery given by Irfan Habib.[12] That the slave procurement was one of the objects of military expeditions of Delhi Sultanates is documented by contemporary Persian sources. The rebellious local chiefs who were not always ready to yield to royal extortions were usually forced to supply slaves to a conquering Sultan. Sultan Alauddin Khalji had reportedly procured as many as 50,000 slaves. Sultan Firuz could raise the number to 180,000 of which 12,000 are reported to have been slave artisans. Even the urban nobles or ministers could share the spoils: one minister of Firuz, Jahan Maqbul Khan, possessed no less than 2,000 slave concubines. Other urban Muslim gentry too owned a number of slaves whose toil supplied their masters their means of subsistence.

Fragmentary informations available suggest that men and women slaves working directly in households, harems of the Sultan or his nobles constituted an elite class of slaves. Male slaves working in textile units in towns or in *khalisa* lands were considered inferior slaves. There is no evidence that slaves ever functioned as foot-soldiers under aristocratic Muslim commanders. It is reported that there existed slave markets in towns where during the Khalji period and thereafter, the market price of slaves was lower than that of animals. This explains why a continuous slave export to outside Islamic world became an additional source of revenue for a Khalji treasury.[13]

In one place Irfan Habib explains the decline of Sultanate slavery because of the Mughal emperor Babar's dislike of the custom.[14] But his other explanation seems more plausible: 'By the very nature of the case such use of slave labour [i.e. productive use of labour in Khalisa or town industries] was a transitional phenomenon. Once the new immigrant crafts or skills [imported from the 'Islamic East'] were well established and the slaves turned, after some generation into free artisans,upon obtaining or buying their freedom,the competition of free labour would increasingly inhibit the use of slave labour, which owing to lack of initiative was notoriously inefficient.'[15]

From the above[16] we may conjecture that the number of women slaves was not much lower than that of male slaves. One learns that the price of girl-slaves was lower than even untrained male slaves both in Delhi or Devagiri markets. With the sphere of manufactures or crafts being still narrow and *khalisa* land being concentrated in the relatively small zone around Delhi,one can hardly account for high price of male slaves only in terms of their diverse productive uses.One may hypothesise that a relatively high number of female slaves of the Sultanate period contributed, by and large, to the enormous increase in civilian population among Muslims by the time the Mughals came to enjoy supreme political authority. There may have been other factors that can account for the extension of Muslim society.

In the extreme northern region, Muslim civil society was the outcome of a direct transition from its tribal past, as they were allowed to retain many tribal norms of land allocation and land inheritance. Baden Powell writes, "the tribes though Mohammedan, are mostly ignorant of the regular legal system of Mohammedan creed (especially of inheritance), and they follow customs of their own."[17] In the southern peninsular region Muslim society had its origin from the descendants of Arab merchants in the Coromandel and Malabar co asts. Besides Arab seafarers of pre-Portuguese days, the Afgan Sultanates of Bijapur and Bahamani kingdom must have had their Muslim nobilities settled in agriculture after they were eclipsed by the Mughal and Maratha principalities in the late 16th and early 17th centuries. But we have no socio-historical evidence to explain the emergence of well-organised Muslim civil societies in the Kaveri basin.

In our view the emergence of Muslim civil society had produced a further destabilising effect on the ongoing social restlessness among sharply stratified rural societies of brahmanic order. If the period before 15th century is taken to be the period that witnessed severe, but silent, instability within a brahmanic social order which encouraged Hindu elites to ally with Delhi Sultanates. Such instability, reinforced by the rise of Muslim civil society, can explain why, during the period from the 15th century to the 18th, India witnessed almost continuous intra-social religious revolts against the brahmanic social order.[18]

In the South, the Lingayat movement caused a major rupture in the brahmanic social order, which ultimately relapsed into the brahmanic social fold. The North found the emergence of Sikhism as a challenge to Hindu caste society. In the East, a new Vaishnavite movement under Sri Chaitanya challenged the brahmanical social order. There is no doubt that nascent Islamic civil societies – whatever their prime origin – reinforced unrest in the brahmanic order of civil society. This contributed to the growth of pluralism and sectarianism within the brahmanical social and cultural structure.[19] Such divisions had perhaps their maximum impact on Hindu agricultural castes. The brahmans in many areas of North India, were dislodged from their superior social position.

In a setting of short-lived imperial dominance of Sultanates, social synthesis as well as social decomposition within the macro-society of the North Indian subcontinent became the main feature of the pre-Mughal period of medieval Indian history. At the height of Mughal imperial power the sharpened socio-ideological contradiction within the extant village community manifested itself in various religious movements. But somehow the Mughal rule of the 17th century forced such intra-communal contradiction to be marginalised and paved the way for the emergence of sharper contradictions between the imperial state power and village communities.

Notes

1 The period between Harsha's decline and the rise of the 'slave' dynasty marked the rise of innumerable external invasions and local kings in the north and east of the subcontinent. The transient rise of local kings of aboriginal or tribal lineage in many regions indicates perhaps a tussle for power among brahmanic social order and other autochthonous orders. The period witnessed at the same time innumerable religious scriptures, social and other

norms of brahmanic variety that indicate brahmanic kshatriya axis, its superiority over other non-Aryan social orders and their chiefs, Cf Kosambi, *op. cit.*, Ch. X.

2 Mahammed Habib, *Politics and Society during the Early Medieval Period* (Bombay 1974), pp. 60-77.

3 Unlike a medieval Indian town, a town in West European feudalism grew up as the antithesis to countryside owing to former's virtual autonomy as centres of manufacture and long distance trade, 'Thus a dynamic opposition between an economy of increasing commodity exchange [and manufacture]. . . . and rural economy of natural exchange controlled by nobles was alone possible in the feudal mode of production'. In contrast, in India in matters of production and scale of exchange, there existed a kind of undifferentiated unity of town and country. The contradiction between town and country, as pointed out by Habib in early medieval India, was essentially a reflection of the contradiction between state as a surplus appropriator and civil society in the rural areas as exclusive producer of that surplus. Cf. P. Anderson, *op. cit.*, p.150.

4 Irfan Habib, 'Agrarian Economy', *op. cit.*, Chap. III, pp. 63-67.

5 *Ibid.*, pp. 70-71.

6 *Ibid.*, p. 72, Habib cites an important Arabic source to contend that 'troops are said to have been always paid in cash by the treasury and that *iqtas* were given only in lieu of the Commanders's personal salaries.'

7 P. Anderson, *op. cit.*, Ch. 2, pp. 112-27, *passim.*

8 From I. Habib, 'Agrarian Economy', *op. cit.*, p. 74.

9 Cf. M. Habib, *op. cit.*, pp. 68-78.

10 This is supported also from M. Habib, *ibid.*

11 Cf. M. Yasin, *A Social History of Islamic India 1665-1748* (Lucknow, 1958), pp. 5-26.

12 Cf. I. Habib, 'Economic History of Delhi Sultanate – An Essay in Interpretation'. *The Indian Historical Review* Vol. IV, No. 2, 1978, pp.287-303.
The substance of the article is repeated in Habib's contribution on slavery in the *Cambridge Economic History of India*, Vol. I (Ch. III, Sec. 3, pp. 89-93) with more elaboration and documentation of sources. But strangely enough, he does not include this article in the bibliography of the *Cambridge Economic History of India,*. Volume I of which he is one of the editors.

13 I. Habib, 'Agrarian Economy', *op. cit.*, p. 91.

14 *Ibid.*

15 Cf. I. Habib, 'Economic History of Delhi Sultanate : An Essay in Interpretation', *op. cit.*, pp. 287-303.

16 I. Habib, 'Agrarian Economy', *op. cit.*

17 Baden Powell, *Lard Systems of British India.* Vol. II (Oxford, 1897), p. 633, fn. 2.

18 In fact, the revolts against the brahmanic oppression had started from the days of early Buddhism, Jainism, Saivism and Vaishnavism. But the revolts

were confined to the elitist segments of the brahmanic society itself. As a consequence all such revolts could spell no disruptive influence on the brahmanic order which had its main target of oppression in Sudra peasants and artisans – the sections totally neglected by such revolts. On the contrary, religious rebels were divided into various sects with different degrees of loyalty to the brahmanic order and scriptures. Trevor Ling, *A History of Religion – East and West* (Macmillan, 1968), Sections 2.40 and 2.41, 3.3. and 5.25, *passim.*

What, however, distinguishes the earlier religious revolts against the brahmanic order from the later ones was that the later revolts were not only against brahmanic ritual superiority but also against the oppressive caste order of brahmanic traditions. The most widespread movement, no doubt within the orbit of brahmanic order was of *Nath* religion,propelled mainly by low caste peasants and artisans. Although this movement later degenerated into a kind of non-brahmanic Tantric mode of salvation and discovered a power of the Almighty within an individual follower, the movement for the first time in the history of indian socio-religious movements discarded the need for brahmanic ritual for salvation and fought against the so-called brahmanic cult of the *Avatar.*

While Naths did not constitute an independent social community distinctly outside the Hindu community, Sikhism had its followers from Hindu or Muslim agricultural castes and created an independent community with radical set of social practices of brotherhood and unity which were distinctly different from those of caste-based communities of the period.It is well-known that the Granth Sahib – the main religious scripture of Sikhs – incorporated in itself not only the holy messages of Guru Nanak and other Sikh Gurus but also those of non-Sikhs like Kabir, Farid, Namdeb, Dhanna, Surdas Pip, Ramananda and Mardan. Cf. N.N. Bhattacharya, *Bharatiya Dharmer Itihas (History of India Religions)* (Calcutta, 1384 B.S., 1976) Chapter X.

19 'The sixteenth century was a period in North Indian history witnessing the rise of a multitude of sects which combined devotional fervour with social protest [against brahmanic caste structure of Hindu society]. The best known sects are perhaps those of Kabir (1440-1518). Namdeb (b. 1470), Vallabha (dates uncertain),Nanak (1469-1538). Chaitanya (1485-1533), Tulsidass (1532-1620). Rui Dasa (dates uncertain) and Dadu (1544-1603). 'Cf Trevor Ling, *op. cit.*, p. 325.

Ling however does not mention another notable name of the period, Ramananda, a follower of Vaishnavism of Ramanuja, having two disciples, namely Kabir and Rabidas. Two famous disciples of Ramananda were from low caste Hindus, the first, the son of a weaver, the second, the son of a barber. In fact, most of his disciples came from low caste Hindu artisans and Muslim peasants.Cf. N.N. Bhattacharyya, *op. cit.*, p. 354.

3.4: Emergence of Contradiction Between Protofeudal Imperial Claim on Village Output and a Self-sustaining Social Production Base of a Village Community

The basic difference between the Mughal state craft of Akbar's period or thereafter, and that of Delhi Sultanates, lay in the installation of a through mechanism of surplus appropriation by the former. This difference surfaced since the period of Sher Shah.

During the Mughal period, the size of the land cultivated by a village community became the unit of surplus assessment of a village. By establishing a hierarchical control structure on cultivated land it unleashed the growth of protofeudal rights on village output. The similarity between feudal and protofeudal rights lies in the use of direct coercion to acquire surplus, but the difference between the two lies in the spheres on which such coercion is imposed. In the case of protofeudalism, peasant labour remained outside the pale of coercion of a powerful statepower. In the case of feudalism, it is firstly coercive occupation of cultivable land by a civilian class of armed powerbrokers, by which the latter enforces enserfment of peasant labour, whether the state power approves of it or not is a matter of secondary importance. The concept of protofeudalism as developed above, under scores a relation of coercion between the village community as a unit and State power or its agent as usurper of village surplus.

In all parts of the world, where Feudalism became a stage of evolution, protofeudalism built up by a powerful state power was its precursor. If in medieval Indian history, one cannot witness a transition of Mughal period's protofeudalism to the feudalism of the West European variant, it is due to the peculiar specifics of land relations within an Indian village community. Such land relations were the outcome, as Plekhanov suggests, of the geographical specificities of the natural material condition of labour in Indian village communities. We do not suggest that only the areas where feudalism was developed as a historical stage of development witnessed massive dismemberment of preexisting village communities. Even in areas where similar development did not take place, wholesale dismemberment of extant village communities took place. In the former case, dismemberment was propelled by a civilian class of individual property holders, in the later dismemberment of preexisting village communities was caused by the socio-religious contradiction between labouring and non-labouring members of a community. However, the geographical specifics of the latter areas acted as barriers to the rise of a coercive power, independent of state power, of a civilian class, that could control the material condition of labour.

A review of the dialectics of social production relations within a Mughal Indian village community interacting with an immensely powerful state power and with the relations among state, bureaucracy and village communities of Mughal India could lay bare why the structural evolution of Indian economy traded this peculiar path. Here protofeudalism failed to pave the way for the rise of the feudal type of dismemberment of a village community. In the Indian situation socio-religious dismemberment of a village community led to its eclipse in a locality and to the *pari passu* rise of a new village community in another. In medieval India a rebellious peasantry who refused to pay taxes rarely succeeded but it never lost its sovereign right on land.

Following the death of Firuz Shah and ascendancy of the Lodhis and the Babar, the hitherto existing mechanism of imperial dependance on local potentates for surplus appropriation began to be replaced by a firmer control mechanism of state power on village output.

Before the introduction of the Mughal land revenue system two kinds of development had already taken place. The first was the development of a class of Muslim and non-Muslim aristocrats at the supravillage level. The second was the emergence of Muslim civil societies at the village level with the relative decline of importance of town economies of the Sultanate period.

Throughout the 15th century the chronic political instability of the Delhi Sultanates caused transformation of their immigrant Afgan, Persian or Turkmanian officials into aristocratic settlers in towns and cities, living on patronage from the imperial ruling clique and on plunder of slaves acquired from successive war campaigns of the Sultans. Besides, they began to function as a new class of armed Muslim nobility in rural areas.

Alongwith this development there was a parallel process of acquisition of power by a supra-village nobility belonging to Hindu and other ethnic groups in the outlying regions. Agricultural regions, for the first time, came to the divided into 'Sarkars' and 'Parganas' in the Lodhi period. They were administered by members of Hindu and Muslim supra-village nobility, patronised by the royal office. While the rise of a Muslim nobility can be explained by the natural inclination on the part of a Sultanate to select coreligionists as his accomplices, the rise of a class of Hindu nobles in distant countrysides was more due to their functioning as buffers between a village community and the external surplus appropriating authority of state power, rather than due to any diplomatic stratagem on the part of a Sultanate to buy the alliance of an alien Hindu countryside. The village communities had to pay tribute to nobles as 'protection fee' and payment was not always voluntary in nature.[1] But such protection fee did not bring with it an entrenched right on village surplus, because membership of nobility was always temporary.

As indicated earlier, the chronic political instability as well as fiscal indiscipline among the late Sultanates provided the village communities a scope to remain more or less free from royal interference in their internal modes of functioning. It has also been observed that such scope paradoxically paved the way for an opposite type of development within a village community, namely, the development of socio-religious conflicts and contradiction between the village peasantry and artisans and intracommunal upper caste privilege and social entitlement. At the same time, a band of Hindu or non-Hindu class of local nobles taking advantage of the extant political chaos, formed their respective areas of influence and sought to survive by collecting tributes.

It is perhaps during this period that there grew a rural community of civilian Muslims. No dependable historical account is available on how these communities grew. It is possible that urban Muslim nobles plagued by political as well as pecuniary uncertainties, organised rural settlement of their slaves in regions close to the city administrative centres. By and large the aristocratic Muslims were fond of living in urban centres and preferred martial occupations.[2]

Since the urban mode of procuring livelihood was inextriably connected with the system of imperial patronage, the uncertainty about such a patronage forced a considerable number of nobles to build their individual sources of income from agriculture. We infer this because during that period, these is no evidence of mass scale of conversion of Hindus into Muslims. Therefore the bulk of Indian Muslims that formed the rural community during he period preceeding Mughals, must have come from the rank of Sultanate slaves – male and female.

Slaves were, in general, low caste Hindus imported into towns by conquering emperors. Irfan Habib testifies to the fact that a substantial number of them was forced to work as labourers under *khalisa* category of cultivation in the Doab region and under few urban craft centres producing luxury goods for urban Muslims nobles. With the gradual weakening of economic and political power of the Delhi Sultanates, either slaves were set free or the slaves themselves by adopting Islam as their religion bought freedom.

We must try to assess the likely impact of the emergence of Muslim communities in the midst of the old caste-stratified brahmanic societies. In fact, during the period between the decline of the Sultanates and the ascendancy of the Mughals, i.e., between the 15th and early half of the 16th centuries - socio religious movements within the Hindu social polity attained their most tempestuous form. The positive outcome for such movements was the birth of new socio-religious groups. The emergence of new socio-religious groups led to multiplication of village communities and extension of cultivation in hitherto virgin land. The socio-religious movements and the subsequent multiplication of religious sects and sub-sects must have caused further extension of agricultural and craft production in rural India.

By the middle of the 16th century when the Mughal empire was consolidated by Akbar, its administrative fiat covered the regions North, East and a part of the Deccan West. Since that period there appeared a process of transition from a predominantly tributary basis of imperial surplus entitlement to a coercive basis of entitlement on which was founded for the first time in India a protofeudal type of landed interest.[3] During the later phase of the Mughal empire, the resultant socio-economic formation came to be consolidated as protofeudal formation. It is true that such protofeudal formation in Mughal Indian agriculture bore elements of *formal* similarity with that of Western Europe during the 10th century.

It is to be remembered that sometimes a *formal* similarity may obscure the *real* difference, as in a different context *formal* difference may obfuscate the *real* similarities. Indeed a *formal* difference existed even between France (the country supposedly witnessing the emergence of feudalism in its classic form) and either the Anglo-Saxon region in North Europe or the Germanic region. But despite this formal difference among these countries, rural societies found similarity among themselves in matters of appropriating the material presupposition of rural labour force as it is found in a feudal mode of production. Even within a country not everywhere can one discover uniform presence of the two most pronounced postulates of European feudalism, viz. private proprietorship in land and the institution of fief-holding and vassalage. There were dissimilarities among the freedom enjoyed by peasants or among trajectories of an evolving relations of state to peasants and landlords. For instance, the southern part of France was less feudalised, 'with a greater proportion of noble estates held outright rather than in fief', and a 'larger non-dependent peasant population'[4].

Let us now cite instances which bore elements of similarity though there existed real differences beneath the surface. The comparable stage is the emergence of protofeudal formations in both Mughal India and west Europe.

West Europe of the 10th century had striking similarities with 16th of Mughal India. In West Europe the centralised power of a Carolingian emperor had, in many respects, strikingly similar mode of functioning, if it is compared to the way a Mughal emperor functioning. Like the carolingian monarch, a Mughal emperor had no hesitation in eliminating any preceding surplus appropriating right of a noble. The carolingian emperor, Charlemagne, assumed so much power that it would appear that a sort of state landlordism had been introduced by him. The power of any Mughal emperor over cultivable land of his territory bears a close resemblance to that of Charlemagne. Charlemagne made tenure of a revenue collecting noble in a region or locality purely temporary, comparable to that of a jagirdar in Mughal India. In both cases, the revenue officials were transferred from one region to the other. With both the carolingians and the Mughals there existed no impersonal mode of recruitment of revenue officials who were recruited by a band of trusted nobles responsible to emperor for their choices.

In spite of all these apparent similarities in appropriation of rural surplus in the form of revenue, while the decline of carolingian empire witnessed the growth of a class of feudal nobles in the countryside, the decline of Mughal in the late 17th century of India did not.

The possible answer brings up to the identification of the real difference between protofeudal formations in the West Europe and India. The real difference lay in processes by which a rural community could be forced to part with its surplus.

The Carolingian empire appeared as a decisive stage in the evolution of private property in West European societies. Since private power of an individual in a society can acquire its material substance only by his property ownership, the development and stability of private property ownership are perpetually shadowed by antagonistic contradiction with labour and assumes a historical course that is far from linear. In the pre Carolingian age various forms of appropriation of conditions of labour had already emerged in West Europe, but no particular form of such appropriation could ensure its stability. This was mainly due to various forms of subsumption of power over conditions of labour by invading groups of nobles, each having its own distinct mode.

The emergence of the centralised Carolingian empire established by the force of arms, acted against this political disorder and chaos among competing modes of appropriating the material condition of labour. Its monarch acquired the supreme private property in land through suspended animation of other forms of property holding. If Charlemagne suspended other property forms so as to consolidate his own, it was not aimed at upsetting the basic social process that tended to beget private individual property rights.He forcefully monopolised all private property rights without upsetting the on going social process. As a result during his reign, private property right of revenue officials was subordinated. After his death such overarching monopolisation came to an end. The class of temporary holders of landed property now began to gain uninhibited articulation. The social process of germinating individual property that lay dormant during the period of Charlemagne, witnessed resurgence after his departure. The only change was that earlier varied property forms came now to be replaced by a similar form of coercive appropriation of the material condition of peasant labour. This, in effect, meant the rise of a new class of landed property owners at the expense of earlier class of heterogeneous categories of property holders. The protofeudal rights on labour set in motion by Charlemagne made the transition to feudal property right on land through universal enserfment of peasant labour.

In the case of the Mughal economy, a village community or society did not witness coercive appropriation of surplus by manifold categories of village land holders. Indeed private property could not germinate within the social fabric of Indian village community. This was in spite of the historical emergence of internally stratified village community that went a long way in upsetting communalisation of landholding and communalisation of labour service. What was then the basis of private labour activity or appropriation of surplus *within* a village community? It was purely a need for consumption on account of which there grew social domination by one group and resistance by another. But such a cleavage ridden community had to confront unitedly an external force such as the town merchants or an external despot - a supra communal king, or a Zamindar/Jagirdar. To the extent, the external surplus usurpation form village was regular and coercive, the intra communal syndrome of social domination and resistance tended to be subsidiary so as to form a communal unity against an external despot. To the extent, a supra village mode of surplus appropriation was erratic, irregular and feeble, the intra village syndrome of domination and resistance came into full play. Again in situations where the despotic usurpation of village surplus was mediated by the capitulation of an intra communal group exercising social domination, the forces of resistance within it tended to wage struggle against both intra communal forces as well as against supra communal despotic usurpation.

Since in Mughal India, the people close to the seat of imperial state power did not arise out of struggle among indigenous power wielding groups, the extant norms of communal labour allocation and surplus distribution in a town or village community had a functional disjunction with the norms that determined the imperial surplus requirement and its disposition. This functional disjunction, paradoxically, acted as a constraint against an imperial despotic exercise of coercive mode of surplus appropriation either from a village community or from an urban merchant community. This is true also in the case of surplus appropriation by a lesser despot (e. g., a zamindar planted on a locality from outside). Since a semi autonomous local king or big jagirdar or zamindar did not always possess a social base in his subordinate communities, it was only an open or veiled coercive authority (not the coercive authority of a social power) that was invoked for surplus appropriation from a village community.

The model of relationship as configurated above, between a social polity and external coercive political authority in the Mughal period did not beget a uniform consequence on the pattern of responses of various village or urban communities, to such relationship. In some areas responses were hostile. This sharply divided civil community and state power or a local despot. Elsewhere,the intra communal syndrome of social domination and resistance made the transition to movements against upper castes and state power. During the Mughal period, the earlier phenomena of irregular and weak mode of surplus appropriation from a community as they were found during the period of Sultanates was rare. Indeed the power of appropriating surplus from a civil community by any external despot was sought to be made regular and thorough during the Mughal period, but it was fettered by the social absence of appropriation of the material condition of labour within a village community.

Thus although a Mughal protofeudal nobility grew during its period similar to what happened during Charlemagne reign, the former did not gain any passage to feudal landownership during the post Mughal period. This was because, unlike early medieval West Europe, Mughal India did not possess the necessary social preconditions for germinating private property in its essential form. While the Carolingian Europe could build up the protofeudal rights on land on a society already exposed to various modes of property formation as the condition of labour, in Mughal India, a village community was liable to surrender surplus to an external interloper, but could not develop the necessary intra communal conditions towards that end. As a consequence, the protofeudal rights on land created in India by successive Mughal emperors, had to swing between the two extremes - the self sustaining autonomy of a communal economy in village and the imperial as well as other external surplus claims.

What then was the specific inbuilt weaknesses of Indian village community that forced it to succumb to coercive claims from the built-in protofeudal interests on village land during the Mughal period ? An autarkic village community had no option but to compromise with the claim from a mightier external despot. But if the autarkical character of a village communal economy was responsible for despotic success in appropriating village surplus, this by itself cannot explain why an external despot stopped short of appropriating the condition of labour in village land. Why did not arise private property in village land of communnity ruled by a despot ? Indeed no historical account of medieval Mughal India can decisively show that a jagirdar or zamindar could appropriate the condition of labour within a village community.

In our view, the proto feudal formation of the Mughal period arose out of a improvised and fragile system of trade off between the imperial mode of surplus acquisition and the social structure of dominance within the stratified civil community.

The Mughal imperial bureaucracy, on its part, followed the Islamic norms of taxation on land imitating the Central Asian model. The Mughal revenue system differed from the model by developing a well organised control structure on surplus appropriation from cultivable village land held by a village community. Although initiated by Sher

Shah, the full flowering of the control structure on village surplus took place during the reign of Akbar. During Akbar's period, a detailed mode of revenue assessment and collection came to be introduced. The total product mix yielded from cultivable land and possessed by a village community, was converted into its money value (by multiplying each crop by the average of prices of preceding five years) and a stipulated portion of this total value (ranging from 50 to 75 percent) was claimed as state revenue. What would be the per household share of the village revenue burden was left to the discretion and consideration of the extant authority within a village community.

In a big landholder's village of *khudkaste* type, each landholder household paid its share of total village revenue according to the size and kind of net output raised from its holding. If it was a pure labourer's village, having no cultivable land to its credit, the village was theoretically free from any imperial revenue assessment. If however a village consisted of only petty peasant landholders who cultivated the village land themselves interhousehold distribution of village tax was according to the amount of output each household raised from their respective holdings.

If it was a mixed village, having both big landholders and petty ones, with a sizable bulk of landless menial population, inter household distribution of village revenue burden was bound to be unequal. Here the big landholders cultivating with hired labour paid less of village revenue than the petty landholders who cultivated with family labour. In this sense, incidence of state revenue burden on a household was decided by its labour-non labour status within a village community. A socially dominant household belonging to the non labouring social stratum of a village community had to pay less share of the total village revenue than that by a peasant landholding household cultivating with family labour.[5] Thus a system of extant social stratification based on labour non labour dichotomy within a village could shift major revenue burden on the petty landholding members who, in general, belonged to the intra village structure of social inferiors, cultivating land with their labour. Had the pre existing village society with its dominant mode of intra social structure of rights and obligations developed an inherent incompatibility with the Mughal system of imposing tax on village output, there would necessarily have arisen situations where proto feudal control structure on land and village output would fail to operate. Since such contradiction was not witnessed in most cases it is presumed that the phenomenon of trade off between the Mughal revenue administration and dominant system of priviledged landholding of social superiors within a village community, became a general trend.

On the other hand a question arises. If the Mughal revenue administration's surplus appropriation faced little or no resistance from a village community what could retain the communal autonomy of a village ? Indeed it can be argued that if a community succumbed to external appropriation of surplus, it was eventually bound to affect the extant intra communal paradigm of distribution of total produce. We have also argued that the Mughal appropriation of village surplus reinforced inequality of income distribution among labouring and non labouring landholders in a village community. If such income inequality could adversely affect the peasant subsistence, there was nothing to prevent an absolute pauperisation of the peasant in the Mughal period. But then why was the preexisting inequality in wealth relations which was intensified by Mughal mode of revenue collection, could not eventually lead to the germination of private property right of village superiors on village land and labour ?

Our answer to the question must necessarily be hypothetical. The actual historical reason that can explain the absence of a rise in private property must lie in the *sovereign right* of a peasant or artisan labour to his minimum livelihood so long as he rendered services on land or craft. Such right could grow in an objective situation where non cooperation from the labourers was liable to put at stake the material reproduction of the village production process. Since *only* the village production process constituted the genesis of wealth relations (whatever the degree of inequality in it) within a village community, the need for its material reproduction was incapable of compromising the sovereign right of peasants and artisans to their minimum livelihood. This formed the dialectical unity of relationship between the socially privileged and the under privileged. Since in an objective situation of high land man ratio and fertile soil conditions, it was only the sovereign *right* of a productive labour that could support extant process of generation and distribution of wealth (or surplus) in a community, village autonomy had to serve as much the primary interest of its own labouring people as that of those village landholders who lived off other's labour. Whenever proto feudal landholding right became overbearing to this sovereign right of peasants or artisans, the standard response of the community as a whole was to resort to various forms of resistance. In fact, Mughal state power was not so myopic as to follow such oppressive policies that could dismantle the extant social basis of peasant mode of production. Because any imperial or any other form of usurpation of peasant right was bound to be self defeating in character.

Therefore the dialectics of unity of the material conditions of reproduction of the Mughal polity was as follows : the state power could not procure its wherewithal without a comprehensive design for revenue collection by planting protofeudal intermediary right, but no protofeudal right on village output could be stretched so much as to cause disruption of the extant social basis of production and distribution within a village community . Again the dialectal unity at each level of the Mughal polity had its opposites. The sum total of such opposites operated around on the one hand, the process of reproduction of the centralised political power and, on the other, that of economic autonomy of the community in a village society. The unity of a village community had its opposites in privileged landholding of the non labouring stratum of big landholders and the subsistence requirement of the direct producers.

In a real life situation, a protofeudal intermediary treaded towards exercising arbitrary power with or without tacit cooperation of the village elites, but such tendency could hardly afford usurpation of peasant autonomy in its own foreseeable interest. In regions where village communities consisted of only peasant households or households with semi tribal social formations of little or no intracommunal stratification, an agent of the Mughal state power could hardly impose even its protofeudal right on the village output. In such a situation regional chief or so called *watan jagirdar* had to pay only a fixed tribute or *peshkash* to the Mughal governor of the province.

The basic component of the Mughal control structure on land in its core regions assumed the form of power-wielding armed intermediary groups that possessed state stipulated 'superior rights' on village level cultivated land and produce. Such an armed intermediary right on village land could, at no stage, assume an unambiguous form of private property in land that could enforce activities of the labouring population of villages. The state sponsored intermediary rights even during their most boisterous phase could hardly disrupt the process of village autonomy in matters of intra village management of social production, distribution and labour engagement. Mughal mode of surplus appropriation by the state power, in this sense, was all along forced to retain its tributary character. It was again not always the size of cultivated land but the number of ploughs used, or the actual amount and kind of crops raised by a village community that decided the size of assessable imperial revenue. But compared to the earlier period of Delhi Sultanates, the Mughal rhythm of tribute collection coincided with the annual rhythm of cultivation. The extent of rights exercised by a particular Mughal intermediary was substantially determined by the power he derived from above. To the extent, the exercise of such power was true to the exact codified norms of state policy, regarding estimation and collection of revenue it lost the arbitrariness inherent in the tributary system of the Delhi Sultanates. It, nevertheless, could assume a protofeudal character because the exercise of such right by a Mughal intermediary reflected surplus entitlement of a coercive variety.

While this intermediary right had an amorphous hierarchical division and heterogeneous nomenclature within itself the principal forms it assumed were many, such as the jagirdars, zamindar, *maadimash* (comparable to Inamholders), taluqdars (during the late Mughal period), etc. None of the above categories could claim, in politico legal terms or in actuality, any absolute or relative proprietary right on the land cultivated by their subordinate villages. Many office holders among these categories, except those comparable to a *maadi mash*, enjoyed a temporary state assignment of a piece of land for their individual upkeep (known as their respective *khas* land). This was in addition to a commission on total revenue collection from their jagirdari jurisdiction. Theoretically, a jagirdar could demand no revenue in excess of what was stipulated by the central administration through state officials like *qanungos* and could not exercise juridical power expect through centrally appointed *qazis*. In practice, however, in many cases the jagirdari powers were much less circumscribed. This happened in case an assignee was a big jagirdar whose power of revenue collection could subsume *fauzdari* or police jurisdiction as well.[6]

Such big *jagirdars* numbering only sixty eight collected 36.6 percent of the imperial revenue from agriculture.[7] They could exercise *de facto* judicial power over their domain and *qazis* and *qanungos* had to acquiesce in their extra legal wishes. It is reported that in some area *jagirdars* were able to chain peasants to their village lands. But this was not a general feature.

With the rise in demand for *jagirs* in the wake of continuously expanding Mughal bureaucracy and military machine, reallocation and redivision of Jagir assigned areas multiplied in order to meet these demands. The imperial method of executing divisions of land among jagirdars was always discriminatory in nature and was never accepted gracefully by all jagirdars. The powerful among them,[9] who held mansab rank as well, could secure bigger *jagirs* and even impose hereditary *jagir* rights on their villages. As a consequence, the relatively smaller *jagirdars* in connivance with powerful enemies of the empire, lost no opportunity of taking advantage of a rebellious situation (in the form of refusal to pay revenue to the imperial treasury). This is shown by the growing frequency of such rebellious activities by senior officials at the supra village level in close connivance with local state officials, particularly in the 16th and 17th centuries.[10] The growing political crisis within the Mughal bureaucracy particularly during the closing years of Mughal centralised power did not stem from any economic crisis at the level of village production as contended by Irfan Habib. Mughal crisis was fundamentally a political crisis resulting from gross inequality in surplus distribution among bureaucrats. While, the political crisis led to armed conflicts and assertion of independence among many regional chiefs and powerful *jagirdars* and zamindars themselves or against the imperial authority, at no stage could it subvert the functional autonomy of village communities. That was why, a protofeudal right in Mughal India could not make a successful transition to feudal mode of production unlike what had happened during post Charlemagne Europe.

If one can empirically substantiate Habib's account of big Mughal jagirdars' capacity to chain labour to land one can hypothesise that during the late Mughal period there emerged, at least in some areas, a semblance of the feudal mode of production. But to which category of land, were the peasants chained? Was it the *khas* land of big jagirdars or the land held by a village which was virtually possessed by the peasants themselves? Since employment of labour in a jagirdar's *khas* land (i.e., land assigned to a *jagirdar* for the upkeep of his household) was exclusively his prerogative, he could force, by virtue of his position, the labourers from a village to cultivate his land. We can concede that some powerful jagirdars could chain peasants to their personal holdings and came to enjoy a sort of *feudal right* on such holding. But what cannot be explained is how could a jagirdar enforce labour in holdings controlled by the subordinate village communities in his domain unless the self-sustaining mechanism of the latter was completely destroyed. The received paradigm of self-sustaining village production base comes into conflict with a coercive use of village labouring population either by an intermediary interloper or by a village oligarch.

What one can observe is that during the interim days of periodic political uncertainty and chaos, a section of powerful Mughal jagirdars could accumulate individual wealth at the expense of imperial revenue entitlements from village communities. But when political stability could be enforced by a Mughal emperor, tenurial reshuffling within the rank of jagirdars followed. Those jagirdars who were found to be defaulters or accomplices of a rebel prince or zamindar, invariably lost their ranks and hoards, if not their heads. Another factor that tended to promote instability within the rank of jagirdars - powerful or not - was their intense rivalry for a coveted position of power within the Mughal bureaucratic set-up. A powerful jagirdar could dislodge his rival from the race if he could buy more favour from an influential member of the Mughal court at Delhi.

Therefore, with so much in-built instability within the rank of powerful jagirdars-cum-mansabdars, their protofeudal status could hardly open up an objective scope for reinforcing their specific powers of usurping land and labour in a village that were possessed virtually by village communities themselves. Even if some jagirdars could weather such occasional instability within their rank, their supposed *feudal* right of hereditary character had to contend with many imponderables brewing up form below namely, the absolute requirements of autonomous functioning of village communities and age-old *functional* (not social) autonomy of Indian peasant or artisan labour.

We have a clearer picture from Nurul Hasan's categorisation of Mughal revenue collectors into the secondary and primary zamindars.[11] According to him by and large most of the secondary zamindars were supra-local chiefs of diverse social or ethnic origins. Many of them also functioned as Mansabdars with access to an extant Mughal court and or matrimonially related to official incumbents holding high ranks in the imperial army. Their power was derived mostly from their proximity to the imperial establishment. A much larger number of revenue collectors belonged to what Nural Hassan calls 'primary zamindars'. Like the secondary zamindars, they also enjoyed a percentage commission on their individual collection and revenue-free personal holding assigned by the imperial establishment, but unlike the former, they had to build up their position and power from below. In other words, the objective situations forced a primary zamindar to rear up close affinity with the village-level intra-communal establishment. Although a primary zamindar always nourished his ambition of becoming a secondary zamindar, the hurdles of his position made him considerably partisan to the interest of his subordinate village communities in a situation characterised by disputes regarding revenue assessment and collection, between the higher level imperial establishment and a village community. While it was the prerogative of a secondary zamindar to choose his subordinate primary zamindars, such choice was never absolute, because a secondary zamindar had revenue obligation to his higher authority. As a consequence, in the selection of a primary zamindar he had to compromise with extant dominant caste or ethnic groups that controlled sizable amount of land in settled village communities in his area. The recruitment of a primary Zamindar was thus governed by primary considerations like who could command loyalty from the dominant landholding caste or ethnic groups.

Hence, unlike the secondary zamindars, who were mostly urban dwellers, the primary zamindars, living in the rural areas, came from dominant ethnic or caste groups of a locality. But even in such situations, cooperation in matters of surplus appropriation between a primary Zamindar and the dominant interest groups among his village communities, virtually amounted to a negation of the interests of labouring population in those communities. Since such negation, could not run its full course by the objective need for natural reproduction of a village community with its unity and opposites, the inalienable contradiction between a primary zamindar's right of encroachment on village surplus and the sovereign right of peasant or artisan labour to a minimum livelihood could hardly attain a level of unresolvable conflict. In this sense the unassailable subsistence requirement of village labourers constituted the basic fulcrum on which the functional autonomy of a village community stood. Thus, the negation of village autonomy by any level of imperial usurpation of village surplus had its barrier in direct producers' unassailable right to subsistence requirement. Therefore, even an arbitrary claim by primary zamindars had to have its limit. The latter could hardly make a revenue demand that was likely to endanger the reproduction of autonomy of the community itself. In fact a primary zamindar hd to work out a balance between two contradictory pulls: on the one hand, his inflexible obligation to collect revenue and on the other, his anxiety to ensure the reproduction of the village production base - his revenue catchment area. While the situational compulsions induced a primary zamindar to chart out a cautious and calculated path, the job of a secondary zamindar had less constraints. A secondary zamindar had to work out an adjustment between the imperial assessment from his region and what primary zamindars could collect as actuals. In case the total collections by primary zamindars fell far short of the assessed revenue and other stipulated cesses, the primary Zamindars were either liable to pay fines or they were forced to revolt against the secondary zamindar. The tyranny of a secondary zamindar can be explained by his built-in alienation from his overlords as well as from village communities. In case they were unable to fulfil revenue obligations, they were thrown out of their jobs and, in such situations, they had nothing to fall back upon for their livelihood. This is probably why during the fiscal crisis of Aurangjeb's reign, many secondary zamindars turned rebels after refusing to pay the exorbitant revenue claims. In such situations, their position, power and aggrandisement had to be constantly reinforced by the material support from their respective subordinate primary zamindars.

Although there existed detailed written codes and regulations that governed the relationship between a Mughal emperor and his Dewan or Mansabdar, or those between a secondary zamindar and a primary one, or those between a local revenue establishment and subordinate village communities, the real life situation was often different. At every level there existed potentialities of conflict and both the dominant authority and dominated subject had to work out a *modus operandi* on the basis of inequality in trade-offs among the parties concerned. That was why an emperor with absolute power in legal terms, had to accommodate, in practice, with hereditarisation of the rights of powerful jagirdars. Under a specifically critical situation sometimes even a secondary zamindar, disobeyed the imperial writ, and made a common cause with his subordinate primary zamindars against a supposedly extortionate revenue demand. In a critical situation, the dominant social elites within a village community fought against the imperial revenue claim. On the other hand, we witness a situation in some regions when the village peasants and artisans had to wage a struggle against both upper caste exploitations within a village as well as exploitations by the imperial order from outside. The unequal trade-offs between an armed authority and its subordinates at every level within the Mughal polity generated perpetual disequilibrium and such disequilibrium precluded the possibility of a rise of an effective absolutist power or right at any level. This state of disequilibrium forced even the supreme imperial authority to pursue different policies in different regions, or in relation to various categories of regional protofeudal interest groups.

There were three fundamental features at any point of time that

There were three fundamental features at any point of time that caused a state of perpetual disequilibrium within a Mughal polity. The first was the absence of appropriation of landed property right (not exactly the right of private surplus entitlement) as a condition of labour at the village or supra village level. The second was an unassailable degree of village-level autonomy of peasant labour's subsistence right that always acted as precondition of material reproduction of social production base. And the third was the uneven contradictions between the imperial requirement of coercive appropriation of village surplus and the assertion of village autonomy in matters of social production and labour use.

If the Mughal polity could build up a semblance of unity within its constituent opposites by over-riding these features it was not on the basis of any written law or centralised coercive machinery but on the basis of mutual trade-offs among its various levels. At the village community level, the labouring stratum could retain its right to subsistence after it agreed to concede surplus to the non-labouring stratum. At the supra-village level, a village community could ensure its reproduction only by buying peace with external powers in exchange of a portion of village surplus either as protection fee or as imperial revenue or both. Similarly within the Mughal official hierarchy, a perpetual conflict at various levels could demonstrate a semblance of unity, however though unstable, by striking, if necessary, unprincipled compromises over relative shares of spoils among themselves. Indeed the imperial surplus requirement that was absolutely necessary to increase its wealth and military power had to buy the loyalty of subordinate village communities and of the not-so-law-abiding mansabdars, jagirdars and zamindars by studied non-interference in their own internal modes of local revenue administration.

Only when a massive enhancement in imperial surplus claim in the wake of its growing fiscal crisis, as it happened during the last days of the empire, tended to overstretch itself at the cost of material reproduction of village communities, that the villagers were forced to resort to either open rebellions or mass scale interregional migration. At no stage during the Mughal period did either a massive peasant revolt or a mass scale peasant immigration in response to extortionate levy attain that tempestuous level that could destroy the Mughal imperial power.

But what could slowly but steadily undermine the Mughal power of surplus appropriation was the eventual growth of mercantile economic power within the polity. The genesis of economic power of the Mughal merchants lay as much in the process of imperial mode of surplus acquisition as in the process by which the empire disbursed its expenditure of acquired surplus. This we shall study further in the Chapter IV.

Notes

1. As we have stated earlier, no early medieval account is available that can precisely indicate the nature of the relationship between a village society and its *khot* or *muquddam* or a local supra-village noble or king. Since the latter in any case could not survive without the economic support from the villages they could hardly afford going against extant socio-economic interests of villages.On the other hand, since a *khot* or a *muquddam* or a local king did not regulate an intra-village economy or its internal mode of surplus distribution among its members, a village society surrendered the surplus to him either involuntarily or voluntarily as a fee for rendering protection service against possible external interference.

2. Cf. M. Habib, *politics and Society during the Early Medieval period* (Bombay, 1974), pp. 10-77.

3. The revenue system under Mughals, for the first time, sought to relate revenue payment to the actual amount of cultivated land with its crop specifications in a village or *mauza*. Since Akbar's time revenue assessment took into account total cultivated land and specific products raised on such land for determining the state's share in it. A certain percentage of collected revenue was allotted to those who, as revenue official or civilian revenue collector or revenue farmer, were vested with the responsibility of collecting assessed state revenue. Accordingly, a jagirdar or a zamindar came to possess an advantage of collecting more revenue from a village than what was legally due or more surplus than what was due, inthe form of *Abwab* or local charge or other imposts. By this procedure the Mughal revenue system could develop a system of coercive extraction of surplus on the basis of the size of land-holding possessed by a village community. We think that this coercive extraction of village surplus was protofeudal in nature. It was not feudal because even during the peak of the Mughal rule, no revenue official or zamindar could establish his proprietary right on land possessed by subordinate villages, although he enjoyed coercive and somewhat arbitrary entitlement to surplus from the subordinate village communities. Since the surplus appropriation right of a zamindar or jagirdar could not act as the condition of labour activity in village land, we cannot treat such surplus appropriating right on village community land as their *property right*.

4. P. Anderson, *op. cit.*, p. 156.

5. Given the social stratification, it can be presumed that the incidence of village revenue burden was more on those within a village community who

were landholder-cultivators. Other things remaining same, the net produce from an acre of land held by peasant-households cultivating with family labour was higher than that from the holdings of elitist households who cultivated their holding with either sharecroppers or village menials. In the latter case, households produce was only the difference between total produce and sharecropper's share or the wages of the hired workers. In the former case, the production of the households included contribution of his own as well as unpaid family labour. This is how, with the introduction of meticulous revenue assessment of Mughal period, inequality of wealth among members of stratified village community was reinforced.

6. Irfan Habib, 'Agrarian Relations and Land Revenue' *Cambridge Economic History of India op.cit.*, Ch. IX,p.242.

7. *Ibid.*

8. "As for peasants, the Jagirdars claimed powers to detain them on the land like serf, and bring them back, if they ran away". Irfan Habib, *Agrarian System of Mughal India,* (Bombay, 1963), pp.115-16.

It is to be remembered that only in *khas* land of a Mughal revenue officer and in *khalisa* areas, the officials could theoretically chain peasants to the land they cultivated. But in the jagirdari areas where village communities were revenue assessment units, even at a theoretical level such possibility could not exist. Because it was not the jagirdar, but the village community which organised production with peasant labour. Even in areas peasants could not be chained to the land simply because there were enough arable land where they could migrate whenever they chose.

9. It appears that Irfan Habib finds two broad categories of jagirdars, the lower class of jagirdars who had to depend on a different group of imperial officials such as *fauzdars* and *mansabdars* for collecting revenue from villagers; and a higher class of jagirdars who procured jagir right from their rank as *Mansabdars*. For the latter, jagir holding became hereditary. Cf. *Ibid.*, p.241.

10.H.K. Naqvi, *Urbanization and Urban Centres under the Great Mughals* (Simla, 1971). Naqvi shows that even under the peaceful administration of Akbar, about 145 cases rebellion, defiance, connivance with imperial enemies took place, most of which were instigated by the members of regional Muslim nobility, Cf. *Appendix*. pp. 160-85.

11.Nural Hasan, *Thoughts on Agrarian Relations in Mughal India* (Delhi, 1973).

3.5: Emergence of Protofeudal Landholding Structures in West Europe and India

A protofeudal mode of surplus entitlement clearly emerged in India during the period of imperial Mughals. Its passage was prepared by the imperial mode of surplus appropriation from village communities since the period of Akbar. We have already explained why we call the Mughal mode of surplus collection from village protofeudal, and not feudal.

Our observation is based on analysis of the dialectical process by which a surplus acquiring Mughal administration was forced by its massive revenue requirement to create a 'hierarchical structure of superior rights on village land'.[1] The imperial process of surplus appropriation had to be executed by a hierarchical structure of superior rights but the latter developed in itself an antithetical force against its progenitor, the Mughal imperial administration. The stronger this antithetical force became, the more independent became the intermediary rights on village produce but paradoxically enough, the assertion of village autonomy became more intense. Apparently within a Mughal polity we can discern two distinctly different mutually reinforcing sets of unity and contradiction. The first one was between the Mughal state power and its essential revenue acquiring arm, the protofeudal intermediary interest, and the second one was between the latter as the symbol of coercive state power, and the centre of social production base, i.e., a village community. In reality however, both the sets of unity and contradiction had their genesis in the basic unity and contradiction between the Mughal imperial power, on the one hand, and the village social economy, on the other. It was the coercive unity imposed by the centralised state policy that invariably unleashed the growth of antagonistic contradictions between it and the direct producers. From this enforced unity and its resultant contradiction was derived the other sets of unity and contradiction, namely, those between the state power and its builtin intermediary interests and those between the village direct producers and others, namely, village level non labouring group of surplus apprropriators on the one and supra village intermediary interests on the other.*Without a centralised state power, group of protofeudal interests in land either in Mughal India or even in Charlemagne's empire in Europe could not rise.*

The process of materialist dialectics manifested in a historical movement of state formations is usually overlooked by many Marxist and non Marxist scholars. That is why it appears to many that 'political decentralisation' was one of the prime requisites for the development of vassalage and fief holding rights typical of many regions of West European feudalism.[2] The thesis on political decentralization as a necessary variable for the growth of feudal economy implicitly suggests that a centralised state polity is a negative historical force that was arrayed against the eventual rise of feudal social and economic formation in the premodern Asia. It is interesting that a unique viewpoint is emphasised by Coulborn to whom "feudalism is primarily a method of government, *not an economic or a social system,* through it obviously modifies and is modified by the social and economic environment. It is a method of government in which the *essential* relation is not that between ruler and subject, *not [between] state and citizen but between lord and vassal"* (italics added.)[3] Coulborn's observation is not on how feudal right could make historical emergence from the pores of prefeudal epoch, but on the essential property of feudal governance of society and economy say as manifested in West Europe. In the political decentralisation thesis, society not the state, should be the point of departure for discovering the genesis of feudal property right. In Coulborn's view it is not the society as such but the method of governance of it by a lord that caused the genesis of feudal property right. In our view, both the above view points are *ahistorical* enough to make departure only from the narrow empirical postulates of history of some European regions where feudal society of governance came into being. In Coulborn's view, since in India or China, feudal governance of society did not arise as a received paradigm, it is absent in India or China. He does not raise the question as to why India or China could not witness the rise of feudal governance of society. What is, in fact necessary is to perceive a period of history of a society not as mere reflection of extant empirical phenomena but as a process of dialectical transition of the past into its present. There can be no disagreement on the fact that during the period of feudal consolidation of property right and enserfment of peasant labour, political decentralisation in West Europe became the resultant *historico-empirical* process. But how this process came into being, or what were the prior historical forces that set such process in motion as the dialectical consequence of an earlier historical process are questions that are still to be answered. Coulborn does not examine the incipient historical specifics that brought feudal governance of vassals in West Europe into being and the differential objective specifics that blocked a similar development in India or China. In the case of West Europe the historical forces that constituted the dynamics of pre feudal state formations and formations of society in their mutual interactional relationship, are required to be probed so as to explain why political decentralisation during the period of feudal consolidation became the consequence. A similar analytical exercise is required to explain why in India or China feudal consolidation could not take place.

In our view, it is the specific nature of reproduction of state as well as civil society and their specific mode of mutual interaction that can explain why apparently even a similar historical paradigm of development does not produce the same consequence on the different states and societies belonging to various regions. In all regions or continents the state power of a government possessed, in general, certain common attributes, e. g., force as its basis and extraction of surplus as its objective. But how could its mode of subsumption of power or surplus extraction be materialised is determined by the nature and dynamics of the civil society it confronts. Therefore, specificity in the mode of materialisation of coercive basis by a system of government assumes significance in explaining a specific paradigm of interaction between a state formation and its subordinate social formation that sustains both. Since a specific mode of materialising a state system and its perpetuation can hardly be delinked from the peculiarity of the historical preconditions of the relevant society, neither mere political decentralisation as such nor a particular system of governance of peasant producers by a landholding interest can be treated as explanatory variables for grasping either a rise of feudal property right or its absence in a country or continent.

Let us now closely examine the comparable developments in the state system as well as the social formations in West Europe and India.

In India the period between the Ghori conquest and the Lodhi Sultanates is roughly comparable to that period of West European state formations that had to face two waves of Germanic invasions against the Roman empire in the context of the rising Christianity. However, in neither situation could the conquerors dismantle the pre existing social modes of production.

In West Europe, after the first wave of Germanic invasions, the only change witnessed by the Roman 'Villa' system, or the system of latifundia based slave mode of production, was a discreet replacement of some Roman latifundia owners by the invading warlords in the conquered regions. The bondsmen soldiers of the invading warlords were subsequently reduced to peasant slaves. That was because the invaders in many regions could make production in their own estates feasible only by transforming their bondsmen soldiers into slave labour. As a consequence, a racially dualistic administration governed a similar mode of cultivation by slave labour and executed an identical mode of surplus appropriation. Following the more massive phase of Germanic invasions, which Anderson calls the 'second wave', the Merovingian empire came into being in the 5th or 6th century A. D. But the Merovingian monarchy did not disturb the slave mode of production (despite the fact that, by that time, slave mode began to show signs of exhaustion) but sought to buy political stability. It failed to do this due to Byzantine and other external attacks, plunder and territorial occupations. The empire sought to maintain its power by directing its war campaigns against politically weaker regions as if to make up for the losses it suffered elsewhere because of external invasions. Out of the resultant political anarchy the landholding structures manned by the Merovingian nobility were forced into a state of flux. Successive invaders implanted their own nobles on land by driving out the existing ones and began to extract surplus from slave labour. While the slave mode of production was not disturbed, the mode of procuring and supervising slave labour assumed multitudinous forms. For instance, the Anglo saxon system suspended Roman villa system after England fell to the Germanic invaders, but could not correspondingly develop a new mode of exploiting peasant labour by replacing the worn out slave mode. Frankish Gaul, Visgothic Itlay and France under the Lombards witnessed only fleeting changes in the basic form of using slave labour in landholding in the wake of the second Germanic invasion, Byzantine attacks and the Arab conquest of Mediterranean worlds. None of these changes represented a major departure from the slave mode of production. Therefore the Merovingian period can broadly be characterised by the persistence of a socio political instability and diversity in social production relation or property forms with slave labour. The coexistence of the truncated slave mode with the production of peasant allods might have the caused discreet emergence of differential status groups among the invaders-turned-landholders or among the peasant producers themselves, but it was still far from the birth pangs of a feudal mode of production.[4]

Similarly in India Delhi Sultanates without disturbing the village control on social production base, frequently changed the taxation measures. It is true that quite a few among them sought to instal a stable form of control structure on supra village chiefs or even *Balahars,* in their anxiety to acquire village surplus, but did not achieve durable success. The allodial character of functioning of village cultivators within intracommunal specifics of rights and obligations of an autonomous village community did not undergo basic transformation. The slavery enforced by the Sultanates could not bring about any effective change either within the village mode of cultivation or within the pattern of supra village mode of surplus distribution. The prevailing system was of communal administration of village production base, and its alienation from the external modes of surplus acquisition (which included tribute payment by a village to outside despots or interlopers as the marked feature during the entire pre Mughal period). Surplus acquisition from royal *Iqta* assignment (which itself underwent several structural changes under successive Sultans) could not help a Sultan build up the sustainable type of intermediary land holding structure in the rural areas. Since a Sultanate imperial system possessed only a fluid bureaucracy and a fatigued militia,the *Iqta* holders witnessed frequent changes in the individual command structure of each Sultanate. The resultant political instability and social restlessness could bring about Taimur's invasion in the 14th century, and the diversionary defiance of a Sultan's writ by any regional raja. Nor did a Sultan dare to venture war campaign against the Chola kingdom or emerging Vijaynagar empire in the South. Just like a Merovingian monarch, a Delhi Sultan had to acquire wealth by plunder, and had to face at the same time pilferage of his wealth by royal servants or its plunder by an external invader.

However, the difference between the rural civil societies of the two continents is more significant for an understanding of the differential processes of evolution in their respective historical contexts. While in the case of the Merovingian empire Christianity began to usher in a socio political synthesis between paganism and politico cultural sophistication of the Roman nobility, in the case of the Delhi Sultanates, or even the early Mughals, the religio culture system of ruler's religion, Islam, failed to execute a similar socio political synthesis between sharply antagonistic natures of social formations under the extant Indian social order and the egalitarian social ethos of the Islamic theological prescriptions. This differential process of historical evolution between the two continents can be explained, not so much by the relative synthetic potential of alternative religio social orders, as by intercontinental differences in modes of interaction between a state power and its subordinate rural society. It is true that brahmanic social order of the pre Sultanate period was apparently far more internally articulate than the pre Merovingian socio cultural order of paganism in West Europe. But this supposed internal articulation of the brahmanic religio social order stemmed not so much from its inner strength, as from the fact that at no stage of Indian history a state power headed by a non brahmanic or brahmanic religious persuation was functionally integrated with the internal dynamics of a civil community in village. In contrast a civil society in pagan Europe was always sought to be integrated with the requirements of the state and its dominant classes. This explains why the religious faith of a Buddhist emperor or a Muslim Sultan in India found it objectively expedient not to disturb or distort the extant religiosocial and economic order within a civil society and economy. This is a contrast with the ease with which the Roman conquest engulfed the entire Western Europe during the height of its power and the much easier modes by which Christianity, a completely alien religion, could sweep the entire pagan Europe. The reason is that in West Europe rural societies lost their individual socio collective identity even before the beginning of the medieval period and were disintegrated according to the requirements of a powerful centralised state power of Rome. This did not happen in India since here distinct functional communality of economic reproduction of a civil society could never be usurped either by an ubiquitous growth of private property or any centralised state power that could dismantle a village community so as to facilitate the conversion of village labour or land, the material condition of labour, into private property.

In West Europe, the end of the Roman imperial economic order was expedited by the first wave of Germanic invasion, because that opened a new epoch of political confusion and disarticulation of the slave mode. The first Germanic invasion reduced the Roman imperial power to a new configuration of 'barbarian'provincial powers in Spain, Itlay, France, England, etc. The second wave of Germanic invasions completed the course of decline of the classical age with its empire, legal network and cultural idioms. Beneath this tumultuous course of political turmoil and economic disarticulation of slavery, a new process of synthesis between the elements of Roman latifundia based slave mode and those of Germanic home bred tradition began. But the course of synthesis advanced very slowly and almost imperceptibly.[5] The political anarchy of the Dark Ages and the attendant instability in the ranks of village chiefs, local lords and others to whom surplus appropriation from dependent tenures was the means of survival, germinated a trend towards complete disruption of extant modes of production. The successive migrations only reinforced this trend which was characterised by heterogeneous categories of rights on land, namely, the rights exercised by Germanic noble state, dependent tenures, small peasant holdings, communal lands, survival of truncated Roman villa system and rural slavery. During this period, 'the Germanic law became progressively dominant', while 'the system of land taxes inherited from Rome broke down' in the face of resistance from landholders, the peasantry as well as the church. The Merovingian rulers had to make two ends meet by plunder of regional lords outside their territory and by imposing tithes on the churches.[6] Eventually a new supra ethnic category of rural aristocrats emerged in Gaul through a steady process of inter marriage and mutual assimilation among member households of the Germanic and Roman landed classes. But neither in the sphere of peasant rights and of surplus appropriating rights of the landed classes, nor in the process of political subsumption of power by the Merovingian rulers could there emerge a stable politico economic basis.

As a consequence, the entire tenure of the Merovingian rulers was characterised by a weak state power confronting a relatively stronger landed class and by a transitional phase of mutual acculturation and social intercourse among landed interests belonging to the church, the nobility and the peasant producers of two ethnic origins - Germanic and Roman. Since this synthesising process could make only a halting advance owing to the political uncertainty and chaos in the midst of armed invasions from outside, from the Byzantine power and the Arbas, a political vacuum developed that paved the way for the rise of the new political power of Carolingians from the rank of Frankish aristocrats. This empire was founded by Charlemagne in the first decade of the 9th century.

The Carolingian empire, unlike that of Merovingians, quickly brought about a political and military unification of West Europe by ruthless imposition of its writ on various categories of private holders of land. The entire empire was divided into many counties and the governance of each county was vested with a trusted noble. The officially sponsored county noble (the tenure of nobility being revocable only by the Emperor himself) was installed into power at the expense of the older landholding groups (new nobles became *de jure* agents of Carolingian monarch assuming the power of a supreme landlord). These Carolongian landowners were not paid salaries but were instead assigned huge territory and a certain percentage of royal revenue to be collected. But such assignments were subject to transfer and constant watch by a smaller central group of supra noble magnates belonging mainly to the personal entourage of the emperor himself.

Beneath this royal organisation of revenue catchment areas lay the development of a well defined land control structure in which royal assignment of lands was rigorously synthesised with bonds of service to be rendered by the assignees. By the end of the 9th century, 'grants of land by rulers ceased to be gifts, to become conditional tenures, held in exchange for sworn service[7] civil, military or extra economic. The lower administrative positions were similarly structured combining tenure of service with manifold obligations to the upper layer of county nobles. The result of this evolution was the emergence of 'fief' as a delegated grant of land vested with juridical and political powers (codified in written forms) in exchange for military service. This is a briefly outlined account of how the elements of landholding structure and enserfed labour services of a future feudal mode of production, came to be germinated under a highly centralised but politically peaceful administration of the Carolingian empire. At the same time it is to be pointed out that the after the death of Charlemagne, the power of the empire began to be substituted by the local landholding elites.

The collapse of the empire was brought about more by the internal consolidation among county nobles in terms of power and absolute land right, rather than by external attacks from Viking, Saracen of Magyar invaders. 'By 850 benefices were virtually everywhere, inheritable, by 870, the last *missi dominici* had vanished, by the 880's the *vassi dominici* were mediatized to local potentates; by the 890's counts had effectively became hereditary regional lords'.[8] Anderson is correct in pointing out that the unweildy Carolingian state apparatus outlived its effectiveness by 'the rapid spread of benefices', and 'their increasing hereditability', 'growing regionalisation of magnate class' was presided over by dynastic civil wars among the heirs of Charlemagne.

We have not suggested a mechanical comparison between the Carolingian empire of early 9th century with the Mughal empire since Akbar's consolidation of power in 1570. It is only aimed at laying bare a comparative process by which a highly centralised imperial control structure and materialised labour could historically cause the establishment and consolidation of a class of protofeudal landed interests or owners of estates. That an imperial control structure and its mode of subsumption of power act as antithetical force driving the centralised authority to its *de facto* decentralisation and ultimate collapse is, however, more evident in European history than in Mughal history. What is, therefore, not evident is why, in West Europe, out of the ruins of Carolingian empire, the imperial control structure (i.e., its mode of subsumption of power by the institution of heritable benefices enjoyed by landholding potentates) made transition to the rise of feudal landownership and peasant enserfment between the 10th and 12th century, but with almost a similar centralised control structure of the Mughals on village land and materialised labour in the 16th and 17th centuries failed to execute a similar transition.

Notes

1. In fact, to the Mughal administration of Akbar, it was an inescapable need. Unlike his predecessors, Akbar's need for having fiscal stability could hardly depend either on an unstable tide and flow of revenue from villages or on war booty or wealth from slave trade as it was the case of the Sultanates. In fact, the size of empire and its growing establishment forced his predecessor, Sher Shah, to mop up a higher amount of village surplus through meticulous survey and revenue settlement of village land used for cultivation. Akbar inherited not only Sher Shah's empire but also his comprehensive land revenue system. While Sher Shah laid down a comprehensive basis of revenue assessment and collection, Akbar made an improvement upon them thanks to the ingenuity of his revenue minister, Todarmal. It is, however, to be pointed out that imperial right on village labour, though mediated only by a claim on a portion of assessable village income, it was exercised more thoroughly and coercively by the Mughals than what was under the Sultanates.

2. Dobb and Sweezy differed from each other on the very definition of feudalism. But both seem to have reached an agreement on the point that other differences remaining as they were, 'political decentralisation' of 11th-12th century Europe was instrumental in the growth of feudal mode productions over the ruins of Roman imperial order.
Cf. *Transition from Feudalism to Capitalism : a Symposium* (Calcutta, 1957).

3. Rushton Coulborn (Ed.), *op. cit.*, pp. 2-4

4. We here differ from the thesis on 'Morovingian Feudalism' propounded by Alfous Dopsch and D.H.Green to whom feudalism means "the status and rite of commendation of one freeman to another". Cf. A. Dopsch, *The Economic and Social Foundations of European Civilization* trans. E. patzelt (London, 1937), pp. 387-88, and D.H. Green, *The Carolingian Lord* (Cambridge, 1965),

Ch. 5.

5. Cf. E.A. Thompson, *The Goths in Spain* (Oxford, 1969), pp. 305-12 and P. Anderson, *op. cit.*, pp. 120-26.

6. The founder of Merovingian empire, Colvis, was a baptised Catholic who lorded over the entire church system spread over Gaul, Spain and the region around the old seat of the Roman empire.

7. P. Anderson, *op. cit.*, pp. 138-140.

The subsequent history of Carolingian empire or its collapse has been analysed on the basis of accounts supplied by P. Anderson and D. Bullough. Cf. D. Bullough, *The Age of Charlrmagne* (London, 1965).

8. P. Anderson, *op. cit., p.142.*

3.6: Constraints of Growth of Protofeudal landholding in Mughal India and the Historical Premise of Mughal Decline

Why the once powerful Mughal imperial control structure on village output could not germinate feudal property rights in land? This question is itself based on two hypotheses developed earlier. Under Mughal land revenue system, although the exact control structure on cultivated land might have contained the phenomenon of hereditary (supra-village or intra-village) non-productive entitlement[1] to a stipulated portion of village output certainly such entitlement was not ground rent as such; and secondly, since any category of supra-village or intra-village non-productive surplus entitlement in pre-British India had to exclude from its formal or actual ambit the mechanism of labour control, no kind of enserfment of village labour could follow directly from either protofeudal landholding of supra-village power groups or from intra-village big landholding of non-labouring stratum as were developed. Indeed, there existed land parcels temporarily assigned to Mughal intermediaries as their *khas* to which labour could perhaps be forcibly attached, as Habib or Kosambi have mentioned. But this was not the general picture of the Mughal control structure either on land (cultivated or not) or on labour services in jagirdari/zamindari areas or in khalisa areas. Firstly, a coercive attachment of labour to the *khas* land of a jagirdar, mansabdar or a zamindar could be materialised only by the force of arms, but in a community of villagers no such coercive use of labour as a regular phenomenon was feasible. Secondly, there is historical evidence to suggest that the main plank of social production was constituted of land and labour of village communities, not of *khas* land and forcible use of labour. Historians, nevertheless, have shown that there existed sporadic sale, purchase or gift of surplus entitlement of zamindar (hereditary or not) at the supra-village level. But any such transfer of surplus entitlement did not necessarily reflect a proprietary character of such transferred entitlement. At no stage of pre-British development, could general categories of social or political entitlement of a portion of village output involve a *direct control* of labour services on cultivable land. From our hypothesis it follows that in Mughal India production decisions were taken not by the village superiors or by the tribute-receiving agents of imperial control structure on an area of cultivated land. A production decision was the prerogative of a village community and such communal prerogative was to be carried out by individualised labour activity of labourers belonging to the community.

Since individualised activity of a labourer was motivated by his production for self-consumption as well as village use, the latter was by and large activated not by a pure external demand of commercial nature for village goods but by internal subsistence requirement. If a village community exported its good, such export was governed more by import requirement of essential consumer goods. In this sense *a Mughal village community was of self-sustaining character not exactly a self-sufficient one.*

The question is how were the communal production decisions arrived at, or to be more specific, who determined the extent of labour use in a particular branch of social production in a village? In our view, the production decisions of the labouring members of a village community were the cumulative aggregate of individualised production decisions of community labourers. Since every individualised production decision had to take into account individual direct producer's subsistence need as well as the need for material reproduction of his communal entity there was no scope for conflict between community decisions and individual decisions. Only when the structure of such rights and obligations manifested sharp mutual contradiction that a conflict developed between the interest of the dominant social group and productive labourers within a community.

It is now acknowledged that Mughal village communities themselves were not of a homogeneous category. Some possessed joint control over so much land that its members could not cultivate it without outside labour. On the other hand, there were communities which had so little cultivable land that unless the surplus labourers of those land poor villages worked in the land possessed by a neighbouring community, they could not survive.

In the case of village communities vesting their power in a chief, there also existed various categories. In some, chiefs were elected from among the elderly and experienced members, and in others, chieftainship was either hereditary or lineage based. Besides, there existed village communities where a chief could command loyalty of kindred ethnic groups forming a majority among community members. Again there were village communities which among themselves (with one or more clusters of settlement in each) did not have any uniform mechanism of surplus entitlements and distribution of land among labouring population. But defying all such differences, village level collectivity of settled households was the unit of social production and distribution and the imperial control structure claimed its share not from an individual household but from the village community or society as a unit.

Within the level of community a non-labouring entitlement to a portion of village surplus was derived not from his *individual power* but from his being a member of a kindred group that could exercise the dominant group power. Since the basic premise for consolidation of an intermediary protofeudal landholding right in Mughal India was the imposition of claim on a stipulated portion of output produced by the village community as a unit, the latter was ready to honour such external claim only when the claim was not unrealistic in magnitude and the community could retain its autonomy in all intra-communal matters relating to its extant mode of land and labour allocation, production and distribution. Similarly at the level of a village community, the non-productive land holders' claim to surplus had to be bought on their part by conceding autonomy of peasant possessions in their holdings. In other words, a village community despite unequal distribution of holdings among members had to guarantee the sovereign right of an active labourer to his subsistence.

In this sense, the basic propeller of social production process during the Mughal period was the labourer's need for subsistence along with latters' communal need for reproducing the village community. While the communal identity and functional interdependence between labourers, including the direct producers, and non-labouring members formed the basis of unity, such unity had its incipient opposites in the objective inequality in intra-communal distribution of produce between labouring and non-labouring members. So long as the direct producers (independent of whether they possessed personal holdings or not) could reproduce their sovereign rights of livelihood in exchange for their labour services, they developed no resistance to either communal inequalities in wealth and entitlement relations or in communal inequality in the distribution of landholdings among members. The wealth or surplus acquisition by those community members who did not render labour services was used only to satisfy their present or future consumption needs and not for controlling means of labour. That was why village inequality in wealth relations could not produce any growth impact on the social production base. In Mughal India social production could grow only as a direct consequence of increase in labour population or in the area of cultivated land, the latter being a free gift of nature. The Mughal system of revenue on its part possessed no in-built mechanism for raising the level of labour productivity. This explains why the social production base of Mughal India, despite its potentiality of productive diversifications, was as a rule, stagnant.

Then why could the village communal system of production as postulated above, generate contradiction with the imperial revenue system? The main reason lay in an ever increasing absorption of men and materials within the imperial power nexus of Mughals so as to warrant an increasing intensity of their coercive appropriation of village output. But the village output could be expanded only by bringing new areas under cultivation with additional employment of labour force. Therefore, all other things (the size of imperial establishment, its nobility, armed troops, etc.) remaining the same, any excess in the rate of growth of consumption requirement of the non-productive segments of Mughal polity, over and above the rate of growth of productive labour in a village economy, was bound to cause manifestation of the basic contradiction between villages as centres of social production and the Mughal establishment functioning as the coercive appropriation power.

Since the basis of surplus entitlement of the Mughal state power was its power of coercion, its hunger for wealth and aggrandisement had no escape from its innate logic, namely, an enlargement of the size of its establishment, parasitic nobility, war machinery, etc. On the other hand, it had at its disposal little or no social mode of executing this power. Therefore, the Mughal state power resting as it did only on its growing revenue requirement, had to confront the system of social production that had no endogenous or exogenous dynamic of its own for its secular expansion (except through an increased size of population growth and/or the area of cultivated land). As a result the basic contradiction between a naked power of an emperor and its armed retinues, with its despotic mode of procuring surplus and the village labourers with their stagnant productivity, had to be more and more reinforced in course of time if the former's surplus claim was boundless.

How did this contradiction within the Mughal polity shape its configuration? First, in the relation of unity and contradiction between the Mughal imperial power and its institution of protofeudal rights of jagirdars, zamindars, talukdars, isaradars, etc; second, in the relation of unity and contradiction between the protofeudal surplus appropriating rights of the Mughal imperial system and the village communities, the exclusive centres of social production base. As a consequence of the above two, the contradiction between a village community and the imperial revenue system could cast its shadow on the relation of unity and contradiction between intra-communal structure of social dominance and servitude. If the first two constituted the dual facets of the basic contradiction, the third appeared as the resultant one.

Without stipulating detailed laws of revenue assessment and collection, the Mughals, unlike the Sultans could hardly reproduce itself. In this sense the protofeudal hierarchy among jagirdars, zamindars and others, had a bond of unity of interest with the Mughal imperial power. It is true that the Mughal hierarchy of revenue collection had the opportunity of appropriating more surplus than what was legally stipulated by imperial laws. But there was the problem of reconciling its claim with such village communities where the rule of the game was social mutuality among the non-labouring strata and the labouring one, armed power being a completely alien instrument in social relations. On the other hand there developed a new contradiction between the revenue hierarchy and the supreme imperial power, in general and between the lower echelons of such hierarchy and the higher ones, in particular. The lower echelons of this hierarchy, namely, the primary zamindars and small jagirdars, with their village or pargana level kanungoes and Amins, had to face the most difficult problems of reconciliation between the revenue claims and the capacity of a village to meet such claims. Frequently, reconciliation was not feasible and the inevitable consequence was conflicts, either among different levels of Mughal revenue hierarchy, or between the revenue hierarchy as a whole and the supreme imperial office. The conflicts became more pronounced in those regions where the secondary zamindars' claim exceeded even the royal stipulations in the wake of consolidation and augmentation of their private power and wealth.

The above contradictions within the Mughal revenue hierarchy or those between the emperor and his establishment as a whole could cast their shadow within the intra-communal relations of a village. As we have argued earlier the imperial assessment hit peasants and artisans more adversely than village landholders cultivating with hired or tenant labour, and that the Mughal revenue administration had by its mode of assessment and collection accelerated the already existing trend towards inequality in wealth relations within a village community. In response to these developments imposed from above there grew in some areas a relation of mutually gainful trade-off between village big landholders and the local establishment of Mughal revenue hierarchy. But this trade-off had its barrier in the sovereign social right of the village community labourers to their subsistence earning in exchange of their services. Since no amount of social enserfment in a caste stratified village community could ever destroy the inflexible right of subsistence by transforming the village material condition of labour, the relation of the trade-off between a group of big non-productive landholders and the local revenue establishment was necessarily limited. An appropriation of village output beyond this limit by any power-wielding group within or outside a village not only endangered the material reproduction of the social production process but also created, in its wake, an uncertainty in the well-being of non-productive big landholders themselves, i.e., their communal process of augmenting their own means of livelihood, wealth, etc. In this sense the autonomy of direct producers' right to subsist in lieu of their labour services, acted as the fulcrum on which the self-sustaining autonomy of a village economy stood. It is this autonomy that forced a village group of non-productive landholders not to capitulate to an unlimited extent on the basis of the said trade-off between itself and local revenue establishment. In some cases, the village non-productive landholders' trade-off with a local revenue establishment endangered the subsistence of village level labouring strata, the situations begot either a trend towards massive migration of direct producers from the locality, or outright confrontations in the form of peasant or artisan revolt.

As a whole, Mughal Indian polity characterised a good number of paradoxes within itself. On the one hand, the polity tended to reinforce the interest of its growing revenue requirement and hence to back the power of protofeudal interests over village output. The effect of this was a sharpening of social as well as economic contradictions within a village community, i.e., a weakening of communal solidarity. On the other hand, a coercive imposition of excessive revenue claim on village tended to germinate, in general, a syndrome of total resistance, not merely from the direct producers, but from the village community as a whole that in most cases included its non-productive big landholders.

While in essence, the Mughal coercive power of the state or that of protofeudal intermediary groups of landholders appeared as an antithesis of the self-sustaining autonomy of a village economy in Mughal India, in reality however, an execution of Mughal coercive power had its limit in communal or supra-communal absence of individual ownership of the material conditions of labour.

This is why the basic postulates that governed the relationship between the Mughal state and a village community were fundamentally different from those that governed the relationship between a protofeudal landholding right of nobles in Charlemagne's empire and the community of direct producers in the rural areas. Under Carolingian empire, the rural societies had never possessed nor inherited an well-orchestrated functional autonomy since the days of Grecian slavery or the Roman empire which had already built up the social premise of individual ownership of the material conditions of labour.

In West Europe, growth and consolidation of protofeudal landholding structure organised by the Carolingian empire did not face insurmountable barriers in a universal social autonomy of peasant right to subsistence within a village society. The differential Indian postulates of the relationship between Mughal imperial state or its official and village community must have arisen from the historical inheritance of an unassailable self-sustaining autonomy of the functioning of village labourers. This is evident from a brief account of Indian evolution that characterised the genesis of the Mughal landholding structure of the protofeudal type and the constraints of its growth that had its manifestation in the evolutionary process of 16th-17th century Mughal jagirdari system of revenue collection.[2]

The imperial administration of Akbar distinguished him from the others. His administrative norms were not based merely on his desire or will, but on codified laws, public as well as civil. His scheme of assigning jagirs, or modes of collecting or remitting revenue, or his mode of differential assessment of taxes on crop (food or nonfood) in rebel or loyal villages, pure jagir lands or khalisa lands, tribute paying zamindars or jagir-assignee zamindaris, etc., were based on a set of codified norms prepared by his revenue minister, Todarmal. Because of these written laws his revenue bureaucracy could manage, apart from the general village land, a huge area of khalisa category of cultivation spread over the entire empire including outlying areas like Bengal and Gujarat.[3]

As we have suggested earlier, from the point of view of State's role in building protofeudal intermediary holding rights on village land, Akbar's empire is only superficially comparable to the Carolingian empire under Charlemagne. Indeed the distinctive feature of the Mughal administrative apparatus since the period of Akbar was the innovation and imposition of a new comprehensively designed codified rights of intermediaries for acquiring surplus from villages and codified laws of assessment of village output so as to decide the state's share in it. Not that the widespread jagir assignments constituted a Mughal innovation, jagir assignments had their historical ancestry in *Iqta* assignments begun by the Delhi Sultanates. However, the Mughal innovation lay in meticulous organisation of the intermediary rights and privileges of heterogeneous categories. It is the superior statecraft of the Mughals, compared to that of the Delhi Sultanate, that helped each Mughal emperor to command a much larger land tract than any Delhi Sultanate had done and to show a better semblance of unitary administrative set-up despite chronic instability and conflicts that characterised each building block of the Mughal power edifice. Moreover, the Muslim or Hindu war veterans on the pay-roll of the Mughals were assigned jagirs and *not the other way round* as was the case with *Iqta* holders (under a Delhi Sultanate) who had to raise most troops for imperial defence from capitulating *rajas*, *rais*, etc.

It is true that Charlemagne's empire also had to recruit trusted nobles with military background for the collection of revenue in alien rural districts. But these Carolingian nobles were assigned intra-county landholdings for the purpose, provided they could assure obligatory military and civil service to the Carolingian monarch. Similarly, a chain of multi-strata as well as multi-ethnic *conditional* tenures or assignments on village cultivated land had been created under the imperial initiative of Akbar. The various categories of official tenure-holders within the hierarchy of Mughal revenue administration ranging from *Dewan*, *Subedar*, *Fauzdar*, etc. to its lowest stratum of primary zamindars of different nomenclatures in revenue circles were never content merely with what they secured in terms of stipulated personal pay and allowances.

They were also assigned personal land or a certain percentage share of collection from a revenue circle consisting in general of a cluster of villages. In most cases, actual acquisition by a primary zamindar or petty revenue official far exceeded what was warranted as legal entitlements. Citing Abul Fazal's evidence. T. Ray Chaudhuri observes: 'the employees of the Mughal state and nobility included a vast array of lesser functionaries ranging from *ahadis* and revenue officials to petty clerks and accountants attached to every department of the administration and every noble's establishment. . . . Many of them could aspire to a lifestyle modelled on that of the Amirs. . . . At one level they were petty exploiters adding through their extra legal exactions to the burden of the [village level] producers. At another, they too, like the armed forces, were an essential prop of the structure of empire.[4]

What was true about the petty Mughal administrative functionaries was truer in case of various categories of upper level holders of intermediary rights. While the incidence of taxes on village producers were, according to Habib, 'regressive' in nature, 'the larger landholders' as village zamindars, or headmen, or as powerful members of a socially privileged segment of a village community, were required to pay less revenue per unit of assessed area under their individual control. Since the incidence of tax per unit of village cultivated land varied according to the nature of the crop raised, the total amount of revenue raised from a village land was not proportional to the size of cultivated land possessed by it. A village land yielding different crops (ranging from 10 to 41) had to bear diverse categories of crop-cum-yield wise tax incidences. Therefore under the given principles of assessment, the actual amount of assessed revenue to be paid by a village left much scope for arbitrariness on the part of intermediaries or revenue officials or zamindars. The extent of arbitrariness in revenue assessment was not, theoretically, designed by officials, as a *pargana* assigned to a jagir-holder contained villages with overlapping tenurial forms such as *khalisa, jagir, zamindari* and *Raiyati* holdings, subject to different stipulated principles of taxation.[5]

But this complexity in the mode of revenue assessment arising out of diverse principles of crop-wise, yield-wise and tenure wise assessment offered official or semi-official intermediaries enough scope for arbitrariness through extra-legal manoeuvres. The codified Mughal principles of taxation always provided a scope for acting on the part of an official in favour of or against a village community, or for shifting on the part of a higher official his revenue commitment through extra-legal manoeuvres on the shoulders of his subordinates. For instance, a sworn revenue obligation of a North Indian zamindar to the imperial administration entitled him to a 25 per cent remission, but in practice, he could manipulate a cent per cent remission for himself provided he could successfully shift his remittable share on subordinate officers and villages by imposing an additional 75 p.c. obligations on them. Similarly, a jagirdar who might prefer to be partisan to the villages under his pargana, could understate production on some pretext or the other so that the incidence of taxes on village communities was less than what would actually be due. This was possible when the jagirdar could secure support from petty revenue officials under him. By and large, the watan jagirdars belonged to this category.

Within a village community a similar manipulation of shifting village revenue burden from one household to the other was not possible. The total revenue burden borne by a village was distributed among households producing aliquot parts of total taxable surplus. Such surplus per unit of cultivated land was greater for village peasant household working with family labour than for large landholders working with wage labour or tenants. Thus, the distribution of intra-village revenue burden was more on the labouring households cultivating small holdings with family labour than on the non-labouring household mostly cultivating large holdings with tenant or hired labour. Therefore the difference between an intra-village mode of distribution of revenue obligations among houscholds and a supra-village tendency of shifting revenue burden from a higher echelon to a lower one was that while at the intra-village level, the total obligation of village revenue was distributed among households in proportion to the taxable surplus generated by a peasant or non-peasant household without any interference from outside, at the supra-village level, in general, the lower office-holders compared to the higher ones had to proportionately bear a larger share of a total imperial revenue claim.

While the Mughal system of revenue assessment was the basis by which inequality was fostered within a village community, the Mughal officialdom of centralised bureaucracy bred many types of such extra-economic manoeuvres and corruption that begot the pervasive modes of supra-village inequalities in wealth accumulation. It is true that a Mughal office- holder of any rank enjoyed many concessions that could help him to accumulate personal wealth, but these concessions corresponding to his status often forced him to part with a portion of his wealth in order to meet the extra-economic obligations to his immediate or ultimate superior. In fact the emperor himself with his military generals, ministers and others, commanded by virtue of power, an inflexible size of extra- economic benefits supplied by his lower level officialdom. The net consequence was that within the Mughal bureaucracy itself there developed an in-built trend towards mutual conflict and competition for favour so as to particularly make the tenures of lower level officials extremely unstable.

This chronic instability within the rank of the various strata of Mughal officials (particularly those who had no personal connection with powerful members of the imperial court or anyone belonging to Emperor's personal entourage) bred among the members of diverse strata a tendency towards social (e.g., matrimonial) or armed alliance so as to protect one's individual position or to ensure one's ascendancy to a higher position in the hierarchy at the cost of a competing rival. Another type of cushion against the chronic instability in the rank of office- holders grew in the form of local or provincial alliances of some of them against the power of the emperor or his cohort. Since the acquisition of power was the only answer to an inherent trend towards instability among office-holders, forcible violation of law at the various levels of Mughal hierarchy so as to acquire power and wealth appeared as a dialectical opposite to frequent imperial arbitrariness in matters of punishing or rewarding an office-holder. This is why the imperial rule that mansab-holding or jagir-holding tenure of an official in a locality must be temporary in nature, became 'largely theoretical'. Irfan Habib says, 'the *mansab* was not inheritable; though *it was normally conferred* [in our view the emperor was forced to confer] *upon sons or relations of higher mansab-holders* thus creating whole-families of khanazads who subsisted on mansabs from generation to generation' (italics added).

A large majority of Muslim mansabdars or jagirdars came from the rank of old immigrants (Turanis, Iranis, Afgans, etc.) and a large majority of zamindars[6] (including the *watan* jagirdars) were Hindus. While big jagirdars or mansabholders could flout imperial law by establishing inheritance right so as to use it as a cushion against the insecurity of their position, their inheritance right was not only not negotiable in the eye of law, but also had no marketability.[7] But the Hindu zamindars could resort to sale,transfer and inherit their positions, because their local roots often helped them to procure means of livelihood even without holding an office.

However, neither the jagirdars or mansabdars (big or small) with absence or presence of their *de facto* rights of inheritance, nor the zamindars with their negotiable right of selling and inheriting the office, could develop within their respective domain any kind of stable machanism of control over village land and labour. Whatever the apparent stability in the inheritance right of a jagirdar/ zamindar, such right and its seeming stability had no social dimension. In this sense any social supra-communal right of surplus appropriation had to be based on striking a trade-off between itself and the subordinate village community as a whole (or its dominant interest group). This is where the fate of post Corolingian West Europe differed from that of India immediately after the decline of the Mughals.

During the Carolingian period the rising nobility could subsume power in proportion to the degree of negation of the interest of direct producers, but even during the heyday of Mughal power, the protofeudal rights on village surplus had to delimit the exercise of such right so as not to disturb the autonomy of peasant labourers' right to subsist. In the former case, the absolutist power of Charlemagne could never subvert the pre-existing social process of germinating private rights on land and labour in the rural areas or substitute the latter by an alternative social process that could create new norms of social right. What Charlemagne did was to enforce the superiority of the private property right of the emperor by ensuring the animated suspension of the extant social process of germinating other private rights on land and labour. As a consequence, after his death private right on land could easily resurrect itself in the form of fief-holding right of the new nobility. In contrast, the Mughal power of surplus appropriation never sought to dismantle the extant process of self-sustaining village autonomy, although the Mughal mode of surplus appropriation appeared in essence as a clear negation of the self-sustaining right of a village autonomy. The *khots* or *muquddams* of Irfan Habib[8] or Nurul Hasan's primary zamindars,[9] – the supposedly lowest level functionaries of Mughal revenue establishment on whom was vested the actual Mughal power of negating village autonomy,could hardly risk a total usurpation of the sovereign subsistence right of peasant and artisan labour. On the contrary, a village *khot* or even a primary zamindar of a revenue circle in the interest of his job had to depend on a closer rapport with the subordinate community establishments in a village rather than with his superiors, i.e., a supra-village jagirdar or mansabdar or 'a secondary-zamindar'. What a lowest level functionary of the Mughal revenue establishment could at best achieve for himself, was to negotiate an individual trade-off between himself and the dominant interest group within a set of his subordinate villages.

One may not dispute that a primary zamindar (not exactly the village chief), as claimed by Nurul Hasan, constantly endeavoured to ascend to the position of higher class of privilege holders such as *khidmatguzari* zamindar or *chaudhari* or talukdars or ijaradars, etc. But it is doubtful whether any such endeavour on his part could, at any stage, compromise the interests of subordinate peasant populations, particularly in a situation where the latter belonged to his own clan, caste or race. How the superior jagirdars with mansab holding right that formed the superior class of landed gentry could avoid transfer, while the smaller jagirdars were subject to constant transfers from one region to another is not clearly analysed by any historian of medieval India.

According to Irfan Habib and T. Raychaudhuri, the superior jagirdars were engaged in the practice of revenue farming which eventually created a class of Isaradars throughout their domains.[10] That the number of such powerful revenue farming jagirdars or mansabdars was few is evident from the fact that they contributed about 36 per cent of the total *jama* of the empire (as acknowledged by Habib and others). It shows how powerful and indispensable they were vis-a-vis the imperial state. What is, however not clear from their evidence is, how could the growth of power of a big jagirdar (hereditary or not) lead to a 'rising intensity of exploitation of village labourers'. Since a high level of intensity of labour exploitation could exclusively be determined either by the growing retrogression of intra-communal processes of social relations of production or by a high degree of intra-communal distributive inequality that drove village labourers toward complete destitution, it is not evident how a growing power of a jagirdar or a zamindar or any other supra-village authority could materialise a new dimension of itself within the complex of communal relations of production in a village. It is only by destroying the self-sustaining autonomy of a village community, or to be more specific by causing the rise of private property as the individual ownership of the material conditions of labour that a peasant labour could be so exploited as to turn him out as an exploitable destitute. In fact, all evidences marshalled by historians show just the opposite, namely that the growth of power of a 'subinfeudatory' supra- village right on village production competed not against the village labour's right to earn subsistence in exchange of his labour but against the imperial power or its local capricious agents entrusted with executing its writ. No historical evidence can cconclusively show that the peasant producers of a village were allegedly exploited more by the accelerated growth of 'subinfeudatory' right of a jagirdar - big or small.[11]

If in the Carolingian West Europe the wealthy trusted nobles received discriminatory royal patronage against the smaller nobles who were frequently transferred, it only shows that notwithstanding the significant differences between the two situations the fiscal as well as the military imperatives of an overcentralised empire invariably forced it to depend more on a strong and powerful class of big nobles that in return could extract more patronage and license from it. But in the West Europe this growth of imperial necessity reinforced the growth of its opposite, namely, the negation of centralized power and the consequent articulation of the nobles' absolute ownership right on village land and the right to consolidate politico-legal enserfment of peasant labour after the death of Charlemagne. In Mughal India or during its aftermath, similar developments did not take place, as even the most tempestuous power of a Mughal noble operated more as a negation of the centralised empire rather like that in West Europe than as a dissolvent of peasant autonomy in the village production process, unlike that in Carolingian Europe.

By this we do not suggest that wealth differentiation among members of a supra-village revenue hierarchy or a village community or between various village communities themselves did not have an impact on the polity and social economy of the Mughal period. At the level of supra-village authorities accumulation of wealth by anybody found reflection in extravagant lifestyle or in power accretions. Since in our model, such wealth accumulation and power accretions could take place mainly at the expense of the imperial power, the economic imperative of such development was the eventual rise of non-productive consumption and the proliferation of power brokers in the urban areas.

How did wealth differentiation within a village or among different villages manifest itself within a rural area? To answer this question, let us examine two aspects, first the actual role a village wealth accumulation might have had in the mode of reproduction of a Mughal Indian village; second, whether village inequality in income was a dynamic of reinforcement of contradiction between a village community and the Mughal state power which occasionally caused peasant migration from settled areas to virgin land, or fierce peasant uprisings in Mughal India.

Irfan Habib broadly finds three categories of people in a representative Mughal village community. They are, (*a*) large cultivators who used 'hired labour' for cultivation (Nurul Hasan's *khudkhastes*?) and raise crops for the market; (*b*) 'Small peasants who could barely produce their subsistence'; (*c*) a vast bulk of 'menial' population constituting one-fourth or more of total village population.[12] He contends that the first group grew up as a consequence of 'economic differentiation' undergone by a Mughal Indian village community.

Habib is not specific about how through differentiation the first 'class' of cultivators (i.e., large cultivators) came to control big landholdings of a village or whether those holdings were their virtual property or not. Since the big holders used hired labour for cultivation, one may argue that they had *de facto* property right on land. But even a *de facto* property right of a non-cultivating landholder could not reproduce or materialise itself unless peasant labour remained attached to land. More important, in such situations there must arise scopes within a village community for hereditarisation and alienability (not to speak of controlling conditions of labour) of such *de facto* right. He, however, supplies no evidence to show that the class of large cultivators (who, in his view did not engage themselves in cultivation work and had to depend on 'hired labour' for cultivation of their holdings) had alienable and hereditary right on their holdings. Even if they had, such right cannot be deemed as property right. Because as Habib himself admits, peasant labour did not remain perpetually attached to land held by any category of landholders.[13]

Apart from what Habib admits, there are three reasons that go against the theory of heredity and alienability of land held by big landholders. First, no historical evidence shows that *social* enserfment of village menial population was virtually the *economic* enserfment within a socially stratified village community. Had it not been so,there would not have arisen the phenomenon of employing 'hired labour' rather than attached labour by big landholders for cultivating their holdings. Second, attachment of labour to land possessed by a non-cultivator could, in general, arise in a situation of either competition among labour for a plot of land or absolute scarcity of arable land. That there was no such scarcity in Mughal India, can be cited by its two widely acknowledged features, namely, there existed so much cultivable waste in many villages that the Mughal mode of revenue assessment stipulated a light burden of assessment on crops in case the latter were raised by bringing cultivable waste under cultivation. The other was the sizable amount of village land possessed by a village community for communal use as village pasture or as sources of energy consumption or for defraying village expenses of service caste people. Third, even if one assumed that labour remained attached to land held by an elitist big landholder, such 'attachment' reflected more the heredity and transferability of land parcels possessed by peasant cultivators among themselves rather than among the elitist landholders. In other words, a big landholding of the non-cultivator village elite does not amount to his appropriation of the material condition of labour in Mughal India.[14]

In Nurul Hasan's account there is a broad hint that even the affluent segment of a village community often voluntarily entered into the supra-village power game. If this is true, our hypothesis of functional disjunction between supra-village mechanism of acquiring power and the self-sustaining mechanism of village autonomy becomes untenable. Nurul Hasan suggests a trade-off between the Mughal need for searching out a primary zamindar and the big village landholder's tendency towards gaining extra-village power for furthering his surplus acquisition.[15] But this suggestion must have its basis on two implicit assumptions : first, all big non-cultivating landholders in a community vied against each other for securing the office of power of a primary zamindar; second, a primary zamindar of a revenue circle so selected, must have enough power to enforce his personal as well as official claim over his fellow members of the community, particularly the peasant labour.

The first assumption can hold good only on the basis of a presupposition that a chronic instability arising out of rivalry for Mughal office within the rank of big landholders was the characteristic feature within a village community and the second assumption virtually stipulates the capacity of a primary zamindar to enserf the direct producers in his subordinate village. Both assumptions taken together drive us to an anachronistic conclusion namely, that the big non-cultivating landholders who by the first assumption were in a continous state of flux owing to mutual rivalry and respective individual efforts towards jockeying for an office of power could, nonetheless seek to acquire enserfment of peasant labour in their holdings. But an unstable privilege-holder that a big non-cultivating landholder was, could impose enserfment on peasant labour only at his peril. Again a primary zamindar had no objective reason for acquiring absolute power of imposing peasant enserfment in landholdings other than (if at all possible) strictly in his own *khas*. On the other hand, the producers had no material reason to put up with their enserfment when they had enough scope for starting cultivation in a fresh virgin land. Without acquiring the power of controlling the means of labour, i.e., land, no economic enserfment of peasant labour was feasible. Thus neither a big landholder nor even a primary or secondary zamindar of Mughal India could enhance its surplus acquisition just by usurping peasants' subsistence earning. In our reckoning, if a non-cultivating holder of village land enjoyed the social entitlement to surplus from his holding, he had to concede at the same time a social obligation of ensuring a corresponding right of a labour to his necessary subsistence. Otherwise, in a situation where a given control over landholding could not be materialised as a condition of labour, and productive labour was relatively scarce, the system of hired labour or crop-sharing could not rear up.

This is, however, not to deny that a village community had its own power structure within it so as to devise a social hierarchy of rights and obligations among members. What is important to stress is that an *intra-communal hierarchy of rights and obligations was independent of the political hierarchy of rights and obligations among officials, nobles and other members operating at the instance of the Mughal imperial establishment or any other supra-village political authority.* While an intra-communal hierarchy of rights and obligations had its genesis from a voluntary or involuntary mutualism within a community itself and not exactly from wealth inequalities among community members, at the supra-communal level political rights and obligations or their associated distribution of power among persons had feedbacks only from their relative capacities of appropriating surplus or wealth.[16]

It cannot be denied that, in general, the upper caste people in a village enjoyed the economic benefit from a given structure of social indignity of menial caste people. On the other hand, the menial caste people possessed a perception of social obligations of the wealthier sections of the community towards them. The dominant communal ethos of such reciprocity sought constantly to strike a balance between the economic disability of upper caste landholders in matters of performing cultivation work by their own labour in their assigned holdings and the social inability of lower caste people in matters of holding land. This is why, as Irfan Habib finds, a village community with a few larger landholders retained about a fifth or fourth of its members as landless menial population.[17] Therefore the phenomenon of landlessness among menial population did not grow up from any economic differentiations within a village but owed its genesis to extant socio-ideologically divisive customs. However, when the intensity of supra-communal surplus appropriation accentuated the intra-village wealth inequalities of retrograde consequence to make the reproduction of labour activity precarious, the intra-communal village unity tended to erode and to cause the rise of peasant resistance against the intra-communal non-labouring stratum of village society as well as state coercion.

Without showing how big landholders in a village community came into being through 'economic differentiation' . . . 'among peasantry', Irfan Habib implicitly uses a concept of peasant that includes both '*khudkaste* and *pyekaste* category of landholders. The former engaged merely in management functions and the latter in direct cultivation work. The concept of the peasant as we have used it here is different. We have defined peasant activity as one of the village labour activity engaged in agricultural production. While we may not dispute his concept, it does not help him to lay bare the process of economic differentiation, if there existed any in Mughal Indian agriculture. He only postulates a village community that contained 'large cultivators', used hired labour for procuring marketable surplus and juxtaposes such 'large cultivators' against a numerically larger group of small subsistence-producing peasants who always suffered from the problem of subsistence. But he analyses neither the relation between large landholders and small subsistence earing cultivators, nor investigates how the large landholders of *khudkaste* or any other variety could materialise their social or economic genesis. His 'economic differentiation' suggests only such wealth differentiation among large landholders themselves that reduces quite a few of them to be *pyekaste* or similar subsistence-producing small holders in course of time. Without making such exercise, he only supplies data on 'cash crops' and food crops so as to prove his thesis of economic differentiation and the commercial character of Mughal agricultural production.

Since Mughal India had to rest on a very large tract of settled cultivation in the continent, a high degree of heterogeneity among soil types and local consumption habits by themselves promised a diversification of crop production in Mughal agriculture. Therefore, it is presumable that the imperial anxiety to procure revenue in cash from settled agriculture must have acted as an instrument of inter village commerce on grains, animal husbandry products and sundry agricultural crops and of a village raising exportable crops in order to import crops required by it.

The most dominant aspect of commercialisation of Mughal agriculture was the growth of inter-village commerce on such diversifed crops and artisan goods that was erected on a stagnant production base. The intra-communal accentuation of inequality in income in a village, that was the gift of the Mughal revenue system itself, might have a subsidiary role in such commercialisation. Again such inequality could, by itself, cause no expansion of village production base, because a village wealth could not be fructified into ownership of the village level material conditions of labour, namely land or crafts.

Irfan Habib's *khudkaste* landholders seem to be none other than the upper caste big landholders and the *pyekaste* ones appear to be low caste small landholders as well as landless cultivators. That the *khudkaste* category of tenure-holders earned more income and accumulated more wealth compared to others in a community does not by itself, indicate the nature of the process of commercialisaion of agricultural production or that of economic differentiation within the Mughal peasantry as a whole unless it is shown how such income and wealth acquisition involved a redistribution of either economic benefit or village land in favour of *khudkaste* at the expense of *pyekaste* categories of peasants. Unless a process of economic differentiation in peasant agriculture does not demonstrate how the dynamics of wealth accumulation arising out of it involve income and land transfer from one group to the other within it, its existence can not be identified. But he does not show how a small peasant-holding could be appropriated by a wealthy landed elite of *khudkaste* or any other variety, or how a zamindar or anybody else having village political or economic power could evict a peasant from his holding either by force or by any other means.

On the contrary, Habib observes that in zamindari areas a zamindar belonged to the dominant caste or clan, needing 'not only the support of his kinsmen but also . . . to protect and enforce his claims'.[18] Apart from zamindari villages there were other villages which, in his view, were largely peasant-held 'with no recognisable persons as zamindars'. On the one hand, the Mughal administration not only supplanted old zamindars but even created new ones over peasant villages and, on the other hand,'there are numerous instances of fresh villages being settled without intermediation of zamindars', it does not follow that 'the zamindari right was, in itself' an article of property'. Moreover, the large cultivators[19] 'remained the claimant[s] to the harvest, irrespective of the labour done on his [their] fields by the hired watchmen'. The peasants were 'said to be the masters at whose behest the reapers worked' on their fields. 'But these separate holdings *implied more the claims to harvests upon them than claims for the permanent possession of particular plots of land.* Once the harvest was removed, the peasant felt no longer tied to the land' (italics added).[20]

From the above review of Irfan Habib's postulates of agricultural commercialisation and economic differentiation within the Mughal village production and peasantry and his account of heterogeneous village categories we can observe that during the Mughal period (*a*) in all village communities, no clear proprietary right on land could emerge; (*b*) the peasant cultivators could not be evicted from land they cultivated even by 'the large cultivators'; (*c*) appropriation of harvest by a non-cultivator was functionally dissociated with any permanent possessing right either on agricultural land or on labour; (*d*) commercialisation of Mughal agriculture or a possible growth of income differentiation and/or wealth accumulation by large cultivators within a village community might have led to diversification of the structure of village production but would not liberate village production from the extant cycle of stagnation.

Let us now examine whether accentuation of income inequality or the resultant wealth accumulation on the part of large landholders within a village community could be instrumental in sharpening the contradiction between the 'self-sufficient entity' (in the tradition of Habib)'.[21] and 'the despotic regime' of the Mughals. In our judgement, any understanding of the dialectical interconnections between the large landholders and the labouring population within a surplus producing village community is essential for grasping the dialectical unity and opposition between a village community and the despotic Mughal mode of supra-communal surplus appropriation.

We have already argued that the inequalities in wealth relations within a village community could not transform the land possessed by a small holder of a village into land to be acquired by a 'large cultivator' nor could it reduce village small holders' possession to be an 'article of property' of village or supra-village local chief or zamindar. The landlessness of a massive segment of village population could not therefore be the outcome of the so-called economic differentiation within a village peasantry. However, the wealth of an affluent member could, apart from having a consumption outlet, find a profitable outlet in investment in village usury or trade in money or goods, either among villages themselves or between a village and a town. In this sense, accumulated wealth in Indian villages of the medieval epoch might have formed the embryo of the rise of trading capital that, independently though during the last century of Mughal rule could assume a gigantic magnitude. Although the village wealth that acted as miniscule capital of village level sahukar or pedlars operating in intra-country commodity trade, the prosperity of trading capital in the later phase of Mughal rule could not be fostered by wealth inequalities among villages. This was because, in absence of rapid expansion of village production and of the size of disposable surplus (that could be used as merchandise) within a self sustaining community, wealth inequality could not accelerate itself beyond a limit. In the rural world of Mughal India the wealth inequality its degree or magnitude - moved around a stationary level.

Since the productive activity of labour was the essential communal condition of surplus entitlement to a large landholder and not the vice versa, wealth inequality within a village community had to have its barrier in the peasant labour's absolute right to reproduce his productive capacity i.e. to his subsistence. That was why, despite the fact that an increase in despotic claims by a jagirdar or fauzdar tended to reinforce wealth inequality in a village community, one finds the strange spectacle that the community as a whole had a hostile response to increased incidence of imperial taxation.

We do not suggest that a supra-village imperial authority or a village group of non-cultivating large landholders, either independently or in mutual connivance, did nowhere try to acquire an absolute power of imposing an arbitrary extortions of subsistence earnings of village level peasantry and artisans. In Mughal India, the paradigms of village community formation and individual communal articulations of peasant right to subsistence in a village were far from uniform. Thus one can witness both the phenomena of a communal solidarity in matters of protecting the village economic interests against an increased taxation of village surplus by the despotic regime and those of only direct producers' revolt as much against the intra-communal social oligarchs as against the imperial authority that sought to enhance taxes on a village.

In fact we find that in some localities, the peasants and artisans under the garb of anti-brahmanic religious movements, had, as their focal point of attack, the local alliance and the trade-off between an intra-communal structure of social dominance and the imperial agents' effort to enhance taxes.[22] Broadly, this can explain why the Sikh uprisings turned against the Mughal power as well as its backyard patronage by local protofeudal Hindu potentates. Even earlier, following Akbar's death in 1605, there were a large number of peasant uprisings in Agra and Patna region in 1610, and in Thatta (Sind) in 1612. In the heartland of Mughal power which was again the heartland of brahmanic social order, such peasant uprisings reflected the assertion of peasant autonomy of its subsistence right and that of landless menial population within a village community against the intra-communal social oligarchs and imperial usurpers.

From a study of the nature of peasant uprisings of this period, it appears that they were dissimilar in degree of mobilisation and extent of ferocity. Some were of a small-scale and sporadic type simply reacting to immediate economic issues, some were led by village headmen or local rajas against the Mughal revenue assessment and then there was still another category of peasant resistance which was well organised and of a sustained type not only as a reaction to imperial exploitation in connivance with the local elitist order, but also as one that focused on an alternative political and socio-economic programme of a group claiming distinct religious or ethnic identity. The chroniclers are usually silent about the first type, the second and third types could force their attention because they involved the Mughal army in a big way.

The first type of 'uprising' assumed the form of passive resistance through migration from settled villages to areas of new settlement. There were many such passive resistances. Passive resistance, apart from its endogenous reason, was reinforced by the fact that Mughal taxation on cultivable waste or new cultivation was lower than on the settled areas.

Although the causes of peasant migration in Mughal India have not been adequately studied, it is certain that migration was a collective response to the inability of a local zamindar or *khot* to ensure subsistence earning. That peasant migration was a widespread practice, can be cited from a peculiar finding (attested to by all medieval historians) that between the period of *Aìn-i-Akbari* and Aurangzeb, 'the overall increase in cultivation . . . could not have been considerable', although during this intervening period 'the measured area [of cultivated land] shows great advance'. This means that some of the settled areas of cultivation mentioned by Abul Fazal, must have been decultivated by the time Aurangzeb's measurement of total cultivated area was completed.[24] This is the only way to explain the discrepancy between the actual area of cultivation at the time of Aurangzeb and the updated measured area indicated by *Ain* and the post-*Ain* new areas of cultivation during the period between Akbar and Aurangzeb. Even Babar was surprised by the agility and expertise of Indian peasants in intra-regional migration.[25]

Since no historian has claimed that peasant migration from one settled area to another occurred due to population growth (in fact, Irfan Habib computes the rate of growth of population for the entire Mughal period to be of the order of 0.14 per cent per annum, and thereby suggests almost a stationary population)[26] the sporadic recurrence of local depopulation and migration that we find in Mughal India, can be explained as the manifestation of passive peasant resistance to extortions by local as well as imperial oligarchs.

The second type of uprisings was also numerous throughout the Mughal period. This was another kind of uprisings which took place in the outlying regions of the empire where the regional Mughal establishment failed to forge a working alliance between itself and the local rajas or village zamindars and headmen. Here a Mughal protofeudal lord deliberately or inadvertently sought to replace the older arrangement.[27] In many of the tribal or semi-tribal areas of northern and western India, this type of uprisings took place, when the tributary relation between a local raja having ethnic fraternity with the local dominant peasant castes and the Mughal fauzdar or the high official, was sought to be unilaterally changed by an absolute enhancement of imperial revenue claim on the former.[28]

The third type of uprisings under the leadership of peasants themselves were found both in the outlying regions as well as in the core regions of the Mughal empire. Broadly, these uprisings were directed as much against the local social oligarchs as against the imperial agents. In the outlying regions of Bengal-Assam border, the Hatikheda uprising led by low caste elephant-catchers and peasantry against the machination of local Hindu potentates and their local Mughal patrons was essentially a pure peasant uprising.[29] The rebellion of Kurmis, Sikhs and Satnamis in the Mughal heartland were uprisings led by the peasants themselves. Peasantry as a heterogeneous caste entity, rather than as a pure class entity conducted those upheavals under the garb of a religious or ethnic resurrection. This was because a peasant movement on a religious, ethnic or caste line could broaden the base of mobilisation and its area of operation during the period.

All these types of peasant rebellions do not indicate that growth of income inequality or wealth accumulation by a few large landholders within a village community or in a cluster of village communities in a region operated as their focal point of attack. Even in regions where peasant movements started as anti-brahmanic or anti-oligarchic social uprisings, they soon acquired an anti-imperial dimension against local fauzdars and other high ranking Mughal despots. Sometimes a pure economic movement against imperial exploitation tended to embrace new egalitarian programme of social and economic reforms with strong denouncement of the extant upper caste oligarchy.

The two way transformation undergone by a peasant movement either from an egalitarian social movement to anti-state movement or the vice versa, demonstrates that in the perception of the village labouring populations the social oppression of non-labouring caste elites tended to fructify itself into a content similar to the politico-economic oppression of the imperial establishment. Nevertheless, often the community elites owing to their *immediate interest* made a common cause with village labour against the imperial tax authority or its local agents and formed an united front of community members as a whole against the latter. In such situations the labouring population of villages not only spared the oppressive local elites but also accepted their leadership in community's struggle against the imperial exploitation. For instance, one cannot deny the basic peasant character of the Sikh religious uprising or the uprising of Satnamis, but such uprising never culminated in the rise of a peasant authority but religio-social kingdoms of Sikhs or Satnami elites with all their religious as well as military consolidation of power. A similar consequence followed from Gujar, Rohilla and Jat uprisings which in the name of upholding the cause of ethnic labourers were actually led by respective ethnic leaders of peasants but they culminated in the establishment of ethnic kingdom of such leaders that ultimately subjugated fellow ethnic peasants so as to procure from them in each case necessary 'protection fee' for keeping the leader in politico military power.

While, therefore, the passive localised and confrontationist peasant uprisings of various sorts reflected in no uncertain terms the basic contradiction within the Mughal polity between the peasant power and the coercive state power, or in general, the contradiction between a village autonomy and supra-village coercive mode of surplus appropriation, the non-emergence of individual private property in land as appropriation of the material condition of labour in Mughal India could not lead to the resolution of this contradiction so as to take Indian social economy to its new stage of development. On the other hand, the Mughal machinery of multi-level coercive use of power itself did not represent a well-orchestrated identity. Internal strife, rivalry and discord among members of Mughal bureaucracy as we have pointed out earlier were its in-built properties. A *de facto* parcellisation of coercive authorities and power machinery of Mughals reinforced those endogenous properties that made such coercive use of power totally incapable of dismantling the autarchic character of peasant communal autonomy and replace the latter by general peasant enserfment.

Therefore it can be observed that the extant income inequality or wealth appropriation by a few within a village community could neither act by itself as a dissolvent of labour's autonomy in matters of village production or its subsistence right, nor could it transform itself within or outside villages as individual ownership of the material condition of labour.

A wealthy villager however found multiple uses of his wealth, namely, in pushing up his level of household consumption or in demonstrating loyalty (by gift-making or paying prestations) to extant institutions or individuals belonging to a local political or social elite groups or simply in buying peace with village-level direct producers through rendering services of ritual charity and ceremonial feasts to village poor, or more commonly lending money to village people engaged in trade. Besides, use of wealth, e.g., in charity towards poor, in gift-making or forging matrimonial alliances with those who were superior by birth or lineage etc., could occasionally help a wealthy villager with lowly social status to gain a high social status. This is attested to by Kosambi and Thapar in their individual accounts of ancient Indian village communities. It is likely that with greater increase in social production and growing inequalities in income distribution in Mughal Indian village similar uses of wealth in buying superior social status were more common. But none of them could cite a single instance of a reverse process of social mobility, namely, that a villager inheriting a high social birth lost his social status owing to his abysmal poverty. From this one can conclude that in general, the use of village wealth for making gifts or for charitable purposes was for buying social security for wealthy status of a person.

One can, therefore, postulate that there were three ways in which accumulated wealth was spent. The first was payment of individual bribe or tribute to an external political or coercive authority so as to buy placement in the lower levels of Mughal administration or simply to avoid his lustful encroachment; the second was gratuitous expenditure in redistributive mechanism within the community members; and the third, was expenditure of wealth as invested capital for export-import business of the village undertaken either by wealthy persons themselves or by interest-paying trading caste people. But none of these uses, however, had a feedback effect on the production base of a village community.

However to the extent, a village wealth of an individual could function as his investment fund for trading in exports or imports of a village, its growth fostered an incipient contradiction between trading wealth as a money command over social good and wares and the wealth possessed by the imperial establishment. Village wealth, though not capable of appropriating its full preconditions in the Mughal period, could form parallel centre of stored-up money value in the rural areas with a rivalry poised against the wealth of imperial establishment. It is true that a rural trading wealth was incapable of appropriating its full preconditions and the extent of rival power it could command was not significant. But as a method of surplus appropriation, it was far superior to its rival. Between the two rivals, one can mutiply wealth through an unequal exchange between supply and demand for wares, the other can achieve the same only by brute force.

While the basic contradiction between the direct producers and the coercive authority of state could not precipitate a change in the destiny of the Mughal empire, a subsidiary contradiction between the Indian mercantile wealth and the wealth acquired by the state power though sheer force could transform itself as a major contradiction of the polity. In this connection it is necessary to stress that Mughal economic bankruptcy did not arise out of agrarian economic crisis, as Irfan Habib infers.[30] The economic bankruptcy of Mughal empire arose out of commercial prosperity of Indian mercantile wealth that slowly and surreptitiously eroded the economic axles of the Mughal state power. The Mughal political crisis was a definite outcome of this slow but steady growth of prosperity of merchants. On the other hand, the social production process under village communities, instead of showing any sign of crisis or decline, showed a tendency towards a degree of diversification by materialising a differentiation among villages in response to prosperity of Mughal commerce. Quite a few villages around important centres of entrepot trade began to specialise in production for roadside markets, though a large number of them were locked up in the production for village use.

Notes

1 The term 'non-productive entitlement' means entitlement of those people who are not directly or indirectly associated with productive labour activity or its intra-structural upkeep. In this sense, the term has its opposite in 'productive entitlement'.

2 The difference between Europe and India is significant in that the Mughal state power, just like the state power of Charlemagne, theoretically or legally owned all the land in its empire. While in West Europe, from such supposed state ownership (manifested in the form of royal surplus entitlement) of land, there arose the feudal ownership of village land and feudal labour enserfment. In India a similar development did not take place following the decline of the Mughals.

3 On Mughal revenue administration and bureaucracy, we use, unless specifically mentioned, the following sources :

(a) Irfan Habib, ' Pre British Land Settlements', *op. cit.*

(b) I. Habib, *Agrarian System of Mughal India (Bombay*, 1962).

(c) I. Habib, 'Potentialities of Capitalistic Development in the Economy of Mughal India' in *Enquiry* (New Series). Vol. 3, No. 3, 1971.

(d) I. Habib, 'Agrarian Relations and Land Revenue', *Cambridge Economic History of India,* Vol. 1, pp. 235-58.

(e) W.H. Moreland, *India at the Death of Akbar* (London, 1910).

(f) W.H. Moreland, *Agrarian System of Moslem India* (Allahabad, 1929).

(g) W.H. Moreland, *From Akbar to Aurangjeb* (London, 1943).

4 Tapan Ray Choudhuri, 'The State and the Economy under Mughal Empire', *Cambridge Economic History of India. Vol.* 1, *op. cit.*, p.181.

5 Ibid., p.176.

6 Here we are not following Nurul Hasan's summary classification of supra-village rights, and distinguish the zamindar nomenclature from the nomenclature of jagirdars and mansabdars for clarifying their respective relation

to the imperial establishment. While a jagirdar or a mansabdar was the necessary adjunct of the Mughal revenue cum army establishment, a village or even a supra-local primary zamindar of a revenure circle was not. The latter were not always appointed by the emperor. The tenure of a primary Hindu zamindar in a revenue circle was in many cases contractual. A zamindari tenure came into being owing to actual or supposed support from subordinate village communities. A zamindar had to pay revenue to the Mughal establishment on behalf of those communities. In case he was not assigned a jagir right in his area, he had no obligations to the establishment for deciding who would inherit or succeed his position, provided the revenue payment was regular.

7 A more correct statement is that Muslim mansabholders or jagirdars could hardly afford selling their positions simply because by doing so they could hardly earn income from any other source. That was why, they were interested not so much in selling their position as in gaining inheritance rights on their positions.

8 Irfan Habib, 'Agrarian Relations', *op.cit.*, pp. 244-47, *passim.*

9 Nurul Hasan, *Thought on Agrarian Relations in Mughal India* (Delhi, 1973), Ch.III, *passim.*

10 T. Ray Chaudhury, *op. cit.*, p.178.

11 We have already observed that norms of Mughal revenue assessment and collection tended to widen inequality in wealth relations among members of a village community. Therefore, if Mughal assessment became heavier, peasant members of a community were bound to suffer more than the nonpeasant ones. But no medieval historian heeds this possibility. We have also shown how a countervailing trend was bound to arise within a village community against supra-village exploitation of peasantry.

12 I. Habib, 'Agrarian Relations' Cambridg*e Economic History of India.* Vol.I. *op.cit.*, pp.247-49, *passim.*

13 'The peasants carried on cultivation in separate fields. The *khasam,* landholder, remained the claimant to the harvest irrespective of the labour done on his field by the hired watchmen. The peasant, or *kirsan* was similarly said to be the master at whose behest . . . the reapers worked on his field. But these separate holdings implied *more than claims to harvests upon them than claims for the permanent possession of particular plots of land.Once the harvest was removed the peasant felt no longer tied to land*' (italics added) *Ibid.*, pp. 247-48.

14 From the early reports of British land revenue settlement officers, it is discerned that there existed two broad spectrum of village-based tenures in the North Western provinces just before the introduction of ad hoc settlement of British rulers. They are *bhaiachara* and *pattidari* tenures. Each of them contained different sub-features, namely, mixed *bhaiachara* and pure *bhaiachara,* or mixed *pattidari* and pure *pattidari,* etc. In general, a *bhaiachara* tenure was characterised by what British historians would call the tenure of 'joint land holdership' or 'joint landholders' villages and the *pattidari* tenure

of single landholder village. While both such nomenclatures were invented by British revenue officials from the point of view of their revenue administration (i.e., whether a village paid revenue to the state jointly by its inhabitants or through a chief), they underscore the age-old Indian tradition of revenue payment by the village as a unit and do not indicate the existence of joint or single proprietorship on village land.

15 Nurul Hasan, *op. cit.,* Ch. III.

16 Most scholars explain this dichotomy between political and social power mechanisms in medieval (if not modern) India in terms of self propelling communal ideology of the a brahmanic social order (by which the social status of a communal individual is defined more by his birth rather than by his deeds). But in our view, it was not the pure ideology of the brahmanic social order (in fact, most of the non brahmanic social orders developed a similar ideology of social stratification on the basis of birth) *but* the specific material conditions of life that provided the scope for the growth of such an ideology of stratification based on birth rather than on deeds. If such a socially divisive ideology did not come to an end, it was because the material conditions of life, that once caused its genesis, did not undergo any radical change.

17 Irfan Habib, 'Agrarin Relations and Land Revenue', *Cambridge Economic History of India,* Vol.I, *op. cit.*, p.249.

18 *Ibid.*, p. 246.

19 Irfan Habib includes within *khudkaste* category of land holders, the following : 'the zamindars, and village Headman' 'revenue grantees and revenue officials'. Apart from investing in field crops, they made capital intensive investment 'in laying out orchards and cultivating fruit production. Cf. I. Habib, *Potentialities of Change in the Economy of Mughal India (mimeo)*, pp. 20-21.

20 Irfan Habib, 'Agrarian Relations and Land Revenue', *op. cit.,* pp.247-48.

21 *Ibid.*, p.247

22 Unfortunately there exist very few empirical studies on Mughal Indian peasant uprisings. For this we depend on Gautam Bhadra's *Mughal Juge Krishak Bidroha (Peasant Revolts during the Mughal Age)* (Calcutta, 1981).

23 This phenomenon may explain why local zamindars were, at times, forced to sell their zamindaris in situations of general absence of marketability of zamindari entitlements. Ch. Irfan Habib, 'Agrarian Relations and Land Revenue', *Cambridge Economic History of India,* Vol.1, p. 246.

24 Cf. Irfan Habib, 'The System of Agricultural Production' (Mughal India), *Cambridge Economic History, Vol.* I, op. cit., p. 225.

25 Cited by Irfan Habib, *Ibid.*, p.218.

26 Irfan Habib. 'Population [c. 1500-1750]' *Cambridge Economic History of India,* Vol.I. *op. cit.*, p. 167.

27 The relation of Paiks under their headman, Sanaton Sardar in the modern

Goalpara Kamrup region of Assam is one of illustrations of this type. Cf Gautam Bhadra, 'Two Frontier Uprisings in Mughal India', R. Guha (ed), *Subaltern Studies* Vol.II (Delhi, 1983), pp.44-49.

28 In fact most of the peasant upsurges in the remote areas of North India that found their entry into the well-known accounts of chroniclers belong to this type.

29 Gautam Bhadra, *op.cit.*, pp. 49-50.

30 Irfan Habib, 'Potentialities of Capitalist Development in Mughal India', *op.cit.*

3.7: The Different Course of Development in Non-Mughal India

South India or, to be more specific, peninsular India had a pattern of development that was distinctly different from the Mughal Indian pattern. Before we take up our analysis of society, economy and state power in the post-Vijayanagar period–a period that marks, for the first time in the peninsula, a rise of such state powers that began to claim regular land revenue for their subsistence and grandeur– some prefatory observations on the earlier period, i.e. on ancient south India, are necessary for grasping the differential tenet of its evolutionary process.

It is necessary to recall that after brahmanic social order gained ascendancy in South India, no supra-social or supra-village system of revenue obligations either to the small kingdom of *Cheras*, *Pandyas*, or *Chalukyas* or to the Pallava or Chola overlordship could emerge. According to some historians, all the localised south Indian societies in Telegu and Tamil areas were governed by various kinds of caste assemblies or simply non-caste village assemblies. But the dominance of the brahman caste assembly over other caste assemblies was conspicuous. In Telegu areas, the brahman assembly known as *sabha* was vested with the power to decide as to how agrarian resources of a locality were to be allocated among various requirements of hundreds of *Brahmadeyas* or non-*Brahmadeya* villages. In Tamil areas, similar assemblies of brahmans are reported to have governed the local village societies.

But there is an alternative view that since the early period, two dominant caste groups, brahmans and Sat Surdas, dominated the peasant and artisan caste villagers throughout peninsular India.

However, we are not absolutely certain whether the Chera, Pandya or Chalukya kings or, for that matter, evén the Chola or Vijayanagar emperors in the south had any non-brahmanic lineage. It is possible to assume that caste lineage of any local or supra-local king cannot even remotely be traced to non-brahmanic origins. The ongoing paradigm was that a local king could assume political power only by virtue of his superior socio-ritual status. What is significant for our purpose is to note that unlike the pattern in North India, in South Indian kingdoms–big or small – the king invariably came from the ranks of the highest caste prevailing in a locality or a sub-region and a king did not impose any secular tributary claim or levy on subordinate village societies. On the contrary, it is pointed out, the subsistence of local kings was dependent on the one hand on the *ritual* prestations from local societies and, on the other, on *ritual* sanction from a Pallava or Chola imperial lord.

The question that arises is how such an imperial overlordship arose? The answers are highly speculative in nature and are in sharp contrast to each other. We can add only our inference. It seems that an imperial overlordship in early South India came into being essentially as the product of competition of armed power and aggrandisement on the part of smaller localised 'segmentary' kingdoms. From this we should not conclude that the power of an imperial overlord had its genesis from military victory or in plunder of other kingdom (like what happened in contemporary North India). The early imperial overlordship grew up out of the unrivalled capacity of a small king to conduct predatory campaigns beyond the coasts of peninsular India to regions as far as Ceylon, Cambodia. Malayasia etc.[1] In this process a small king by demonstrating his military expertise and achievement could push himself to the level of an overlord so as to command awe and ritual obedience from fellow kings.

From this method of acquiring overlordship, Burton Stein generalises the medieval paradigm of growth of an Indian overlordship. He asserts: [In] South far-ranging predation was a part of the pattern of Indian overlordship and a central, though neglected, aspect of Indian kingship, [as a whole]. Where there was neither the tradition of, nor the apparatus suited to, the realisation of state revenue through an ordered administrative system, except in quite localized territories, Indian rulers, great or small, depended for a portion of their income on raids upon neighbours, or in some cases, upon distant, rich overlords.[2] This formulation may be correct about the early South Indian Chola overlords, or even earlier ones to whom 'the sea provided the opportunity and the means to extend the region from which wealth could be extracted beyond the *peninsula itself* [3] (italics added). But it is doubtful whether the formulation is entirely valid in the case of Delhi Sultanates or earlier overlords in the North. The formulation is invalid also in the case of South's Vijayanagar imperial overlordship.[4]

A credible formulation to explain this plundering propensity of early empires can be made: up to a particular stage when the acquisition of agricultural surplus by an imperial administrative machinery was small or not feasible at all, collection of rich booty through predatory raids and plunderous conquest is found as imperial means of subsistence and power aggrandisement. This trend can he traced even among European empires and it possesses, by itself, nothing of an Indian character. The Macedonian conquest of Central or East Asia, or the earlier Athenian or Spartan conquest in Europe, can be cited as illustrations. In every continent's early history we find instances of how an empire that could not develop a dependable system of revenue collection from its agriculture, took recourse to external raids or conquest to acquire booty for the imperial treasury. A despotic power always assumes its crude form in plunder of wealth possessed by others.

In any case, by the time Vijayanagar empire could entrench itself firmly into the Tamil core region in its southern part, agrarian societies and sub-societies already proliferated themselves in the deltaic areas of Godavari and Krishna in the north, in the Tamil plains in the south, in the monsoon-fed tracts of Karnataka and Kerala bordering the west coast and even in the arid uplands of Salem and Coimbatore regions.

The relevant question is whether the modality of acquiring wealth and treasure for an empire underwent any change in the course of South Indian transition of overlordship from Cholas to Vijayanagar empire during the 15th century. It is self-evident from historical accounts that the imperial political organisation witnessed almost a sea-saw change during this period. This was notwithstanding a number of crucial similarities between the Chola empire and its Vijayanagar counterpart. Indeed both were strong 'war states' engaged in upholding and extending the spiritual and material cause of brahmanic order at two different points of time. There existed, however, the apparent politico-organisational differences between these two empires. We are to identify the objective compulsive force that paved the way for these differences.

From the historical accounts of the Gupta period of North India, we find that kshatriya emperors, including Harsha, undertook massive land grants to brahmans to extend agricultural cultivation with sudra labour. What however is less evident is despotic raids outside their political sphere of influence to acquire booty. The attitude of the state towards brahmanic patronage under the Guptas is only roughly comparable with that under Chola overlordship in the South in matters of massive land grants to brahmans.[5] The dissimilarities between them were, however, more important.

In the South, the early states – segmentary as well as imperial ones–set out as their principal objective, the extension and consolidation of brahmanic civil power. Temple construction and landgrants to brahmans came in the wake of implementing such an objective. In contrast, in North India no such objective of state power can be evidenced. On the other hand, the Guptas collected revenue through *Sita* and *Rastra* management of agricultural production, whereas the Cholas, to the best of our knowledge, had no definite system of revenue collection.

D.N. Jha notes that in the South, the practice of *Devanan* gifts to temples started from pre-Chola-Pallava period but landgrants to brahmans during that period were not a popular practice. The brahmans under Pallava overlordship were provided only with gifts of corn (paddy), cows, etc. From his study of the Chola period Jha finds that landgrants were made more to individual brahmans than to temples. He cites an extract from N. Karashima, 'brahmadeya villages [villages donated to powerful brahmins of the time] were the local nuclei of the Cola [Chola] power structure, their [brahmins,] function being to integrate and control the surrounding non-brahmadeya villages.[6] But what is striking is that whereas the North Indian kshatriya emperors made massive landgrants not exactly to enhance the brahmanic social power but to extend the imperial base of revenue collection, the Chola landgrants to brahmans were geared mainly to extend brahmanic social power.

Burtan Stein's hypothesis on the rise of individual brahmans as landed magnates during the Chola period comes very close to N. Karashima's hypothesis as cited by Jha. Stein, however, does not find slackening of landgrants made by Cholas to temples during their rule. He cites the period c.1300-1650 as that which found the highest number of temple constructions in South India and tries to develop, in this connection, the following points in his observations on South Indian polity.[7]

(1) Tamil plains constituted by the core region of the south Indian macro-economy and consisting of *Cholamandalam* (wet region of *Kaveri* basin) and *Tondaimandalam* (tank-based ecotypic region of semi-arid type) were 'from the 5th century civilization developed . . . whose social and cultural forms profoundly influenced people over a great portion of the Southern Peninsula' extending up to '*Pandimandalam*' (the southernmost portion of the peninsula) and '*Karaman-*

dalam' (a substantial part of the modern state of Karnataka).

(2) Where irrigated rice cultivation (by river water, monsoon water and tank-based irrigation) was routinised and the risk or uncertainty of return was low, one finds a relatively high density of settlement of brahman villages (*brahmadeyas*), their 'major tasks' being maintenance of control over land and labour of all villages (including non-*brahmadeya* ones) and extension of 'hydro-agricultural' type of irrigation system.

(3) The 'distribution of brahmin villages serves as a matter of reliable irrigated cultivation and its attendant social and cultural configurations, including relationships between the dominant high status social groups and those of lower status [of right and left variety] dependent upon them'. While brahmans had their own assemblies, the Sabha, the other people in Tamil plains had their locality-based (or village-based) assemblies called *nadus*, the human and natural resources of which were controlled by (what Stein identifies as) *Nattar*, 'a ruling class.[8] The supreme decision-maker relating to agricultural resources (their mode of use and management) of *brahmadeya* villages was the *Sabha*, but in regard to non-*brahmadeya* villages similar responsibility was vested in the *Nattar* over which again 'landed Brahmins exercised maximum control'. Under both categories of brahmanic local powerbase, *Sabhas* and *Nattars*, with its subordinate *Nadus* (the local assemblies of non-brahmans), decision-making power was not vested with non-brahmans, the latter had to carry out orders from the brahman authority of *Nattar*. Therefore, no direct economic patronage (such as forwarding loans to peasant-producers in distress) or obligations (such as payment of taxes or revenue) existed between members of *Nadus* and regional kings or Chola overlords. Stein says that in peninsular India no revenue flow from villages to town or to state-authority can be traced. What is discernible is the practice of revenue payment to a *Nattar* or a *Sabha* by peasant producers among villages against the formers' social as well as management governance to which the latter was subjected. Regarding allocation of water from rivers, tanks or wells (which were, however, to be dug, channelised, or constructed using free labour of peasant producers), a *Nattar* was the most powerful. But a *Sabha* or a Nattar never made investment in improving techniques of cultivation or for digging wells, tanks or irrigation channels from river. Stein further observes, that all local taxes and tributary payments in South Indian

region were in kind or in terms of labour services and not in cash.

(4) In the arid regions with scanty rainfall and hazardous modes of cultivation, where only millets and no rice could be raised, the population density was the lowest, and brahmanical institutions of dominance and management, or the corresponding practice of brahmanic appropriation of peasant surplus, were almost non-existent. Such regions, 'cover the Maravar and Kallar people of Ramnad, Madurai and *Pudduk Kotai* at times and *Reddis* of parts of Royalseema'. Along with these arid regions there existed semi-arid tracts where the agrarian economy contained a precarious balance between livestock production and the production of millet. Such semi-arid tracts were found in regions belonging to modern Coimbatore, Salem and in the upland semi-dry regions of modern Karnataka.

In this region too, brahmanic institutional settlement could not make much inroad. Here landholders belonged, by and large, to low castes and tended to defy external threat and domination. 'As peasant cultivators they displayed extraordinary initiative and enterprise and were able to move their flock and herds as well as their skills', in order to thwart external threat. Such arid or semi-arid regions were inhabited mainly by semi-tribal societies. The fertile plains of the peninsula were characteristically inhabited by populous agrarian societies of brahmanic order and dominance.

From the two principal socio-cultural configurations of South Indian macro-society, as drawn up by Stein and outlined above, one may observe that during the Chola period brahmanic socio-feudatory rights began to consolidate in the fertile tracts of the peninsular India and could attain their height by the time Vijayanagar empire of the fifteenth century came to reign supreme. The Chola overlordship did not figure out itself as an well-orchestrated state power. Its internal power base had to sustain itself from the support of the *nattars* and its power of overlordship rested on its capacity to execute external plunders. Therefore, in terms of regional power equations, the Chola overlordship was nothing more than a blown-up version of a *nattar* power base to which other *nattars* rendered the service of loyal supporters perhaps in order to share the direct and indirect spoils from external plunder. In this sense the claim of overlordship could be decided not by its ritual superiority over other *nattars* but from its unrivalled despotic capacity to plunder distant neighbours. Thus the Chola overlordship was exercised not so much for its own sake as to construct temples with a part of acquired treasure from external aggressions. Its twofold job of temple construction and landgrants to powerful brahmans enhanced the general social power of a *nattar* landed interest over a *nadu* locality. When the Chola overlordship failed to reward its rural base of clients, i.e., the ruling class of *nattars*, the system began to corrode within itself. The muscle power of *nattars* in general, i.e., brahmanic ruling stratum in the rural areas, began to expand at this phase in opposition to declining Chola overlordship. In this way, the historical mission of the Chola dynasty to enhance brahmanic consolidation came to an end.

By the mid-14th century the rival brahmanic kingdoms of *Hoyasalas* and *Pandyas* grew in strength. They had their genesis, respectively, in the expanding socio-ritualistic power of local *Ukkulas* in Karnataka and of *nattars* in the Tamil areas.

The above account explains only the external factor that led to the deterioration of the relationship between the *nattars* in general and the Chola overlordship (no longer capable of delivering goods to the cause of the brahmanic social power). Inability to face the advancing Arabian Sea power cannot alone explain the reality that led to Chola decline. The reality lay in the growing challenge to brahmanic supremacy in general. Such challenges had indeed their dialectical genesis from the modes by which the Cholas sought to extend as well as cause expansion of the social power of brahmans in South India. The mode of extension was, as we have stated, construction of new temples and installation of new deities, and the mode of expanding superior social power of brahmans was making landgrants to powerful brahman elites who, as grantees could impose ritual prestation or gift obligations on low caste peasants and artisans. The South Indian challenges to brahmanic supremacy in economic and social matters assumed two forms. The first followed the economic consequences of temple constructions, and the second form manifested in the socio-religious movements of Lingayats that sought to curb the social dominance of the brahmanic order.

While temple construction under Chola overlordship was motivated as the instrument of extending and consolidating the brahmanic socio-economic power, the growth of innumerable temples and associated townships began to produce, by the 13th century, its adverse impact on the brahmanic domination over village production base and commerce. The multiplication of temple towns augmented town-trade on commodities produced by village artisans which eventually 'freed many commercial and artisan groups in villages from older social constraints imposed by the agrarian-centred concerns of the Nadu localities'.[9] In this sense the rise of innumerable temple towns began to corrode the brahmanic monopoly of inland commerce by the emergence of Sat Sudra traders who now began to operate from artisan centres of the temple towns. The *nattar* ruling stratum of brahmans or its Chola patronage possessed nothing to arrest this growth. The growing rise of Arab merchants appeared as an obstacle to the plundering expedition of Cholas. And the brahmanic commercial monopoly began to be circumscribed by the rise of Sat Sudra artisan-merchants in inland commerce and by the rise of Muslim traders in coastal commerce. In fact, the emergence of Muslim traders in the coastal areas coincided with the rise of a new class of inland commercial entrepreneurs from the ranks of Sat Sudras. The Sat Sudra traders, operating from temple towns, could now bypass the Tamil commercial interest of brahmans and earn commercial profit by supplying directly to the Muslim traders, the merchandise like pepper, clove, sugar, dyestuff, etc. Now even the village artisan wares such as fine and coarse varieties of cloth could be procured by Muslim traders form Sat Sudra merchants of temple towns. This development indicates little or no change in the commodity structure of peninsular export and import trade. The only change it brought about, was in the caste or racial configuration of the community of merchants that now engaged itself in inland town-based commerce and overseas trade. The most significant consequence of this development was, however, on the countryside. Now, the hitherto existing centripetal trend, within a local village society began to disappear and the supra-local organisation of *nadus* called *mahanadus* in Karnataka region and *Periyanadus* in Tamil region began to appear. 'Inscriptions of these enlarged localities mark them as instruments of dominant cultivating group . . . and they refer to themselves as prosperous sons of soil . . . sons of earth goddess'.[10]

This relative socio-economic emancipation of the dominant cultivating and artisan groups in villages was accompanied by their socio-religious movement that swept South India during the 12th and 13th centuries. We do not suggest that the socio-religious movement of Shaivites in South India acted as an elixir to the economic emancipation of village artisan merchants. In fact, the socio-religious movement did not stir up the Tamilian labouring populations as much as it did their counterpart in Karnataka. Nevertheless, the socio-religious movement of Shaivites in South India can be viewed as opposition to the brahmanic social hegemonism.

The Lingayat movement was essentially the second form of socio-economic challenge to the brahmanic social power that gained its momentum notwithstanding the Chola patronage of the brahmanic supremacy. In the 12th century one, Basava, himself a brahman, had steered the anti-brahmanic socio-religious movement to preach his gospel of Veer Shaivaism. The movement was popularly known as Lingayat movement. The apparent focal point of this movement was the rejection of ritual superiority of brahmans, and the corresponding brahmanic social stipulation like caste discrimination. The female right to seek salvation from indignities, suspension of animal sacrifice, devotion to secular labour activity as the supreme mode of attaining salvation and that of praying to its deity Shiva, rejection of brahmanic priesthood and practice of vegetarian food habit etc. constituted some of the social objectives preached by the Lingayats. The movement did not spread equally to all regions of South India. After the death of Basava, a section of Lingayats revived some of the old practices of the brahmanic order. However, it is claimed, that in quite a few regions, this movement found its dominant group of followers from among artisans and peasants (viz, tailors, potters, barbers, oilmen, weavers, washermen, itinerant traders, agricultural labourers, etc.), and that the majority of occupational groups in those regions once belonging to inferior caste became Lingayats.[11]

The speed with which the movement was embraced by low caste people, no doubt, indicated a deep social antagonism that was engendered between brahmans and other caste members in contemporary rural societies. It is true that the movement could not substantially undermine the brahmanic power base of *Ukkulus* or *Nattars*. But it is also true that the *ayagar* system of allocating land to the village menial servants (which became widespread later on in the macro-region under Vijayanagar empire of the 16th century) came into force for the first time in one or two regions in the 14th century. The possible impact of the movement was that now a village came to be identified in terms of secular artisan or peasant activity groups. All these changes, by themselves, do not reflect a substantial departure from the mode of exercising brahmanic social power structure in the rural areas of the region.

From the second half of the 13th century to the middle of the 14th century, we find an interregnum of roughly hundred years when one does not find any stable imperial overlordship in the macro-region.

The period witnessed recurring conflicts between the Pandya overlordship in the Tamil regions (that originated from the class of *nattars* powered by their wealth acquired from subordinate village societies and profitable Coromandel coastal trade) and the Hoyasala overlordship in Karnataka. In fact, during this period the political power base of each sub-regional brahmanic overlordship tried to compete with each other for catapulting it into the position of Cholas. While during the last days of Chola rule (c.1180 to 1280), Tamilian *Peryanattars* began to involve themselves in Chola succession wars, they had to contend at the same time with the rival brahmanic power of Hoyasalas that was eager to subjugate the fertile Tamil plains. It was during this period that an independent but a third brahmanic kingdom of Vijayanagar, situated in the northern edge of Tamil region on the bank of Tungabhadra river, grew up. The Vijaynagar kingdom mastered sufficient military strength and discreetly abetted both Hoyasalas and Pandyas.

In its early course of ascendancy, the Vijayanagar kings helped incursions into Tamil plains but at the same time supplied arms to Pandya kings. In its own interest, the Vijayanagar kingdom never aspired total victory of either Pandyas or Hoyasalas but wanted to fuel their mutual rivalry. After both Pandya and Hoyasala kingdoms were militarily exhausted following a prolonged conflict among themselves, the Vijayanagar incursions into the Tamil core territory began during the middle of the 14th century. They quickly established the imperial authority of Vijayanagar empire over both Hoyasala and Pandya kingdoms. Most of the subordinate kings in Andhra, Karnataka and Tamil core region were, however, permitted by the Vijayanagar imperial rulers 'to retain their local control system on the condition [that] they neither constituted a locus of sovereignty to attract allegiance of lesser chiefs, nor granted such recognition to others besides the Vijayanagar rulers'.[12] The transition of the imperial political nerve centre in South India from the Chola's temple town of Thanjavur to a relatively cosmopolitan Vijayanagar, on the banks of Tungabhadra, was marked by no dramatic change in the complex of relations between a contemporary state power and the rural agrarian societies and sub-societies in the South Indian macro-regions. But certainly the statecraft and the mode of exercising power over subordinate landed interests among local brahmanic kings and institutions was far better orchestrated in the case of Vijayanagar imperial overlordship than in the case of any other previous overlordship in South India.

Many historians characterise the rise of Vijayanagar empire either as a political response of 'Hindu' chiefs to the so-called 'Islamic conquest' of the northern India, or as a Hindu 'war state dominated by its military needs'.[13] There are others who find in its emergence a kind of consolidation of feudalism in India on the grounds that the empire created a class of non-brahman military warriors from among Telugu and Karnatic immigrants by assigning land in the Tamil territory. The tenure of these warriors (known as *Nayakas*) is said to have been based on an exchange between the obligatory military service of *Nayaka* to the empire and imperial assignment of land to the former in lieu of his war service to the Vijayanagar king.[14] Following Nilkantha Sastri, Burton Stein calls this empire merely a confederational unity among 'segmentary states'.[15] Stein, however, does not specify the material dynamics that forged such confederational unity that could replace the earlier absolute sovereignty enjoyed by each of the 'segmentary' states.

In our view, the Vijayanagar imperial unity was the product of an alliance forged among the sub-regional political power bases of wealthy ruling stratum of brahmanic origin in a specific historical context. We have already noted how during the 13th and 14th centuries a slow but steady shift in favour of a rising class of non-brahman traders, low caste artisans and cultivating interests, began to gain momentum within the matrix of a local rural society in all three sub-regions of South India–the Tamil core region, the Vaishnavite Telegu region in the north and the Shaivite Karnataka. But the imperial unity could not be maintained only by a few brahman commanders (*Durgadhipatis*) of Vijayanagar imperial forts. To consolidate this imperial unity the brahmanic empire of Vijayanagar undertook two important measures : the first one was an unforeseen extent of organised promotion of brahmanic ideological cause by installing new and newer temple 'deities' around which a number of new urban centres of Vijayanagar empire could develop under royal patronage.[16] The second was a novel measure showing a specific improvement in the statecraft. It was the founding of the *Nayaka* system that could combine obligatory military service of non-brahman war heroes with land assignment. The empire had no other option but to depend on dispersed tribal groups or even Muslims and on arms import for enriching its soldiers and firearms. It was basically the military reason that forced the empire to attract non-brahman warriors (those coming from the Telegu region at the time of military confrontation between early Vijayanagar expansion and the Reddi kingdom of Kondavidu) to act as subordinate war leaders under a brahman commander of the imperial state with tribal foot soldiers or Muslim horsemen.

This class of non-brahman Telegu and Kanara warriors under the command of a brahman Durgadhipati came to be known as *Nayaka*. The Vijayanagar *Nayakas* were not full-time warriors. During times of peace they practiced cultivation on lands assigned to them by the empire. Burton Stein claims that the *Nayakas* originated from the superior peasant castes and that they were assigned land for settlement mostly in Tamilian semi-arid regions. Their familiarity with superior cultivating techniques, compared to that pursued by the peasantry, belonging to the Tamil *Urs* came from their earlier experience of cultivation in inhospitable environment. Since the land assigned to a *nayaka* was cultivated by himself and his family he could not be reckoned as a feudal lord.

Since external plunder had ceased to be the source of treasure, the question arises as to how a Vijayanagar imperial lord procured his required fund to meet its military and administrative expenditure? To answer this question, we must point out that for the first time in the peninsular history the brahmanic overlordship of the Vijayanagar empire sought to tax the *amara* category of villages in order to finance its administrative expenditure.

In fact, *amara*, *bhandaravada* and *manya* were the three main tenurial categories in land under the Vijayanagar empire. The yields from *bhandaravada* tenure, numerically the smallest category, were to support the military forts scattered throughout the empire. The villages under this tenure may have been supervised by the commanders of the forts. But exactly how the administration of the production and governance of the village peasantry and artisan took place under this tenure is not known. The corresponding features of *manya* category of land tenures, covering a somewhat larger number of villages, are not known either. The greater portion of this income went to support the brahmans, temples and immigrant Shaivite *gurus*. The largest number of villages came under the *amara* category (three-fourth of all villages). Under this category, a village had to pay multiple taxes from its surplus (after deducting the cultivators' share, *vellal vaqai* – a system that once fed the *Nattar* rulers). The beneficiaries of system ranged from the imperial authority to war veterans and foot soldiers. It is not known as to how village production process under this category was managed? What is known is that only *Nayakas* and *ayagars* cultivated land in a village of this category. They were assigned land respectively by the imperial ruler and extant village authority. The *ayagars* rendered labour service to the village authority and the *Nayakas* on occasions to an imperial overlord. There is no doubt that they did not have to pay any tax and so they must have enjoyed the rights of free peasants as long as they could render obligatory services.

Therefore, *Nayakas* and *ayagars* were not substantial holders of land, nor were they instruments of imperial surplus appropriation and peasant enserfment. On the other hand, there is evidence that apart from earning by serving as militia to the imperial power, the *Nayakas* could sustain themselves as free cultivating peasants, somewhat comparable to *hoplites* of Ancient Greece. Nevertheless, the multi-ethnic character of the *nayaka* tenure in a village land certainly circumscribed the social dominance of brahmans. This explains why among Tamil village societies of the late Vijayanagar empire the traditional brahmanic ruling stratum represented by the *Nattar* institutions began to disappear.

From our analytical account of the Vijayanagar imperial overlordship and its mode of reproduction, it is evident that the rise of an imperial overlordship purely for protecting the political supremacy of socially powerful brahmanic power could buy stability only by measures which paradoxically tended to undermine the social and political supremacy of that very brahmanic power.

The dialectical movements of history found their clear manifestation at the next phase of development in peninsular India. The brahmanic kingdom of Vijayanagar was replaced by various types of non-brahmanic sub-regional state powers. The decline of Vijayanagar empire and the subsequent rise of smaller sub-regional kingdoms heralded a new epoch in the political and social history of the South India. While this epoch is characterised by the end of brahmanic political supremacy, the reasons that led to the emergence of this epoch were not exactly the changing power equations among brahmanic and non-brahmanic groups of political aspirants. In fact, the system of South Indian imperial overlordship contained certain attributes which were not present in any of its North Indian counterparts. These very attributes made a South Indian overlordship susceptible to collapse. One of them was the abject dependence of the overlordship on the dominant powers in a peninsular civil society. This was clearly absent in North India where a state power– big or small – always stood on its own mode of appropriating politico-economic power.

The militarily powerful northern rulers rarely launched military expeditions against southern empires except to plunder wealth probably because of the difficulty of negotiating the huge mountainous terrain that separated North from the South India. But this apparent security enjoyed by the early South Indian empires of Pallavas, Cholas and Vijayanagar produced a paradigm of political overlordship in the South that rarely could form a base of politico-military power of its own, independent of political supports from the smaller brahmanic kingdoms. The South Indian system of overlordship never transcended its character of confederational unity among smaller, but locally entrenched, brahmanic powers.

This weakness manifested itself in the chromic inability in matters of appropriating an independent basis of surplus appropriation from subordinate village societies. During the Chola period, while the brahmanic ruling stratum of *Nattars* could levy surplus from *Nadu* localities, the Chola overlords had to fend for themselves by overseas plunder and had to supplant the social power of *Nattars* by investing their booty in temple constructions and by making landgrants to individual brahmans.

Again the Vijayanagar empire possessing no scope for external plunder, had to introduce three kinds of land tenures, two of which were meant respectively for brahman commanders in imperial forts and for feeding brahmans and temples in general. The only kind of land tenure from which the Vijayanagar rulers could levy surplus, was not lucrative enough to enable them to raise a professional army for the imperial state. On the contrary, by introducing the *Nayaka* and *Ayagar* systems the imperial overlordship unwittingly acted against an imperial monopoly of appropriating village surplus.

When the Vijayanagar overlordship, despite its mammoth investment on the construction of temples, proved incapable of further enhancing brahmanic interest, its decline became inevitable.

When the political supremacy of the brahmanic system, epitomised by the Vijayanagar empire came to an end, the localised brahmanic powers sought to sustain themselves by collaborating with the emerging non-brahmanic political powers. The latter developed two distinctive features: the first was an absence of any effort either to patronise brahmanic ideology or to promote the social power of the brahmans by landgrants. The second was the dependence of the state system, for its functioning and reproduction on the acquisition of village surplus.

Thus there was a formal end of brahmanic political supremacy in South India. The localised state power now faced the problem of manning its administration with a bureaucracy of non-brahmanic origin. But for its able functioning, the non-brahmanic state power had to depend on brahmanic elites. The second feature directly affected the hitherto undisturbed monopoly of surplus appropriating interests in the rural areas. The earlier ritual garb of brahmanic surplus entitlement from village communities now changed to rigorous social enserfment of the village-level direct producers. The ritual prestations or gifts to brahmans or neo-brahmans (those who claimed brahmanic lineage of this or that kind, but were socially inferior only to brahmans and superior to others) now became a demand which had to be enforced. This type of brahmanic social coercion was exercised not by armed power, but by the manoeuvres and designs of a supra-village political bureaucracy of brahmans.

At this critical juncture in the evolution of peninsular state system, there grew a brahmanic variety of social feudalism in most of the non-Mughal areas of South India. This development in South India contrasted sharply with the development in North India. While a Mughal bureaucracy rarely interfered with extant intra-communal paradigm of rights and obligations of a village community, the objective situation in the non-Mughal South left little scope for a disjuncture between a official bureaucracy and the brahmanic social dominance. Unlike in North, a South Indian village community in the absence of a strong state power that could enforce surplus extraction for it, confronted no secular supra-village political power capable of undermining brahmanic supremacy or in matters of challenging the latter's control over village land and labour. It was the immediate interest of a localised state power that characteristically prevented it from undermining the socially coercive apparatus of brahmanic oligarchs within a village community. The village community could also subsist in South India, but whereas the autonomy of a North Indian village community had its essential base on the secular right of the direct producers to subsist on the basis of their labour activity, the autonomy of a South Indian village community rested on the priority or predominance of socio-oligarchic claim of a brahmanic or neo-brahmanic power on village surplus over the competing claim of the state powers.

Two important questions arise: the first is, what prevented a brahmanic power from assuming a politico-legal right on village land in the form of landed property? and second is what could, in a setting of pervasive dominance of the brahmanic authority, sustain the communal mode of existence of direct producers in South India?

The first question can be answered by the fact that a politico-legal claim on surplus generating labour activity comes into being when the extant extra–economic authority of appropriating surplus outlives its social scope or the direct producers' autonomy of their subsistence right appears as fetter to intra-communal mode of surplus appropriation by the non-productive elites. We have seen that the post-Vijayanagar developments in peninsular political power while formally ending the brahmanic supremacy in political overlordship, paradoxically enhanced the power of the brahmanic social oligarchs. In other words, the objective social reality in peninsular India did not warrant an objective requirement for politico-legal form of appropriation of land as the condition of labour. In Mughal India, on the other hand, the communal right of direct producers to subsist acted as a fetter to politico-legal assumption of power by a village zamindar (or a non-productive elite) for appropriating village land as condition of labour.

The answer to the second question is that unlike in Mughal India, in South India there existed a closer connection between the material reproduction of a village production base and the same of a state power, particularly during the post-Vijayanagar phase. In this sense, notwithstanding the unilateral dependence of a non-brahmanic local state power on the brahmanic socio-oligarchic authority on village land and labour, there persisted a deep antagonism between the two in their respective relations to village production. This antagonism had its repeated political manifestations during the post-Vijayanagar period. This is also the reason why, in contrast to Mughal India, a southern state power helped village peasantry by remission of state tax on villages or by advancing distress loans to villagers or by digging wells or tanks in villages. In contrast, the brahmanic social oligarchs paid special attention to devising diverse means of exploiting social surplus yielded by direct producers in a village. Apart from this chronic contradiction between a state power and its bureaucracy in post-Vijayanagar South India, the other factor that helped a village community (numerically dominated by direct producers) to sustain itself against the interloping authority of brahmans was the mechanism of socio-economic exploitation itself. In absence of politico-legal articulation of the surplus appropriating right of a brahmanic social authority, it was in the interest of the social authority to nourish a community just to exercise its right of appropriation. If the brahmanic right was not codified in politico-legal terms, that was in order to wrap it up in socio-ritual terms and this presupposed the existence of a community. Indeed, unless a village community existed, the social power of a village oligarch – whatever his social identity - could hardly be materialised.

Since most village land in South India was controlled either by a temple or religious establishment or by a brahmanic or neo-brahmanic social elite, and village labour or water was also allocated by them, the labouring population as a whole could develop no independent means of existence. Except in the arid or semi-arid tracts, the history of South India witnessed no peasant migration or founding of villages under the initiative of peasants. The social feudalism of the non-Mughal peninsula region could arise, on the one hand, because of an uninhibited degree of brahmanic or neo-brahmanic social control over means of production and labour power and, on the other, by overbearing dominance of them within the intermediary political set-up of a non-brahmanic state power.

Notes

1. Burton Stein, 'South India : Some General Considerations', *Cambridge Economic History of India,* Vol.I (Ind. edn.), *op. cit.*, pp.14-42.
2. *Ibid.*, p.20.
3. *Ibid.*, *loc. cit.*
4. In fact, in his contribution, 'Vijayanagar c.1350-1564' in the same volume, he cannot cite a single instance to show that Vijayanagar overlordship derived a portion of its income from predatory conquest beyond the peninsula. See Ch.IV, Part I, *op. cit.*, pp.102-24.
5. D.N. Jha, 'Temples as Landed Magnates in Early Medieval South India (c. A.D. 700-1300)' in R.S. Sharma (ed.), *Indian Society : Historical Probings, op. cit.*, pp.202-16.
6. N. Karashima, *Proceedings of Tamil Studies*, pp.233-50, Cf. T.V. Mahalingam, 'Villages Communities in South India', *Transactions of the Archaeological Society of South India,* (1955) 33-46, *ibid.*, p.209, fn.22.
7. B. Stein, 'South India : Some General Considerations', *Cambridge Economic History of India,* Vol.I, *op.cit. passim.*
8. Burton Stein is somewhat ambivalent in his exposition, as he does not probe into the exact relationship among the *Sabha* (the Brahmanic assembly), the Urs, (The peasant association) and the ruling class of *Nattar*. From his findings it appears that all of them having appeared during the *Chol*a period, their functions were overlapping. According to him, 'the Sabha . . . took *responsibility for the decisions* to allocate agrarian resources [obviously including labour and water] to various requirements to hundreds of *brahmadeyas* or *agraharams*. . . and it was locality assemblies (*Nadus*) of non-Brahmans who carried out this function'. On the other hand, the *Nattar* ruling class which included landed brahmans could be controlled by brahmans owing to their 'dominance over the land and people of the locality '. Stein claims that from

among the most powerful *Nattars* of the Kaveri basin, developed the Chola overlordship.

9. Burton Stein, *op. cit.*, p.34.

10. *Ibid.*, p.37.

11 C. Parvathama, 'Role of Protest Movements in Social Transformation', *Proceedings of Indo -Soviet Symposium in Social Sciences* (Santiniketan, 1977) (mimeo).

12. B. Stein, 'Vijayanagar , c.1350-1564', *Cambridge Economic History of India, op. cit.*, Ch.IV, p.103.

13. K.A. Nilkanta Sastri, *A History of South India*, 2nd edn. (Madras, 1958). pp.296-97.

14. D.C. Sarkar, *Indian Epigraphical Glossary* (Delhi, 1966).

15. Cf. Proceedings of Seminar on *Land System and Feudalism in Ancient India.* (Calcutta, 1964).

16. This was, indeed, nothing new. The Chola overlordship, as we have found earlier, pursued the same policy of patronising brahmanic ideological dominance.

17. That the Telegu or Kanara immigrants (including the *nayaka* warriors) invited by the empire did not require Tamilian retreat from land can be explained by two factors: (*a*) the immigrants arriving in the wake of induction of warriors included, among others, merchants and agricultural labourers, were allowed to settle on the black-soil tracts of Tamil country, long neglected by local Tamilians; (*b*) in other regions, i.e., the regions of settled agriculture in the Kaveri delta, local institutions of *Nattar* class and its subordinate *Nadus*, disappeared with the emergence of 'new multi-ethnic local authority of the *Nayakara* and *Ayagar* Systems'. A. Krishnaswami, *The Tamil Country under Vijaynagar* (Annamalainagar, 1964).

There is, however, a controversy among historians as to whether the *Nattar* class authority of Tamil country was entirely replaced by the *Nayakara* system and the *Nadu* by the *Ayagar*-system. But there is less dispute on the fact that during the Vijayanagar period brahmanic monopoly of *Nattar* was circumscribed by the multi-ethnic *Nayakara* authority, and the *Ayagar* system became more widespread in Tamil agrarian societies of the core region.

3.8: The Nature of Protofeudal Exploitation in Non-Mughal India

How the brahmanic variety of 'social and economic exploitation of labour' could sustain itself within the matrix of non-brahmanic political power structure in South India can be illustrated by the pattern of developments under the two most powerful sub-regional state powers that eventually developed in South India – the Golkunda Sultanate and the Maratha kingdom.[1] By the mid-17th century the two state powers divided between themselves the major part of the peninsular India. We shall briefly sketch the relevant features of the internal developments in each to illustrate how the brahmanic socio-economic dominance could persist without facing any threat from a state-sponsored control structure on village land and labour. A state-designed control structure in its own myopic interest allowed the socially dominant groups' absolute control mechanism over land and labour. Indeed the growth of the brahmanic social power within the rural polity could build up its social base so thoroughly that no other rival elitist group could germinate in South India except as a collaborating surrogate of the brahmanic social dominance. This explains why within the rural polity of South India, social enserfment of menial population became virtual economic enserfment of the latter.[2]

Golconda Sultanate emerged as a regional kingdom in the early years of the 16th century under the governance of Qutb Shah, a Shia Muslim of Perso-Islamic origin. As a kingdom in the Telugu-speaking area Golconda initially emerged by combining some of the *Kakatiya* kingdom of Andhra region and the Gajapati kingdom of southern Orissa. Its political centre later shifted from deltaic Andhra to the Telengana region, the homeland of Vijayanagar Telugu *Nayakas*. Two warrior-peasant castes of Reddis and Valamas colonised the arid and inhospitable Telengana plateau in the early medieval period, perhaps because brahmanic elites had earlier occupied the fertile Godavari delta by establishing social dominance on the local labouring population.

In this context, we are to note that, unlike the Tamil fertile regions or Karnataka plains, the agrarian societies of the early medieval Telugu areas were predominantly inhabited by powerful peasant castes of Razus, Valammas, Kammas and Kapus (*Reddis*).[3] E. Thurston wonders how the Valammas and Reddis became superior caste groups and ascended a social hierarchy which placed them next to Telugu brahmans in course of later developments. He conjectures that the two superior Telugu peasant castes originated from two immigrant brahman males (or autochthonous brahmans)[4] and low caste local women.[5] In a village society, there were both these peasant castes of higher social status and village menials who rarely had the right to cultivate land. Telugu Lenkas belonged to one of such left-hand menial caste but in course of time they developed expertise as loyal foot soldiers capable of using firearm under a Reddi or Valamma warrior/cultivator during the days of ancient Kondaividu kingdom of early medieval Telengana.[6]

The Telugu warriors who at the instance of Vijayanagar overlordship, migrated to the Tamil region included among themselves heterogeneous ethnic groups, such as Valammas, Lenkas, Kammas of Rayalseema regions of Telengana plateau and most of them were absorbed within the Vijayanagar Nayakara system. That was how the Vijayanagar *Nayakara* system could develop a multi-caste village authority in the semi-arid tracts of 16th century Tamil country. But Golconda *Nayakas* before immigration continued to remain divided among themselves in matters of retaining their independent caste as well as functional identity. Unlike the Vijayanagar *Nayakas* the Golconda *Nayakas* were extremely loyal to their local brahman patrons.

The reason for the social bond between Telengana Reddis and Valammas on the one hand and the Telugu brahmans on the other was the brahmanic patronage of the former castes so as to establish a kind of rural peasant-cum-warrior aristocracy that actually functioned as a political base of either pre-Vijayanagar *Kakatiya* brahmanic kingdom or neo-brahmanic Kondaividu Reddi kingdom. Either of them had ties of dependence on these warrior peasant castes for war and cultivation. Perhaps expertise at cultivation and warfare made these warrior peasant castes indispensable to the Vijayanagar empire. This also shows that their homeland in the Telengana region was so inhospitable that an assignment in a foreign soil was adequate attraction for those who had no other means of survival. Moreover, in such hostile natural environment, right to occupy a land that could be brought only under labour intensive methods of cultivation, could readily assume an issue of contention among the social and political powers in a Telengana village.

However, with the beginning of the Golconda empire, particularly under Qutb Shah, the local Telugu brahmans began to gain political ascendancy, assuming important bureaucratic positions, and the Telugu peasant warriors had to operate as the main politico-military base of the kingdom.[7] J.F. Richards reports: 'In every type of tax collection the agents who actually made the collection were virtually all brahmans. Brahmans also served as ubiquitous agents (*vakils*) for virtually all greatmen, whether Muslim nobles or Hindu, Armenian or European merchants. In this capacity brahmans often achieved substantial wealth and real, if delegated, power. Numerous, though subordinate, official posts, entrepreneurial opportunities in tax farming, and widespread opportunities as agents and brokers largely counter-balanced the inevitable loss of patronage and worldly influence experienced by temple or priestly brahmins of the region under a Muslim dynasty'.[8] In the earlier period the Telegu Komati merchant castes were the tax-farmers as well as traders in Masulipatnam port. But during the phase of brahmanic ascendancy under Sultanate officialdom, brahman officials could easily replace the Komatis as dominant segment of tax-farmers, if not as coastal traders.

The Golconda Sultans, however, did not initially dislodge the Reddi or Valamma officials from dominant positions in the lower levels of rural administrative hierarchy. In fact, each revenue-yielding zone (pargana) was put under the hereditary administrative control of a powerful Reddi or Valamma family. Such pargana-leval officials called *Deshmukhs* (Persian, *Desai*), were vested with 'the primary task' of 'maintaining armed retainers' and of 'assisting the collection of tax by taxfarmer's (*hawladars*) in lieu of a commission on collection, or a tax free grant of village land in each zone.[9] While the civil administration was vested in Deshmukh families, the fiscal administration lay with brahman *Deshpandes*. The remuneration of Deshpandes was broadly similar to that of Deshmukhs. At the earlier stage the village accountants, the brahman *Kulkarnis*, could not exercise their caste dominance in all parganas, and the Muslim administration lifted a good number of *Kulkarnis* to the position of *Deshpandes*.

The last Sultan of Golconda is reported to have issued a firman directing the appointment of village headmen only from the ranks of brahmans who were still functioning as accountants, namely, the *Muqaddams* and the *Kulkarnis*. A more important official patronage could be appropriated by the elitist segment of brahman officialdom when it was vested with the power of recruiting pargana level chiefs like Deshmukhs and Deshpandes.

This general policy of the later Sultanates towards local brahman elites helped the latter to assume official position ranging from *Deshpandes* or *Deshmukhs* to lower orders such as village headmen and *Kulkarnis*. This was not always due to the fact that brahmans were more efficient than others in matters of literary and administrative experience. Perhaps the institutional reshuffling of personnel, particularly during the period of the last Sultan, was mainly to avoid conflicts between the rural official aristocracy belonging to the dominant peasant castes and the brahman tax farmers like *Deshpandes* who had collaboration from brahman *Kulkarnis*. This made the non-brahmanic officials somewhat superfluous.

Though the local brahman elites could command the loyalty of powerful peasant castes, the caste rivalry between them and the brahmans in the sphere of distribution of patronage and surplus appropriation' ,must have created potential for conflict. Since there existed no uniform principle of taxation, and tax farming had no rules to follow, misappropriation of state revenue or leakage of taxed income in the process of revenue collection caused misuse of fiscal power by brahmans mainly at the expense of those who were vested with civil administration. This perceived need to end the duality in caste dominance in civil and fiscal administration, induced the last Sultan to place the brahmans at the helm of both fiscal as well as administrative affairs in a pargana or village by pushing the Reddi or Valamma officials out.

The power of the local brahmans increased so much under Golconda kingdom that when Abul Hasan, the son-in-law of Qutb Shah, became the Golconda king, a series of conflicts between the Sultanate nobles of Muslim origin and power-hungry brahmans began.[10] In the initial round the brahmans were successful. A Telugu brahman, Madan Pandit, was made the Chief Minister by Abul Hasan. Pandit and his brother, Akkana, soon seized control of key positions in the administration, finance and army, and in the process many Persian and other Muslim noblemen were dislodged from the power structure. It is said that Pandit was not as ruthless as his deputies were, at least, to the indigenous Decanni Muslims. A few among the latter were indeed given, innocuous positions in the administrative structure. Pandit also attempted to create a loyal group of followers among *Deshmukhs* by replacing, with the help of the king, the independent and spirited ones by those who were obedient to him. The various European traders or travellers of the period 'attribute to Mundanna and Akanna increased severity to all non-brahmins'.[11]

Madan extended the boundaries of the empire to include the greater part of Tamil core region including Tanjore. Hence, apart from consolidating a brahmanic supremacy over traditional agrarian societies of Telengana., the old brahmanic domination over Tamil heartland was also reinforced by Madan Pandit. It is likely that during this period the village authority of *Nayakara* system began to disintegrate yielding to the new brahmanic authority of village headmanship in the Tamil regions.

The political power of Madan Pandit, and the power enjoyed by a group of brahman elites under him came to an abrupt end with the victory of Mughals over Golconda Sultanate. The Mughal campaign against Golconda could not be successful without the active collaboration of disgruntled Muslim nobles and the studied indifference of local warrior castes.

After the collapse of the Golconda kingdom, its territories were annexed by Aurangzeb in the last decade of the 17th century. Subsequently the brahmanic political power of patronage-distribution among powerful caste elites came to an abrupt end. But by that time brahmanic elitist domination over village-level agrarian societies and sub-societies became all pervasive and left no room for peasant-castes to resurrect their old economic power. While in the Telengana region itself the number of *agrahara* villages (i.e., tax-free villages granted to brahamans) increased several times, in the agrarian societies of Godavari deltaic regions or in those of fertile Krishna regions or in Tamil core regions, the socio-economic coercive power of brahmans acquired its highest degree of articulation. The brahman elites–irrespective of whether they belonged to Saivite or Vaishnavite sects now had absolute social authority over all categories of village land (*agrahara* or *brahmadeyas*, non-*brahmadeya* or *Mirasi* and *Mugasa* turned zamindari). Apart from an unrivalled social domination by brahmans, a huge amount of revenue-free village land coming as they did under the control of more than 2,000 temples[12] in Tamil region, supplanted the growth of civil power of brahmans over village land in the region.

In the core regions of the Golconda Sultanate, the village societies which were once dominated by the famous *Reddi-Valamma* caste groups were now subjugated by brahmanic elites. During the last days of the Sultanate, the brahmanic coercive authority forced the villagers of other caste groups to contribute liberally to the construction of temples and to donate land for the maintenance of temples.

Following the Mughal annexation of Golconda a change was, no doubt, brought about in the administrative structure and there emerged the Mughal institutions of fauzdars, jagirdars and mansabdars. But the latter functioned according to instructions from the Diwan (the imperial Mughal governor) of Hyderabad. There is, however, no record to testify that the old fiscal administration of Golconda kingdom underwent an abrupt change and was replaced by the Mughal system of revenue assessment. In fact, the only change that the Mughal authority could introduce was suspension of tax-farming and the sale of *Deshmukh* rights. The introduction of Mughal *Jijiya* tax on non-Muslims cannot be treated as an additional burden on local peasantry since under previous rulers villages had to pay heterogeneous categories of unofficial ceses and levies extracted by brahman tax farmers and *Deshmukhs*.

It is more likely that the basic official structure of fiscal or revenue administration of Golconda regime was retained by the political overlordship of the Mughals. It is true that few changes in the racial specifics of administrative personnel were brought about in the upper reaches of the local Mughal machinery of revenue administration, particularly at the level of *Deshmukhs Deshpandes*. But the brahmanic dominance at the level of village *Kulkarnis* and other holders of village office did not undergo any change. An alien jagirdar (i.e., a Muslim *Deshmukh*) could not hope to collect village levy without cooperation from the dominant group of village officials who were none other than locally powerful brahman landholders. The saleability of *Deshmukh* rights under the earlier regime already led to the substitution of non-brahman Deshmukh rights (once enjoyed by a few affluent peasant caste people) by those of wealthy brahmans reducing the non-brahman *Deshmukhs* to the position of village officials under a brahman headman.

The warrior-caste peasants in the new situation began to organise sporadic peasant rebellions against the new Mughal *Deshmukhs* and fauzdars–brahmans or Muslims–this took the form of banditry against wealthy merchants, revenue officials and affluent brahmans. On the other hand the Mughal administration of Hyderabad failed to mobilise any major ethnic group of people in the rural areas who could function as foot soldiers to safeguard Mughal imperial interest.

Mughal insulation from the supra-village polity caused the expansion of Muslim *mansabdars* recruited mostly from the rank of alien Muslim officials or a few urban Deccani Muslims (by the late 18th century,

Muslim nobility were increasingly dominating the emerging urban societies of South India). The growing fiscal crisis of the regional Mughal administration of the Mughal governor in Hyderabad, foreshadowed its doom with the advent of the more militarily agile Maratha chieftains.

It will be too simplistic a view, as Richards appears to hold, that the top-heavy set-up of Mughal mansabdars was the basic cause of the financial crisis that engulfed the South Indian component of the Mughal empire. It is to be admitted that the Mughal Diwan of Hyderabad failed to transplant in South India a North Indian model of dependable protofeudal control structure on village output. This failure can be explained broadly in terms of a differential path of evolution of South Indian polity that found itself totally subdued under brahmanic protofeudal interest by the time Mughals usurped political power in the region. The social precondition that helped Mughal imperial power in the North was largely absent in the 17th century South India. It was only by conceding autonomy to brahmanic protofeudal elements in the South Indian countryside that local Mughal power could sustain itself. This explains why the Golconda machinery of revenue administration could not be replaced by the North Indian model of Mughal administration. Therefore the small amount of revenue that could trickle out from the South Indian countryside to a Mughal Deshmukh was the prime cause of the financial crisis of the local Mughal governor.

It is now widely acknowledged by historians that the South Indian administration had to be financed by Aurangzeb from revenue collected in Bengal. This financial crisis might have had its genesis in an expanding war machinery, but the crisis could not assume the dimension or intensity that it had, if it had not been for the meagreness of local revenue collections. Besides, the repeated predatory incursion by the Marathas into South Indian Mughal territories (not infrequently in cooperation with local rebel groups) made the financial crisis extremely acute. The only outcome of this political chaos and financial disorder was the brahmanic consolidation over local village-based agrarian societies and sub-societies. Here social enserfment of peasants and artisans by supra-village or intra-village brahman elites could assume the form of economic exploitation. The brahmanic command was enforced neither by any intermediary control structure on land nor by any proprietary right on land. It could enforce its entitlement by controlling the major segment of land. The varied landed interests that were engendered around socio-feudatory privileges of brahman elites and temples, were thus able to appropriate surplus from the labouring population of the macro-region.

However, the process by which the protofeudalism of the brahmanic variety could consolidate itself in the heartland of Western Deccan and in Kerala is not similar to that in other parts of the peninsular region. For instance, for the brahman rulers of Travancore (a part of modern Kerala), the political tribute from subordinate village societies was not its only source of royal income. In addition the Travancore rulers could augment royal accumulation of treasure by engaging themselves in overseas trade. In revenue administration and overseas trading activities Travancore rulers found their social (if not political) surrogates from among the dominant local warrior caste, the Nayars. The Nayars, unlike other social groups in South India claimed kshatriya status by virtue of their brahmanic lineage. On the other hand, the Maratha kingdoms with their non-brahmanic origin, also had to succumb to brahmanic political supremacy by the early 18th century owing to internal reasons.

Many political historians have dealt with how the Maratha political power grew from the womb of the Nizamshahi kingdom (1604-26).[13] What needs to be emphasised here is that neither the weak Bahamani Sultanate, nor the Sultanate of Ahmadnagar, nor the Bijapur kingdom possessed the capacity to build an administrative structure once they seceded from Nizamshahi kingdom. Because each had to depend for its survival on a racially alien military bureaucracy manned by local non-brahman peasant-warriors and on fiscal administration controlled by locally powerful brahmanic groups. In this respect their situation bears a close resemblance to that found in Golconda empire under Qutb Shah. A weak state power dominated by local *Deshmukhs* and *Deshpandes* was always liable to collapse particularly when the former found itself caught between Mughal predatory intervention and internal dissensions. While the Golconda *Deshmukhs* under Madan Pandit could not drive their political power to its logical end, namely in the formation of an independent state power, the Maratha non-brahmanic *Deshmukhs* under Shivaji achieved this end.

Under Shivaji, the Maratha kingdom could not gain a high degree of internal political consolidation. The powerful Maratha *Deshmukhs* with their individual war machines could hardly swallow the fact that one of them, by virtue of his military superiority, could declare himself a king and establish his kingdom at Satara with the help of armed unity forged among petty *Deshmukhs*. Had Shivaji not sought to curb the power of his rival *Deshmukhs* by abolishing the latter's source of economic power, i.e., coercive collection of levy from lesser *Deshmukhs* and had been content with a confederational set-up, there would have perhaps been a better prospect of sustained stability after his death. Shivaji with his large armed retinue assumed the role of a king and sought to establish his personal command over other *Deshmukhs*. In his endeavour he had to force obedience from other *Deshmukhs* by virtue of his superior military skill. In order not to allow rival centres of power to develop in his kingdom he scrupulously avoided assigning *jagir* or *deshmukh* rights even to his loyal officials, although there are evidences that he assigned *inam* lands to quite a few in south Konkan.[14]

Faced with the hostility of the brahman and Muslim *Deshmukhs*, Shivaji had to depend more on his military power and skill rather than on diplomatic manoeuvres. After his death the kingdom could not sustain itself owing to its exclusive dependence on arms. It is not suggested that the reason for the constant bickering between Shivaji and the big *Deshmukhs* was just a struggle for power, and that his abolition of tax farming was aimed at cutting the economic power of his rivals. Shivaji wanted to form the basis of a state power with the help of a secular bureaucracy, a professional army and a comprehensive land revenue system. In this sense, Shivaji's state craft is roughly comparable to the Mughal statecraft. His bureaucrats had temporary tenure in a revenue division and he recruited his militia from among the low caste artisans, peasants and agricultural labourers. Indeed, Shivaji sought to establish direct contact with village headmen (*mugasaholders*, *muqquddams*, etc.) through official tax collectors. Besides, he introduced a new measurement of land and its classification into four categories[15] in order to make a realistic assessment of levy. That he did not succeed in these measures because of his preoccupation with war, is also true.[16] As a result the chronic proclivity among hereditary big *Deshmukhs* and jagirdars towards asserting their plunderous prowess remained only temporarily emasculated under Shivaji's governance. In historical terms, Shivaji's measures for building up a well-orchestrated state power are found to be a sheer aberration in the otherwise historically evolved non-Mughal southern state structures dominated by brahmans. While the Satara-based Maratha king was reduced to a titular head after Shivaji's death, the political structure that came into being, assumed the form of a 'confederation' under a Brahman hereditary prime minister, the *Peshwa*. He established his own government at Poona and his generals established their own subinfeudatory domains such as those of the Holkars of Indore, Gaekwad of Baroda and Sindhias of Gwalior. The Peshwa took an independent stance as the chief of these states, and conducted predatory expedition to the Tamil regions and to Rajasthan taking advantage of the political uncertainty of the post-Aurangzeb Mughal empire. Since the Peshwa expeditions could augment less and less booty compared to the amount of expenditure involved in the military expeditions, the tax burden on the peasantry, traders and artisans increased enormously.

The Maratha agrarian society now faced a rapid change in the pre-existing structure on land and labour, when an European trading company began to loom large on the Maratha horizon.

Before the 'reforms in tenurial forms' undertaken by Malik Ambar, Nizamshahi's latest Prime Minister, the peasant community of Maratha villages during the 16th and early 17th centuries were subject to regressive tax farming by brahman, non-brahman (mainly Kunbi peasant castes) and Muslim Deshmukhs. Such tax farming only strengthened the economic as well as military power of the tax farmers, who frequently deprived the royal exchequer of assessed revenue. This was the reason why Malik Ambar was eagar to bypass the defiant *Deshmukh* intermediaries. He sought to collect taxes (through short period employment of royal officials) from hereditary village officers such as *patils* or *muqquddums* on the basis of crop assessment, made by village accountants (*Kulkarni*) and village headmen (*chaugula*).

The traditional village society consisted of those hereditary officials (of whom only the *Kulkarnis* were recruited from among the brahmans), of Kunbi peasant castes, tenant landholders (*upari*) and village servants and artisans (*balutedars* or *bare balutedars*).[17] The *mirasi*-holders and some of the *uparis* initially belonged to *Kunbi* castes. The *balutedars* came mostly from low menial castes. Shivaji once sought to follow Malik Ambar's reforms of revneue administration particularly in his Swarajya. But later, during the reign of Peshwas in the second half of 18th century, most of the *mirasi* landholders or *thalwaks* were found to be brahmans and *uparis* were largely Kunbi peasants, working as tenants on the land of big *thalwaks* (who by that time became a non-cultivating segment of village peasantry). The big brahman *inam* holders, and holders of land assigned to temples and mosques came to be under brahman or Muslim *Deshmukhs* or Deshpandes.[18] Previously, *balutedars* also held small *inam* holdings for their village services, but by the end of the 18th century, they became landless artisan or peasant labour.[19]

Land in Maratha villages, as reported by Fukazawa, had the following tenurial categories, (*a*) *Mirasjamin*, i.e., land directly controlled and cultivated by Kunbi peasants, (*b*) *Inam Jamin*, i.e., private land held as revenue-free gifts by highly heterogeneous landholding groups consisting of *Deshmukhs*, *Deshpandes*, village *Kulkarnis*, village headmen (*Patils* or *Muqquddums*), assistant village headmen, etc. The village *Inam* lands assigned to various service caste groups of *balutedars*, temples, mosques, etc. also fell under this category, (*c*) *Khalisa Jamin*, i.e., treasury land of the government, (d)*Gotkul Jamin*, i.e., lands of extinct families or waste lands.[20]

There is no evidence regarding the proportion of land under the respective tenurial cagegories. We only know that both Shivaji and his successors in Maratha kingdom, including the Maratha principalities under the Peshwas, financially helped a village community to broaden its cultivation base by digging new tanks, wells and by advancing loans (comparable to Mughal *taqqavi*) to the Kunbi village panchayat. The ostensible reason was to broaden the royal tax base in agriculture, as it was in the case of Mughal state investment on building canals in the upper Gangetic basin.

But two features of village surplus appropriation under Maratha confederacy or under Peshwa principalities are important for grasping the reversal in the social control structure on land. The first, as earlier stated, was the resurgence of a more compressive tax farming in village societies under Maratha principalities of the Peshwas. The second was an increase of revenue rates with the onset of growing political instability when the principalities themselves were engaged in bitter hegemonistic conflicts amongst each other. The military expenditure of the *Peshwas* which sometimes took the from of bribing the foreign powers either to desist them from aggression or to crush them militarily began to increase enormously during the period.

In the absence of dependable records, it is difficult to assess the extent of ruination wrought on Maratha peasantry or to delineate the process by which most of the big *inam* holdings came under the control of brahmans and temples or to answer why Kunbi peasants–once the dominant group of *thalwaks* in a Maratha village community–swelled the ranks of *upari* or landless tenantry and could be displaced in the process by brahman *mirasi* holders.

Fukazawa cites changes in land distribution in two Maratha villages, *Pimpal Saudagar* and *Jategaon Budruk* in course of the last quarter of the 18th century (from 1771-72 to 1797-98 in the case of the former, and from 1790 to 1803 in the case of the latter) so as to show how during that period 'economic differentiations' took place among the peasants.[21] He, however, does not define his concept of a 'peasant'. Indeed, a brahman *mamlatdar* or *Deshmukh* or *Deshpande* or a village *Kulkarni* was *not* peasant by any definition unless any of these officials engaged in some form of labour activity either as cultivator or as a supervisor. He finds that in both villages 70 to 80 per cent of land is held under 'peasant' holdings with a farm size of, at least, 10 to 20 acres of land at the end of the 18th century. Since Fukazawa cannot identify the caste or functional specifics of the so-called big or small peasants, one can at best conclude that in the last quarter of the century there was a tendency towards the decline in big landholders and a corresponding rise in the number of middle-order landholders, with little or no land left with small landholders (i.e., holders of less than 5 acres in the first village and their counterparts with less than 20 acres of land in the second village). The only people who can be designated as peasants *per se* are shown to have decreasing or no control over land. Moreover, what Fukazawa completely misses is the fact that in both villages the total area of cultivated land declined.[22] There can, indeed, be no necessary correlation between the absolute decline in the total area under cultivation and the so-called 'economic differentiation among peasants'. If we consider the data as even roughly realistic, the only inference one can draw is that in the last quarter of the 18th century the landholding structures gained greater degree of multiplicity of non-peasant rights by substituting self-cultivating peasant rights on holdings. Fukazawa's theory of economic differentiation among 18th century Maratha peasants is not based on factual analysis, on the other hand, it indicates the actual shift of land from cultivators to non-cultivators.

The above observations on two Maraths villages conform to our broad conclusions, namely that with the decline of Peshwa political rights, once powerful brahman officials fell back on Maratha village society and became non-cultivating *Mirasi* holders or *inam* holders;and that no stable intermediary control structure on village land and labour could develop within the Maratha agrarian polity. As a consequence when the British came they created a new class of brahman landlords by introducing the *Ryotwari* system.

Notes

1. It is however to be remembered that none of the segmentary states mentioned above was politically stable as each had to contend against external attack from the imperial power of the Mughals. Hence, internal political stability was a prime requirement of their existence.

2. One may point out that we have not picked our illustration from the core region of South India, i.e., from the Tamil region. In this connection one has to remember that after the decline of the Vijayanagar empire no state power in South India could originate from either the brahmanic or non-brahmanic political aspirants. It is true that Tanjore brahmanic kingdom in the most fertile track of Tamil plain represented a kind of statehood. But the most important attribute found among the contemporary state powers of the southern Sultanates belonging to Karnataka, modern Andhra or Golconda or of the Marathas in south-west of the peninsula, was not available in Tanjore. The latter had no professional army of its own, nor did it have a suitable bureaucracy for administration and revenue collection. Tanjore kingship was a developed version of social feudalism of a brahmanic power that procured its treasure as much from socially coercive exploitation of the peasantry and artisans of subordinate villages as from prestations or gifts from subordinate brahmanic land grantees.

3. Cf. E. Thurston, *op. cit. Castes and Tribes of Southern India* (7 vols, Madras, 1909), *Raju*, Vol.VI, pp.246-56: *Valama*, Vol.III, pp. 336-42; *Kamma*, Vol.III, pp. 90-104: *Kapu*, Vol.III, pp. 222-49.

4. This is, however, a highly controversial point among historians of South India. Cf. Suvira Jaiswal, 'Studies in the Social Structure of Early Tamils' in R.S. Sarma (ed), *Indian Society : Historical Probings*, *op.cit.*, pp. 124-55.

5. Cf. E. Thurston, *op. cit.* 'Introduction', pp.i-xxviii. Similarly Nayar community in Kerala which claims a kshatriya origin is not found anywhere else in South India. The Nayars are widely believed to be born to sudra women by Namboodri brahmans.

6. This ancient Telugu peasant tradition of mixing the right to war with the right to cultivate land (with the consequent unfettered right to enjoy one's own fruits of his labour activity) in the Telugu areas was completely alien to standard brahmanic tradition as it was developed in ancient North or South of India.

7. J.F. Richards, *Mughal Administration in Golconda* (Oxford univ. Press 1975), pp. 4-5.

8. *Ibid.*, p. 18.

9. *Ibid.*, Ch.II, p. 29.

10. *Ibid.*, Ch.III, *passim.*

11. *Ibid.*, p. 42. In this connection Richard, cites the account of Francois Martin, the French Governor of Pondicherry, who travelled to the Golconda

capital of Hyderabad as late as 1681 and witnessed "ruined villages and towns . . . by the avarice of Brahmins."

12. Burton Stein observes : 'Madras (Tamil Nadu) state conducted a survey of temples enumerating all or most of those consecrated temples possessing substantial structural features (and thus datable by architectural styles) and more than a modest endowment fund. There are many obvious imperfections in these data, yet the resulting enumeration permits a reasonably positive identification of over 2,000 temples whose major structures may have been constructed between *about 1300 and 1750*. . . . Computer analysis of these data indicate that between 1300 and 1450 [i.e. , the period of transition from Chola to Vijayanagar empires] the average number of temples built in the sixty-nine talukas for which there are data, was 0.5 per taluka; between 1450-1550, [the first part of this period found the Vijayanagar power at its peak, the second, however, began to witness signs of its collapse] 0.7 temples per taluka; and between 1550 and 1650 [when Vijayanagar power almost collapsed and sultanate Golconda was at its height of political power] *1.5 temples per taluka*, *op. cit.* , p. 113 (emphasis added).

From the above data it is obvious that even during the reign of the Muslim Sultanate, the Tamil region witnessed the highest rate of new temple constructions. Paradoxical as it is, it clearly indicates, that notwithstanding the racial complexion of the successive political overlordship, the brahmanic civil authority of the Tamil region could grow up at an accelerated pace. Again one can perhaps discern a correlation between the period and the intensity of temple construction in the sub-region and the nature (fertile, arid, semi-arid, etc.) of its soil. That the Thanjavur temples built during the Chola period were located in a fertile tract, indicates brahmanic preference of fertile region as a suitable place for temple construction in the initial phase. It appears that the rate of new temple constructions were not abruptly high when brahmanic domination over state politics was considerable as it was during the period of late Cholas and early Vijayanagar periods. On the contrary, the rate of additional temple constructions began to sharply increase in the arid and semi-arid tracts (i.e. , modern Madurai, Ramanathapuram, Tirunelveli, etc.) and came late in those regions where non-brahmanic state powers emerged, and semi-tribal and peasant-caste villages came under the subjugation of brahmanic social authority.

We have not, however, come across similar data on temple constructions in the Telugu and Kanara speaking regions. Nevertheless, one may discern a correlation between temple constructions and brahmanic political and/or social domination. After the total political decline of brahmanic power with the advent of Mughals, the growth of temple construction attained its peak in all the regions including the arid and semi-arid regions. In other words, temple construction became the brahmanic instrument of exercising sovereign social power even in villages of less fertile regions inhabited by semi-tribal people after the brahmans lost political power. Cf. B. Stein, *loc. cit.* , pp.

113-14.

13. No single source can be cited as adequate for such an account. We refer only to two sources–one comprehensive, the other introductory. Cf. Surendranath Sen, *Administrative System of the Marathas*, 2nd edn. (Calcutta, 1925), pp. 3-45: Satish Chandra, 'Shivaji and the Maratha Landed Elements' in R.S. Sharma (ed.), *Indian Society : Historical Probings*, *op. cit.* , pp. 248-65.

14. Satish Chandra, *op. cit.*, p. 255. H.K. Fukazawa reports that such assignment of jagirs or *inams* took place in regions outside his own kingdom. See note 15 below.

15. H. Fukazawa, 'Maharastra and the Deccan: A Note', *Cambridge Economic History of India*, *op. cit.* , Ch. VII, p.197.

16. *Ibid.*, *loc. cit.*; Satish Chandra, *op. cit.*

17. H. Fukazawa, 'The Medieval Deccan and Maharastra', *Cambridge Economic History of India*, *op. cit.*, Vol. I, Ch.IX, Section 2, pp. 250-51; Ravinder Kumar, *Western India in the Nineteenth Century : A Study in Social History*' (London, 1968) Ch.I.

18. For evidence see Ravinder Kumar, *ibid.* , Ch.I and II.

19 H. Fukazawa *op. cit.* , pp.252-54.

20. *Ibid.*, p.250.

21. His observation is based on studies of two Maratha villages undertaken by Harold H. Mann in *Pimpal Saudagar*, and N.V. Kantikar in *Jotegaon Budruk.* Cf. Fukazawa, *op.cit.* , Table 7. p.253 ; Table 8, p.254.

22. This can be found out when we multiply the average size of holding with the total number of landholders on different dates.

4

Dynamics of Medieval Indian Commerce

4.1: Commerce Under the Sultanates and the Mughals

Before we analyse medieval Indian commerce–inland or overseas–it is necessary to explain our theoretical framework.

In any society–medieval or modern–a commercial activity is one of unequal exchange between the buying prices and selling prices of commodities. However the difference between pre-modern and modern commerce lies in the latter's integration with a production process aimed at the marketing of commodities produced, while in pre-modern commerce the social production process, though meant for consumption, remains independent of commerce, i.e., production is only for use value creation. The money stock possessed by a medieval entrepreneur is his money capital that represents his potential command over the goods he likes to purchase at low prices for subsequent sale at high prices.

Money derives it worth only as a universalised command over goods, thus at a point of time the total money in stock and circulation lying with the state or individuals is theoretically the aggregate money value of the total physical surplus of goods in stock as well as in circulation. In other words, unless a medieval society produces a physical surplus of goods, the direct producers in such society cannot be induced to part with an amount as surplus payable to other members of the society. In such a situation no worthwhile stock of money or investible money capital can arise in the society.

A mercantile activity as a mode of surplus earning has to compete in general with other modes of surplus acquisition in society. This is more so if the growth of surplus in a society is more or less inelastic and, more important, surplus appropriators are not themselves direct producers. A king or a priest or a plunderer directly appropriates surplus from producers, but a merchant or trader appropriates surplus only through an unequal exchange among two distinctly different groups of people. First, *producers* or *actual possessors* of merchantable wares who want to transform these wares into money but cannot achieve it by themselves; and the second, the non-productive consumers, e.g., the emperor with his militia and bureaucracy, despite earning disposable money through revenue collection is not able to negotiate the flow of goods from producers or actual possessors to themselves. The merchants acquire the initial investible money capital either by way of making loan from the state or by converting their precious metal into standard money coins or from any other exogenous occupation or source. Thus, we can conceive of medieval merchants as the distinct functional group of buyers of wares separate from the direct producers/manufacturers themselves or their community overlords.

As a specific form of surplus appropriation, the medieval commerce has contradictions (as co-appropriator of surplus) with other forms of surplus appropriation, but such contradictions remain subdued as long as a commercial entrepreneur extends the cooperation to other forms of appropriation in matters of materialising their substance. On the other hand, the direct appropriation of surplus (either in money or kind) is the historical cradle in which commerce engenders itself as a specialised activity. Rodney Hilton shows how in medieval England, wealth originating from escalating rent from urban real estate formed the money wealth of commercial entrepreneurs engaged in wool trade and production of woollen fabrics.[1] The particular way the medieval European merchant capital or the capital engaged in medieval European commerce had its genesis may not be found in medieval societies in regions where private property in land, or rental form of surplus appropriation, did not emerge. In these societies, although the initial impetus for commercial activity came from inter-village mutuality and interdependence in matters of imports and exports of consumption goods among villages of different agro-climatic regions, the genesis of fund for commercial activity among few villagers can be traced to a village surplus acquired by non-productive members of a village society.[2]

The transformation of subsistence fund needed by the village commercial entrepreneurs into commercial wealth could take place only when a sharp inequality in the distribution of social surplus between the non-productive urban centres of such societies and the centres of social production among village communities developed. Whatever the inter-continental difference between the process of genesis of commercial money capital, it was the direct appropriation of surplus either by village rentiers or by non-productive village elites that universally acted as the initial offspring of money capital of commerce. This historical genesis of commercial money capital in a medieval society of Europe or Asia always made its entrepreneurial activity subservient to the ruling mode of social production and distribution. Again due to this historical reason commercial wealth or capital could multiply itself only to the extent it was allowed to do so by the extant social mode of production. A mercantile money capital did not, by itself, possess the capacity to initiate a change in the social production base nor could it always control or direct the production process towards its own end.

One can cite the instance of sizable commercial activity among Greek city states of classical antiquity based on the slave mode of production that could hardly set in motion a trend towards commodity production *per se*.[3] Commodity production as a dominant phenomenon arises only when both land and labour become commodities. In no medieval economy was either land or labour subservient to money. What were, then, the dynamics of the pre-commodity production phase? The dynamics of commerce during that phase lay in circulation of goods, the social process of production being exogenous to, and independent of, whatever degree of commercial buying and selling of use values was there. It is only under the capitalist production process that commerce motivates the production process or *vice versa*, and commercial activity reaches its peak.

Since pre-capitalist commerce confines itself merely with the circulation of goods as an instrument of real value appropriation, i.e., physical surplus through unequal exchange, the institutions other than merchants which can help commercial activity are the institution of state power that empowers money to be legal tender for transaction of goods. In a non-capitalist setting of natural economy where social production process cannot rear up commodity production, the use value of goods rather than its exchange value remains the basis of commerce.

It is only because goods in a precapitalist economy are produced for use, such 'usefulness' of goods makes them marketable. While the dominant social modes of production and distribution of goods constitute the physical presupposition of commercial activity, its monetary mechanism depends on the state power. Though medieval commerce is the consequence of an unitary mutualism among three distinctly different functional groups in a polity, the basis of such mutualism is the material self interest of each group which can hardly usurp the existential interest of the others. But underneath this apparent mutualism there are mutual contradictions. The temporal movements of these contradictions are the locomotives of historical changes beyond the medieval societies. The trajectory of such changes is bound to be different in a society and polity where private individual property dominates social production from another where this is virtually absent.

In a medieval state formation without private property, the state authority becomes the direct appropriator of a sizable amount of social surplus. If in such societies the direct producers consume out of their produce and do not require to purchase any consumables, it can be shown that direct producers sell their surplus goods to merchants only when it is necessary for them to procure cash so as to enable them to pay revenue in cash and that the cash revenue distributed among imperial officials as their salaried earning prompts its transformation into consumable goods. In such a situation the difference between direct producers' sale value of a consumable good and merchant's sale value of the same consumed by urban non-productive consumers, amounts to profit in value terms or surplus in physical terms appropriated by the merchants. The necessary condition for a positive rate of mercantile profit or surplus appropriation is the excess of merchant's sale price over the price at which a direct producer sells his goods to the merchant. The merchants negotiate through price mechanism, the flow of rural goods to urban centres where the mode of earning livelihood is, by and large, non-productive. Merchants have their return in mercantile appropriation of a portion of surplus produced by the productive members of society in the rural areas.

Within this simple conceptual framework that deals with circulation of social goods among direct producers or actual possessors of goods, merchants and rural-urban non-productive members having various categories of entitlements among themselves, we investigate the dynamics of medieval commerce as it existed in India.

We have little information about the state of commerce in ancient

India except what Kosambi or some other historians supply. From whatever informations one has, it seems that manufacture in ancient Indian towns completely collapsed with the eclipse of ancient Indian empire and that towns' manufacturing crafts migrated to rural areas. Since we come to acquire more information about towns, trades and villages - their mutual relations of the period of Delhi Sultanates, we propose to make the period of Sultanates, as our point of departure for investigation.

Irfan Habib points out that during the period of Delhi Sultanates there grew a number of urban rice traders and grain merchants in towns. But a little reflection suggests that this growth of 'inland commerce' in grains was *not autonomous*. The commerce between town and village was indeed forced upon a village which was under a compulsion to pay 50 per cent or more of its crops as royal tax (on the assumption that an official *iqta* holder or a village headman of that period did not impose any extra claim on village output).

Such compulsion from above imposed on a village community, generated a need for commuting part of village grains so acquired as tax in kind into cash. As we have observed in Chapter II, a Sultanate or its agent had no mechanism of assessing village surplus. Therefore the tax on village was to be borne by heterogeneous forms of supra-village or village power-brokers who already existed during the pre-Sultanate period. The 'commerce' so engendered during the period of Sultanates witnessed a band of caravan traders or wealthy grain merchants who came into being only as by-product of the royal tax policy.[4] It is quite possible that the kind revenue in terms of grains collected by an *iqta*-holder from the *khots*, *rais* or *rajas* found its transformation into extant currencies which were in operation (i.e., silver or copper *tanka*) at prices lower than the prices at which the urban merchant purchasers of village revenue in kind from *iqta*-holder, sold grains in towns, and that this price differential constituted the source of the mercantile profit.

This process of enforced exchange between a town and a rural area further lubricated the mechanism of despotic revenue collection by the Sultanate establishments rather than a free market mechanism that could only ensure an autonomous growth of inland commerce. That the dependence of a Sultanate power on import of foodgrains from rural areas was the basic dynamic of commerce in grain can be illustrated by Irfan Habib's emphasis on the role of coercion in augmenting town supply of grains. He states that the state power of a Sultanate had, on occasions, to imprison caravan traders' families, or their transport animals if the traders failed to procure stipulated grain provisions for Delhi. Had the inland commerce been unfettered and autonomous, there would have been no need for coercion.

This coercion by the state for securing provisions for town populations of North India explains how commerce in grains during the period of Sultanates grew up more as an axle within the imperial modalities of revenue administration and expenditure rather than as the consequence of a supposed pervasiveness of a free socio-occupational pursuit. Indeed commerce does not figure as an independent or voluntary pursuit of caravan traders or merchants. The towns under a sultanate with their fluctuating populations were overwhelmingly *parasitic* in nature.

The contradiction between town and country of the period–as compared by Mohammed Habib[5] with that in feudal Europe–was in essence a contradiction between an alien state and the extant rural agrarian society. Such contradiction during the period of Sultanates is qualitatively different from contradiction between town and country in feudal West Europe, where, 'the paradigmatic medieval towns . . . practised trade and manufactures' and 'were self-governing communes enjoying *corporate political and military autonomy* from the [rural and even urban] nobility and the Church[6] (italics added). In a sense contradiction between town and country in medieval Europe stemmed from more or less independent economic bases of their own that could force an exchange of foodgrain from the feudal countryside for town manufactures and merchandise. Again a medieval town economy of Europe with its independent manufacturing base was in sharp contrast to towns or cities of classical antiquity where the nobles with their massive possessions of land and shave were the most powerful citizens. Luxury manufactures and commerce in classical cities of Europe were developed at the behest and under the stewardship of urban landed nobles.[7]

The modes by which the parasitic towns and state power of Northern India of the 14th century were instrumental in causing the rise of a class of caravan traders and urban grain merchants, and in the process, a civilian mode of mercantile pursuit of profit, necessarily fostered an insulation of urban grain merchants from the closely-knit rural community of *Khots*, peasants, artisans and others. It is possible that many among the urban merchants might have had either kinship ties or active economic relations with the local trading caste people of a rural community engaged in intra-rural peddling trade. But such ties, by themselves, could not necessarily indicate an identity of interest between village-level pedlars and the urban merchants or caravan traders. What this class of town merchants could, at best, achieve was the formation of an urban-based civilian community of town-living grain merchants or small traders. Only this might be a new development as a consequence of the development of the enforced commerce in grains that otherwise inhibited commercial autonomy of merchants during that period. However, the rise of a class of urban grain merchants in 14th-15th century India was circumscribed by two things. First, an inefficient revenue collection mechanism under the Sultanates in matters of augmenting village level demand for liquid cash (as revenue payments by village headman were, in most cases, in kind rather than cash). Second, the absence of a well-regulated monetary system that would cause the expansion of money supply among civilian merchants or traders under their own initiatives (as minting of the ruling currency, *billon* –a copper currency mixed with silver alloy–was permitted only in the capital cities of Delhi and Agra).

The Mughal revenue administration by establishing an elaborate revenue-administrative set-up, became dependent on a civilian category of primary zamindars at the lowest level, or the pargana-level secondary zamindars at the supra-village level, apart from on its own officials like jagirdars, mansabdars, fauzdars, subedars, etc., for the collection of revenue from villages. The relatively efficient set-up of revenue collection under the Mughals with its meticulously detailed modes of assessment of output of a village was characterised by great flexibility as well as rigour. In contrast to the earlier systems of taxation, the Mughal system – as developed under Akbar – was not based on arbitrary plunder. The practice of *zabt* system (taxation on the basis of annual measurement of cultivated land and crops raised) during Akbar's reign, replacing in most places the earlier system of *kankut* (an arbitrary assessment based on visual survey on crops raised) showed the extent of caution and rigour in the Mughal mode of revenue assessment and collection. Droughts, flood, scanty rainfall and frequent famines in a region were taken into account when assessment of revenue claim from a village was finalised. Here lies the flexibility of the system. The more important element of Mughal flexibility lies in its 'positive system of incentives' that characterised the mode of differential tax rates on different crops so as to promote selective crop production and in 'the practice of charging lower rates' on village fallows that was clearly designed as incentive towards a net extension of cultivation.[8] Hence the Mughal system of revenue assessment, though mediated by a no less tyrannical control structure on village output, had to develop the system of built-in incentives for cropping intensity as well as for horizontal extension of cultivation.

In order to achieve its objective the Mughal system of revenue collection had to build a multi-ethnic protofeudal structure of superior legal rights on village cultivated land as well of direct imperial right on an extensive *khalisa* land in the different fertile regions of the empire.[9] This impersonalisation of the legal right of a Mughal empire on village output and on cultivated land freed activities of people with commercial pursuits from coercive manoeuvres that characterised the period of Delhi Sultanates.

While the development of commerce in the rural areas during the Mughal period (from Akbar to Aurangzeb) was the unavoidable outcome of the impersonalisation of a comprehensively designed Mughal system of revenue assessment and collection, the built-in flexibility in matters of permitting public minting of centrally standardised coins in a large number of local mints spread over the various Subas of the Mughal empire facilitated the growth of autonomy in rural commercial transaction.[10]

The other important development that had its genesis from a well-knit revenue administration of the Mughals was the proliferation of urban centres discharging centrally-financed religious or economic administrative and/or police functions for hinterlands. It is true that compared to the pre-Sultanate period, the Sultanate period also witnessed the rise of new towns or reinvigoration of old ones and that the majority of Mughal urban centres like those under the reign of a Delhi Sultanate had revenue collecting functions. But in, at least, one significant respect, an average Mughal urban centre differed from its counterpart under a Delhi Sultanate. A Mughal urban centre, while retaining the character of a headquarter of, at least, one revenue circle grew up as *a feeder of rural commercial transactions* around its neighbourhood. While an average urban centre of the Mughal period collected imperial revenue in cash from the hienterland, not the entire collection was transmitted to the imperial treasury. A portion of collection was retained by local urban centre for defraying the necessary expenses of those who were directly or indirectly connected with the job of revenue assessment and collections, namely, the local zamindar and his retainers, *quajis*, *kanungos*, civilian traders, moneylenders, small shopkeepers, keepers of shrines or mosques, scholars imparting lessons and sundry others, i.e. , all such people who helped the reproduction of the local urban society of the non-productive type. Village headmen of hinterland village communities or individual peasants or artisans of villages found a ready market for their grains and goods in that proximate urban centre. The village pedlars could buy village importables from urban shops and sell the village exportables to them to sustain themselves in their subsistence type occupations. The agents of big interlocal or city merchants bought local merchandise wares from such urban centres. In contrast in an average urban centre of the Sultanate period, the *iqta*-holder collected village revenue in kind, in a situation of prevailing confusion in the market of diverse exchange media, by and large retained a portion of the revenue inkind to meet local expenses and commuted the remaining amount of revenue in kind for transfer to the Sultan's treasury.

If the relatively short tenure of a Delhi Sultanate was found unequal to his need to develop an well-orchestrated monetary system, the shortness of tenure itself was one of the basic consequences of an absence, in general, of an impersonalised revenue and administrative set-up or of ready acquiescence on the part of a Sultanate in a personalised statecraft of the Central Asian variety.

It is true, as pointed out by both Irfan Habib and Tapan Raychaudhuri, that the Mughal emperor, Akbar, also permitted the payment of revenue in grains, but Akbar might have allowed such practice mainly in distant localities such as Bengal or Gujarat where at least during the early period following Mughal occupation, the Mughal revenue system was not yet in operation and the dominant Mughal currency of the time, the copper *dam*, could not replace the earlier currencies in circulation among rural areas, e.g. , Bengal *cowries* and silver *mahmudis* of Gujrat or the old exchange media in the areas of Watan jagirdars having different systems of local weights, measures and currencies.[11]

It was, therefore, the requirement of Mughal revenue system that spearheaded the rise of the Mughal monetary system–its flexibility and rigorous standardisation, its novel changes as well as shifts. Paradoxically enough, the Mughal monetary system with its scope for free minting and its centralised rigour in matters of currency standardisation made the Mughal currency secular enough not to discriminate between the interests of an oligarchic state and that of people in the larger society. It was this secular trait of the Mughal monetary system along with the impersonal laws of revenue assessment and collection under successive Mughal emperors that acted as accelerators of growth of money supply corresponding to the autonomous growth of commercial activities within the empire. If the desire of a Mughal despot to rule by his coercive power a vast empire, initiated the Mughal empire in India, such subjectivity was eventually lost in the spectrum of objective developments that were brought into being as the consequence of the materialisation of such subjective desire. If the imperial need for revenue was absolute, more absolute was the need for a system of impersonal norms of revenue assessment and collection. This objective requirement of revenue collection under impersonal norms paved the way for an well-orchestrated system of monetary integration between the need for imperial revenue appropriation and the need for a thorough monetisation of exchanges not only in the state administration but also in the non-state civilian sectors. Such monetary integration could not be materialised in a standard medieval situation which was why free minting of standard currency appeared as an absolute necessity.[12] It was this Mughal monetary system that activated the growth of independent commercial activity of a new civilian class of commercial entrepreneurs not necessarily enforced or patronised by the imperial power.

The objective presupposition of the autonomous growth of Mughal commercial activities was decided not merely by the civilian scope for augmenting its money supply provided by the imperial monetary system, its basic presupposition lay in the very imperial stratagem by which people at large (civilian zamindars,peasants, artisans, merchants or peddling traders) were to pay their cash dues to the imperial authority.

What was the specific way by which the imperial revenue strategem could be dovetailed into the monetary system in a region? There is not much data on this. However, one can refer to an exercise in this regard by Stephen P. Blake.[13]

By using the revenue circle data as available in the last part of Book 3 of *Ain*, Blake estimates the sums of money generated within a Mughal town of a given hierarchical order to be roughly equal to the sums of the money value of the taxed agricultural surplus yielded by the town's rural hinterland. He proceeds with two assumptions: first, agricultural surplus was the exclusive source of Mughal revenue; second, any Mughal town was the headquarters of, at least one revenue circle, and was therefore provided with an entitlement on a portion of imperial revenue. His investigation was concerned with three large provinces of the empire, Lahore, Agra and Delhi that accounted on the year of study, i.e., 1600, for about 54 per cent of the total cultivated area of the Mughal empire. He categorizes 717 towns and cities in these provinces into four different hierarchical levels, each of which compared to the lower one collected and retained a larger absolute sum of Mughal revenue in cash so as to meet respectively the financial claims of emperor and the versatile financial needs of an urban conglomerate. The status of a level is determined by the number of higher level functions, its member-towns discharged for the upkeep of the Mughal administration, police, revenue collection/assessment and religious activities.

The polar opposites among such levels were the three cities of Lahore, Delhi and Agra that discharged all types of high level functions and the small towns that were headquarters of only a single revenue circle. While Lahore, Delhi and Agra were at one pole, about 80 per cent of Mughal towns that functioned mainly as headquarters of a single revenue circle were at the other pole. Between these two poles there existed other towns, one with two higher level functions, and the other with single higher level function, although towns belonging to both levels had to discharge the functions of headquarters of more than one revenue circle. The second highest number of urban centres (about 18 per cent of the total) belonged to the third hierarchical level having one higher level function. The second hierarchal level vested with more than one higher level function, had very few towns.

Blake shows that cities and towns of the first and the second group could commandeer a relatively greater absolute amount of revenue for their own purpose not only because they serviced a larger hinterland but also because their higher level functions were more diversified. The huge size of resident populations among them, Blake seems to suggest, caused the rise of self-sustaining commercial and manufacturing bases. On the other hand, the urban centres belonging to the third (having only a single higher level function) and the fourth (having no higher level function) groups, although constituted the overwhelming majority of Mughal towns and cities, could individually as well as collectively claim a disproportionately lower amount of Mughal revenue for themselves as they serviced a much less number of revenue-circle hinterlands.[14] What Blake implicitly suggests is that the majority of Mughal towns could not develop enough as to allow them to have independent commercial or manufacturing bases. What is implicit in Blake's findings is that while the Mughal towns and cities lacked in general a base of manufactures and commercial activity of their own, about 2 p. c. of them could somehow develop independent production and commercial bases so as to meet a part of the requirements of their own urban populations.

While we have no general disagreement with Blake's inference, at least, in one respect we should qualify our endorsement of his position. There are no large Mughal towns known to have developed a manufacturing base during the Mughal period, although one should not deny the rise of royal *karkhanas* in Agra and Delhi, employing hired artisans to provide luxury goods meant exclusively for the city nobles. What, however, was a spectacular development was inter-village specialisation of production among villages around city centres or along the important trade-routes. Some villages were developed as 'artisan villages' or villages with horticultural specialisation. But such development had no direct causal factor in the rising wealth of city nobles. It was solely due to rising commercial activities of wealthy civilian merchants engaged in transactions between a town and immediate rural hinterland or in long-distance trade. However, the extent of such production specialisation among villages based on putting out system initiated by merchants, was of enclaved type and was circumscribed by the general character of Mughal villages producing mainly for use.

Our observation is strengthened by Blake's computation of the possible numbers of village-based intermediate and standard marketing centres in the Mughal Indian provinces of Lahore, Delhi and Agra. An intermediate marketing centre close to a town was characterised by its daily commercial transactions in which peasants actively participated either as seller or as buyer; and a Standard Marketing centre was the place for either a bi-weekly or a weekly commercial transaction. Both the varieties of marketing centres located in big villages virtually constituted on the one hand a bridge between intra-village demand and supply of goods and on the other hand–and more significantly–between the urban effective demand for grains and goods and the supply of the same from rural areas. From Blake's estimates, it is evident that in Lahore, Delhi and Agra, the total number of revenue-circle towns with the kind of commerce they had within them was much less than the number of intermediate marketing centres alone. The total of urban commercial centres was around one-fifth of the total number of village-based intermediate as well as standard marketing centres together.[15] From one of Blake's findings, it seems a distinct possibility that within the universe of the Mughal inland commerce, the towns as headquarters of revenue circles and as centres of unproductive social consumption could supply liquid money in exchange of consumables supplied by villages through the mediation of local or extra-local merchants and the variety of marketing centres grown within big villages must have supplied to the towns a portion of transacted goods of themselves.

The inter-village commerce over a wide area on exportable and importable goods was in this sense the main prop of the Mughal Indian commerce. Commercial transactions within an urban conglomerate or that between an urban centre and nearby villages cannot be construed, unlike what a number of historians of medieval India believe, as the driving force of Mughal commerce. The phenomenal development of artisan goods industries in specialised or non-specialised villages had its reinforcement not from the tastes, preference and demand pattern of urban groups such as the Mughal nobility, senior officials and big merchants, but from the integration of creative ingenuity of village artisan labour with its high aesthetic standard.[16] However, although the rural transactions in goods constituted the main dynamic of Mughal commerce, the commercial activity as wealth accumulating venture could shape only when the rural commerce could feed the urban commercial activities.

A series of independent commercial endeavours dealing with 'intra-local', 'inter-local', or 'inter-regional' and 'international' transactions on merchantable wares could grow up as the distinct features of the Mughal commerce by the second half of the 16th century. While mercantile activity was fostered by free minting, the rigorous application of revenue laws on villages reinforced the contradiction between the imperial state power of Mughals and a self-sustaining village community anxious to gain its economic power. The marked unevenness among regions in matters of proficiency and expertise in production of agricultural and artisan goods made certain regions more commercially ebullient and made a few regional village communities more economically powerful than others. To the extent commercial export and import activities within the village economy of Mughal India could gain autonomy due to the rise of rural cash nexus it was a radical departure from the basis of commerce during the period of Sultanates. If one wants a precise formulation of the differential pattern of development in Mughal commerce, it can be observed that the Sultanates enforced commerce on grains from above, while the more diversified productive as well as commercial activities during the Mughal period represented the net outcome of a commerce that grew up from below. By this we do not suggest that peasants and artisans became free agents during the Mughal period and that commercial activities faced no official interference in contrast to what existed earlier, nor do we hold that the Mughal state policies positively encouraged or patronised more independent commercial ventures.[17] Nevertheless, one has to point out two significant aspects of development in state policy in its relation to commercial activities of civilian community of merchants during the Mughal period. First, as a matter of state policy a Mughal emperor neither patronised nor interfered with the commercial activities of civilian traders. Secondly, if a Mughal official indulged in trading activities or taxed the artisans or commodity merchants too much or appropriated their wares or wealth by any foul means, that was clearly beyond the pale of strict imperial norms of functions and duties.

Notes

1. R.H. Hilton contends that among economic historians it is more or less agreed that the initial stock of wealth with which English merchants had started their commercial activities lay in rental accumulation from the feudal landed property; the commercial profit being reinvested in the accumulation of land assets. This is nothing unusual in a setting of hereditarity, transferability and hence, marketability of private property in land. What is further shown by him is the emergence of merchant capital from growing urban real property (houses, buildings, land, etc.) and the incidental ground rent. This finding is significant from the point of view of the nature of genesis of European merchant capital. See R.H. Hilton, 'Some Problems of Urban Property in the Middle Ages', C.H. Feinstein (Ed.), *Socialism, Capitalism and Economic Growth: Essays Presented to Maurice Dobb* (Cambridge, 1967), pp. 326-37.
2. This follows from the assumption we make about such societies where, although no private property in land or labour exists, the merchants of a village (x) may enter in trade on export-import items with merchants of another village (y). The service of merchants of x and y villages is to be remunerated by the members of those villages. The remuneration can be manifested in X villagers agreeing to pay a portion of x surplus to village merchants. The same holds good about y villagers' readiness to pay a portion of y surplus of village merchants.
3. Perry Anderson, *op. cit.* , Ch. 1, pp. 18-26.
4. I. Habib, 'Pre-British Landed Property', *op.cit.*, p. 295. 'Agrarian Economy', *op. cit.* , Ch. III, Sec.3, pp. 82-86. Besides such commerce imposed on villages, there certainly existed commercial activities among villages themselves at the lower level. No historical account on inter-village commerce of early medieval India is available.
5. M. Habib, *op. cit.*, for pagination see Chapter 2 section 2.1.

6. P. Anderson, *op. cit.*, p. 150.

7. Marx gives a memorable expression to this difference between towns of classical antiquity and those of Asian or European Middle Ages: 'Ancient Classical History is the history of cities, but cities based on landownership and agriculture; Asian history is a kind of undifferentiated unity of town and country (the large city, properly speaking, must be regarded merely as a princely camps superimosed on the real Economic Structure); the Middle Ages (Germanic period) starts with the countryside as the locus of history, whose further development then proceeds with the opposition of town and country; modern history is urbanization of the countryside, not as among the ancients, the ruralization of city.' Karl Marx, *Pre-Capitalist Economic Formations,* Ed., E. Hobsbawm (London, 1964), pp. 77-78.

8 Irfan Habib, 'The State and The Economy', *The Cambridge Economic History of India*, Vol. I, *op. cit.*, p. 174.

9 The present para and the subsequent ones, if not otherwise indicated, borrow mainly from the following sources:

(*a*) Irfan Habib, 'The Social Distribution of Landed Property in 'Pre-British India' (in short 'Pre-British Landed Property'), *op. cit.*

(*b*) I.Habib, 'Mughal India', *Cambridge Economic History of India*, Vol.I, *op.cit.*, Ch.VIII, Sec. I.

(*c*) Irfan Habib, 'Agrarian Relations and Land Revenue' *Cambridge Economic History of India*, Vol.I, *op. cit.*

(*d*) Tapan Raychaudhuri, 'The Mughal Empire', *Cambridge Economic History of India*, Vol.I, *op. cit.*, Ch. VII, Sec.1.

(*e*) T.Raychaudhuri 'Inland Trade', *Cambridge Economic History of India*, Vol. I, *op.cit.*, Ch. XI.

10. Although the Mughal monetary system was trimetallic in form, with gold *Muhrs*, silver *rupee* and copper *dams*, in practice the innumerable imperial transactions within the administration or between the former and the public were conducted mainly in copper *dams* or silver *rupees*. Again between the copper *dam* and silver *rupee*, during the greater part of Akbar's reign copper *dam* was the main currency, but from the period of Jahangir, silver *rupee* had found its most pervasive use among the state, officials and civilians alike. What is most notable for our purpose is that 'these coins [gold muhrs, silver rupees and copper dams] were uttered under a system of free coinage which meant that all those [that, of course, included the civilian merchants] who paid the prescribed mint charges and seigniorage could have their bullions coined'.

Cf. Irfan Habib 'A System of Trimetallism in the Age of the Price Revolution' in J.F. Richards (ed.), *The Imperial Monetary System of Mughal India* (Delhi 1987), pp. 137-70.

11. Cf. Irfan Habib, 'Pre British Landed Property', *op. cit.* 'A System of Trimetallism', *ibid.* , p. 143.

12. Om Prakash observes this: 'The absence of the equivalent of modern

monetary management [as found in a capitalist country] also implied that the accretions to the supply of standardized money . . . over any period of time was determined not by the government but by the public itself within, . . .' Om Prakash, 'Foreign Merchants and Indian Mints' in J.F. Richards (ed.), *The Imperial Monetary System of Mughal India*', *op. cit.* p. 173.

13. Stephen P. Blake, 'Structure of Monetary Exchange in North India, in J.F. Richards (ed) *ibid.*., pp. 100-36.

14. *Ibid.*, Table 13, p. 122.

15. See Tables 10,11 and 12. *ibid.*, pp. 120-21.

16. This is evident even today when one finds a craze among urban wealthy people to purchase beautiful but useful cottage industry products (not merely for decorative purpose) designed and produced by illiterate artisans of distant rural areas with no urban sophistication.

17. In fact, by the end of the 17th century Mughal peasants and artisans came under the more widespread usurious and credit nexus of moneylenders, usurers and merchants. Many Mughal state officials not only resorted to individual extortion of mercantile wealth but also interfered occasionally with the activities of commodity merchants. As for illustrations one can cite Shaista Khan's imposition of 'royal monopoly over salt, saltpetre, and beewax and even fodder' or Asaf Khan's investment of Rs.10,000 in the procurement of merchandise and ordering Ahmedabad weavers and dyers not to work for anyone else till the procurement was over, or Shaista Khan's and Prince Azimushshan's forcing merchants "to buy their wares at prices" they themselves dictated. Even if we assume that such reports do not represent the general picture, nonetheless, one must account for even such not-so-frequent conflict between merchants on the one hand and ambitious members of Mughal bureaucracy on the other. One has to concede that there existed great economic freedom for Mughal direct producers or commercial entrepreneurs compared to what they were during the earlier period but on the other hand the theory of Mughal non-interference in mercantile pursuits can hardly reflect the dialectics of the actual situation. In fact, interference with mercantile activities or plunder of merchants appeared as an occasional phenomenon only during the latter period when elasticity of revenue collection became low along with gradual loosening of the grip of imperial administration over provincial bureaucracy and when the commodity trade could easily lead to acquisition of immense treasure.

4.2: Mughal Commerce Since late 16th Century

The Mughal empire witnessed a growing precariousness in revenue collection and in the management of its own revenue administration. By the late 16th and early 17th centuries, the elasticity of direct surplus appropriation in various forms became lower and lower due to factors beyond the control of the imperial administration (e.g. , growing village resistance against additional levy, tolls, cesses, etc., resistance of lower rank officials against the claim of their superiors within the set-up of Mughal revenue administration and above all the inelastic social production base within a village). At the same time, the revenue requirement of the administration went up in absolute terms. A fattened bureaucracy and militia and an increasing number of armed retainers employed by individual nobles in the wake of frequent succession wars were factors that enhanced imperial revenue requirement as well as all categories of financial claims on a village. But such claims could hardly be materialised due to stagnation in social production base. In a sense a relative inelasticity in the growth of actual surplus appropriation by direct coercive measures on the one hand, and the highly elastic growth of claims on villages on the other, tended to create a potentially conflicting situation within the Mughal polity. While the former accentuated inequality among the members of military and civilian bureaucracy, the latter tended to foster financial crisis among all categories of direct surplus appropriators at the supra-village level.

This phenomenon of growing financial crisis was felt more at the various levels of supra-village power structure. It ofen provoked a provincial governor of the commercially rich provinces like Bengal, Agra or Gujarat, or a town governor of busy entrepot centres like Honghly or Surat, to indulge in the plunder of merchants' wares. The interference of Mughal officials with mercantile accumulation of wealth reflected, more than anything else, the relative inadequacy of the mode of direct surplus appropriation (by coercive means) in tiding over a financial crisis.

The greater viability and efficiency of surplus appropriation by the mercantile mode of unequal exchange became conspicuous even to the Mughal officials. This explains why in Bengal quite a few Mughal governors forced the successful commodity merchants to take loans from the former so that the latter could be forced to pay a portion of their profit to governors as interest on loans, or force artisans in local guilds to sell their goods at low prices, to be subsequently sold at a high profit to merchants, or why in Golconda the Mughal Governor, Mir Jumla indulged in private trade, or why a number of Bengal fauzdars were themselves engaged in mercantile occupations so as to accumulate personal wealth despite the official stipulation that prohibited trade by Mughal officials.

The imperial monetary integration and the enforcement of the Mughal laws of revenue assessment and collection, were instrumental in the proliferation of export-import trade among the Mughal villages. The growing income inequality among members of the bureaucracy as well as that between towns and villages, strengthened the commercial viability of surplus appropriation by unequal exchange and weakened the viability of coercion as a method of surplus appropriation.

If the relations of appropriation and acquiescence between the state with all categories of supra-village power authorities began to engender conflict and hostility among them, the mercantile method of surplus appropriation through the mechanism of unequal exchange drove urban merchants to acquire more money wealth than their rural counterparts.

With its canopy of power and the cult of *magnificentia*, a Mughal town could emerge as a dominant buyers' market dependent on urban merchants for both essential and luxury consumer items, and a Mughal Indian village, relegated to the phalanx of imperial obscurities burdened with only obligatory surplus payments emerged as a veritable sellers' market for the entire agricultural produce and manufactures a town needed. The Mughal Indian commerce, though had its main propeller in inter-village commerce, the commerce between a town and rural area could beget more urban commercial wealth than could commerce among mercantile enterprises in the rural areas. This was due to two reasons: the first was a pervasive absence of a good bulk of non-productive but financially well-off consumers of mercantile wares in the rural areas; the second was a heavy concentration of non-productive well-off people in and around the Mughal towns that characteristically suffered from a chronic disability in matters of producing not only the items for essential consumption to be imported from the rural areas but also those luxurious consumption goods needed by their own resident populations.

Therefore, two cardinal features of the Mughal market acted as planks for the autonomy of Mughal Indian commerce as a whole. They were: (*a*) the emergence of towns as a dominant buyers' market; and (*b*) the emergence of villages as mainly a sellers market for agricultural produce and diversified manufactures. Together they constituted the basic *sine qua non* of late 16th and 17th century development of Mughal inland commerce. In a similar sense the growing overseas demand for Indian mercantile wares, particularly from the mid-16th century onward, might have supplanted the growth of inland commerce of Mughal India, but it certainly was not a decisive factor. During the Mughal period relative political stability and peace promoted overland commodity trade. Kabul and Kandahar were connected in the trade network to Lahore, Multan, Pali, Agra, Delhi, Patna, Kasimbazar and Banaras, etc. on the northern and eastern trade routes, and Ahmedabad, Burhanpur and Cambay on the western overland trade route. Most of the above trading centres at the same time were centres of inter-Asiatic entrepot trade. As such these centres were involved in considerable exchange of important wares between Persia, Egypt and the Gulf countries and those coming from the west of the Indian peninsula. If Indian entrepots gained importance in the commercial map of contemporary Asia it was mainly due to its geophysical location. While Indian coastal and land routes gave her the advantage to reap the benefit of augmenting its supply of silver within the country, it is doubtful how far this could stimulate inland production. If the fabulous money wealth of Indian merchants could transmit an expansive effect on Mughal production base, in general, and the growth of mercantile production, in particular, the general configuration of Mughal industry and agriculture as epitomes of stagnation and low productivity would be a dispensable myth.

At this stage we need to point out that during the 17th century, the prosperity of inland urban and sea merchants was a sharp contrast to the growing fiscal crisis of the imperial Mughal establishments. This broadly explains why the later Mughal Imperial powers ignored the harassment of small commodity merchants by the imperial officials or preferred not to interfere with the increasing poll taxes and other cesses on small or middle category merchants.While the late 17th century Mughal administration silently witnessed the harassment and plunder of money wealth and wares of intra-local and inter-local merchants of modest means, a category of very rich merchants ('comparable to Europe's merchant princes in wealth and power') could develop a workable rapport with the local or provincial princes of the Mughal empire. This relation between the urban rich merchants and the power-wielding Mughal officials underscored a new phase of development in the late 16th and 17th century commerce.

The contention of many historians that the Mughal officials were always hostile to any kind of mercantile activities, seems to be based more on the assumption that Mughal officials were lustful and indiscriminate devourers of mercantile wealth than on a careful scrutiny of facts. It is acknowledged that an average Mughal official with delegated imperial power was anxious to increase his personal wealth. But it must also be acknowledged that there was cooperation between Mughal high officials and big urban commodity merchants. In fact, such cooperation subsumed various forms of mutual dependence and had its two stages of evolution during the entire Mughal period. In the first stage two aspects should be noted: one was the Mughal chief's need for revenue from port commerce, and urban nobility's need for essential as well as luxury goods. On the other hand, during the first stage indigenous town merchants, big or small, had the problem of procuring finances for trade. Sometimes local princes supplied credit to chosen urban merchants at high rates of interest or on a promise to supply rare luxury goods, either indigenously produced or imported. This was before the 17th century commercial prosperity of Indian urban commerce. At that stage 'the long distance trade, in its Asian context, was an object of interest to indigenous [local] rulers and governments... for levies and tolls' to be procured from merchants.[1]

At the second stage, i.e., at the stage when inland urban commerce gained a substantial financial autonomy and access to innumerable centres of entrepot trade, the creditor-debtor relation between big urban merchants and the Mughal princes was, in general, reversed. In this situation, the growing fiscal crisis engulfing the entire polity was in sharp contrast to the high degree of profitability of an urban commercial pursuit, and in the accumulation of money wealth, particularly by the urban substantial merchants. The concentration of wealth among a few at the top of the administrative hierarchy could take place through growing inequalities of distributions of appropriated surplus. But this income inequality made a substantial section of Mughal officials (provincial governors or dewans, local fauzdars, petty jagirdars, mansabdars, etc.) dependent on credit from merchant magnates as means of making two ends meet. In general, affluent urban merchants of the time supplied credit to them. The big merchants in return earned not only interest but also the privilege of toll-free procurement of merchandise from the rural areas under a debtor-official.

Thus on the one hand, the relation between big merchants and Mughal officials was characterised by mutual dependence, the relation between ordinary rural or semi-urban merchants of modest means and the petty officials of the empire, on the other, became more and more hostile particularly when the latter were in financial difficulties. Many European travellers of early half of the 17th century narrate accounts of how small commodity merchants were fleeced by petty Mughal officials. But such accounts are biased as they are unable to explain how, in spite of such harassment and plunder, almost uninterrupted growth of inland commerce took place in India during the 17th century. The growth of inland commerce had to depend on that section of the inter-local commodity traders who were relatively bigger commodity merchants operating from cities or big towns. Moreover, the supply of essential and luxury items of consumption for town could be augmented only by those substantial merchants. Again under the initiative of big merchants diversification of production of inferior and superior varieties of artisan goods, jewellery, and various luxury wares took place which found ready customers among the urban Mughal nobility, high officials and even among petty officials (usually 'earning more than their regular salaries and wages').

While the fiscal crisis of the 17th century Mughal administration[2] forced it to borrow from substantial merchants dealing with supply of emergency provisions and liquid credit, the Indian merchant community as a whole underwent a degree of urban-rural wealth differentiation within its rank.

However, the growth of silver money-wealth-itself a product of a higher mercantile command over silver from overseas-and urban transactions among big urban merchants, from the late 16th century onwards, could embrace not only the transactions between urban and rural India, but also the more innumerable and sizable commercial transactions among the villages themselves. This explains why the copper *dam* as the ruling medium of exchange came to be replaced by silver *rupee* and its smaller denominations. The rise of mercantile money wealth could not however, cause a revolutionary change in the extant structure of social production or a change in the elasticity of supply of mercantile wares. As a consequence, there was increase in mercantile money wealth and corresponding scarcity of merchantable goods.[3] The rise of commercial money wealth outstripping the supply of goods must have been the reason for mid-17th century price rise.[4] The terms of trade between transaction demand for goods either from money wealth of foreign buyers or from money income of town-living people (largely derived from directly appropriated surplus) and the transacted supply of wares by big urban merchants, who could effectively control the supply of goods in towns and trade centres, must have turned in favour of the latter. Again among the merchants themselves those who could command more money power, (i.e. , the richer merchants) could control bigger portion of available wares. As a consequence, the merchants of moderate means operating in small towns and in the rural areas were forced to enter into competition for village wares with the bigger ones operating from important trade centres.

While financial crisis at the various local levels of Mughal bureaucracy tended to make small merchants the easy targets of plunder by officials, it paradoxically offered scopes to the urban living richer merchants for operating locally through agents and bankers. A substantially rich merchant, in an urban centre could, on the one hand, earn dividend from his credit business among members of local urban bureaucracy and procure, on the other hand, more merchandise from villages so as to feed his growing commercial network. The consequence of such differentiation among individual scales of merchandise procurement and business turnover within the Indian mercantile community, as noted by N. Streensgaard and others, was the gradual disappearance from urban areas of the village peddling traders and small merchants in the second half of the 17th century.[5] The other factor that accounts for a higher increase in wealth of urban big merchants, as Irfan Habib points out is the growing urban mercantile practice of procuring merchandise for urban or foreign consumption through, what he calls, 'commodity production' or production of artisan goods in newly developing artisan villages through `the putting out system'.[6] Habib suggests that urban mercantile wealth had a spectacular rise owing to urban big merchants' 'more intensive exploitation' of artisan labour employed under the putting out systems. But this suggestion is valid only when one could show that there was a highly elastic supply of unemployed artisan labour in Mughal India, in a setting of relatively inelastic supply of merchant capital that could be available for investment in 'putting out system' of organising artisan production.[7]

Even if one concedes that there was indeed a putting out system of artisan production, particularly in rural artisan villages located near the prosperous trade centres of Gujarat and Bengal it is difficult to accept the theory of 'intensive exploitation' of artisan labour by merchant employers or merchant creditors.[8] A more viable proposition is that since urban merchants minted more money wealth than their rural counterparts by investing in urban commerce and credit business, it was in their commercial interest than in the interest of artisan labourers themselves that caused the rise of the putting out system and/or artisan villages.[9]

The financial crisis of a vast segment of the urban nobles and aristocrats during the later Mughal period arose as much from its parasitic dependence on highly differentiated shares of total imperial income that could be extracted from a relatively inelastic social production base as from its consumption expenditure. This crisis virtually paved the way for the growing leakage of a considerable portion of imperial surplus to merchants in general, and to urban wealthy merchants, in particular.

In a way the alienation of a Mughal state power from growing rural-urban or overseas commercial activities helped Mughal merchants. The wealthy merchants dealing with both money-changing as well as commodity or credit businesses, as well as such export merchants as Virji Vora of early 17th century Surat; Abdul Gaffar and Ahmed Chellabi of the late 17th century Surat; Mir Jumla of Golconda Sultanate and Kasi Viranna of the Coromandel region of mid-17th century, faced no interference from either local governors or from foreign merchants. Had there been no insulation of mercantile activities in India from Mughal machinery of administration, or had there been a close identification of commercial interest with the dominant political interest of the local or imperial state power (as it was the case in the late medieval Europe) prosperity of inland commerce would not have taken place in Mughal India. The Indian situation contrasts with that of medieval Europe where the so-called rise of commercial capitalism had its plank more on the external trade of a nation rather on the richness of inland commerce. Inland commerce in a European nation could not make headway until its town economy could destabilise feudal agriculture. The rise of commercial prosperity in West Europe was dependent on how much one nation could sell another, inland commerce, by and large, being *nonsequiter* in the process.

Indian commercial prosperity during the Mughal period of the 17th century, in contrast had its initial spurt not from what it could export but from what villages of one region could export to villages and towns of other regions. Therefore, in the case of Mughal India, it was the inland commerce in her rural and urban areas that played the pivotal role in her commercial ebullience. Indian towns being, by and large, centres of consumption (not of social production), it was the size of village goods and the amount of urban demand that could be satisfied by the countryside that determined affluence of urban mercantile interests in Mughal India.

We have so far examined how in Mughal India, within a framework of mutual inter-dependence between the political power of the imperial establishment and the money power of wealthy merchants, a process of wealth accumulation of the latter and a corresponding decline in the economic power of the former was promoted. One can witness a roughly similar process also in Western Europe. By the middle of the 17th century, the sovereigns of the nations of West Europe came to identify their own interests with that of a monopolistic mercantile house. But in India, we do not witness similar identity of interests between those of the sovereign and the merchants which would help to promote export trade or forge an alliance against an external mercantile power. Instead, what is found is that the prosperous Mughal merchants who were so influential in the later Mughal period had to retreat from mercantile world of India with the advent of European commercial powers. Why this happened is a question we shall answer in the following sections.

Notes

1. K.N. Chaudhury, 'European Trade with India', *Cambridge Economic History of India, op.cit.*, Ch. XIII, Sec. 1, pp.184-85. Chaudhury, however, calls it 'cost of state protection'. But there are others who think that it was the growing greed of Mughal state officials that made them fleece the wealthy merchants so much that 'transactions among merchants themselves used to take place under cover of darkness'. Cf. Fray Sebastian Manrique, *Travels of Fray Sebastian Manrique (1928-41)*, Trans. C.E. Luard and H. Hosten, 2 vols. (London 1927). John Fryer, *A New Account of East India being Nine Years' Travels.* Ed. W.Crooke, 3 vols. (London, 1909, 1912 and 1915).

2. We do not suggest that the growth of directly appropriated surplus came to an end. In fact, there are instances of various imposts and cesses during the period of Shahjahan and Aurangzeb which were over above land revenue.

But the frequency of peasant resistances of imperial taxation increased during the period. The imperial efforts to quell the disturbances reinforced the financial crisis of the empire.

3. This was perhaps the period when wealthy urban merchants were instrumental either in establishing or patronising a self-propelled growth of artisan villages around the busy centres of entrepot trade and the Mughal emperors anxious to have luxury wares of choice established *karkhanas* in a number of Mughal towns.

4. We, therefore, do not accept Irfan Habib's assumption that one of the important factors that accounted for 17th century price rise was simply a rising import of silver by Mughal India from abroad. It is necessary for any one to locate the reason for such price rise in the domestic sphere of the Mughal economy. A mere rise in the amount of silver currency in circulation or the relative depreciation of value of silver relative to the values of the metal, say copper or gold, cannot be deemed as the causal factor of inflation in the goods market unless one establishes
(*a*) that as a consequence of the increased import of silver currency (with its smaller denominations), the aggregate money supply in circulation during the 17th century went up more than what was warranted by the rise in output or the velocity of silver money in transactions on output during that period; or (*b*) that the terms of exchange between a village, the main centre of social production and an urban conglomerate, that could procure consumables by paying liquid silver cash could turn in favour of the former or merchant. Indeed, mere evidences on increased transactions in silver *rupee* as medium of exchange and on relative absence of transaction in copper *dam* in a situation of increased silver supply cannot be construed as decisive indicators that use of silver currency was the cause of price rise. Cf. Irfan Habib, 'A System of Trimetallism', *op. cit.* We have more to say on the cause of 17th century price rise.

5. How such economic differentiation could adjust with traditional bondage within a mercantile community? Since a community network among merchants (that was largely absent among European merchants of the 17th century) underscored their mutual interdependence in matters of supplying credit and saleable wares, it may be pointed out that such community network militated against economic differentiation among members. But if we hold that the sole dynamic of such differentiation was the amount of business in money and wares a community member could command, the amount of interest and profit earned by different members were bound to be unequal. The inequality in business incomes among members of a particular mercantile community does not necessarily destroy community bondage among themselves. A small merchant could act as an agent or a broker of a wealthy merchant of the same community, or a big merchant struck by misfortune could act as a surrogate of a successful merchant who through perseverence and skill could rise to his present position from that of a small merchant. Community interdepend-

ence among members of a mercantile community could not act as a barrier to economic differentiation among themselves.

6. Cf. Irfan Habib, ' Potentialities of Capitalistic Development', *op. cit.*

7. Irfan Habib appears to have made a distinction between the village artisans who under the jajmani system only produced for use (i.e., for local consumption) and the artisans producing for market under the putting out system. But he is not explicit about the social form of existence of the second category of artisans in Mughal India. Did the artisans producing for market constitute an integral part of a village community? Or did they have their own villages around the urban centres or centres of entrepot trade? He gives no answer, nor does he suggest any inference. From the historical accounts of various authors it appears that by the end of the 17th century, there were cotton weavers' or silk weavers' villages around Surat and Ahmedabad, and around Patna, Hooghly and Satgaon. If this is so, the question arises, how such artisan villages were governed or who dominated the artisan community? Did the artisans contract credit individually or collectively through a master craftsman or an artisan guild? Or were the artisans merely debt-serfs of merchant creditors? Unless one knows what was the condition of labour in artisan villages, it is difficult to contend that artisan labourers were exploited by powerful merchants or that they produced of their own for an unknown market. In ancient Greece, slaves produced artisan goods for markets under the stewardship of slave owners, but that was not 'commodity production'.

8. Indeed any stage of commodity production presupposes that capital as property in its material form, appropriates so much the conditions of labour that labourers having no other means of livelihood, are forced to sell their labour to capital at a value less than the value of their labour. In other words, in Habib's reckoning, the merchant capital in Mughal India could appropriate so much the conditions of artisan labour that unemployed labourers were large enough to be forced to sell their labour power to merchant capital (for their livelihood), so as to part with a surplus that eventually could be transformed into further accumulation of merchant capital. Thus it has been suggested by Habib that in Mughal India the merchant capital was the initiator of commodity production or the production for market:

The system of production under the 'putting out system' does not necessarily indicate complete usurption of condition of labour by those who invest capital in supplying raw materials, nor does it necessarily indicate an unequal exchange between owners of labour power and the owners of capital that is invested in supplying raw materials to artisans. The basic objective of capital investment in the 'putting out system' in the context of the absence of private property cannot be meant to transform the surplus labour hours of the artisans into profit, but to procure merchandise so as to make profit in the market at the expense of consumers. Indeed an investor in the 'putting out system' could reap mercantile profit even after paying the *customary* wage (i.e., the wage received by artisans without entering into the 'putting out system') to employed artisans and selling their wares at high price to urban or overseas purchasers.

4.3: Nature of Unity and Differentiation Among Mughal Merchants

The question raised at the end of the preceding section can be reformulated as follows: (*a*) given the nature of commercial prosperity during the 17th century what was its impact on the intra-communal business propensities within the broad community of Mughal Indian merchants; and (*b*) what explains the general trend towards mutual cooperation between the wealthy merchants of India and any group of incoming European shore merchants?

Answering the first question is more crucial as it has to unfold on the one hand the nature of prosperity itself of Indian commerce, and on the other, the consequence of such prosperity on intra-communal *mores* of interdependence among members of a mercantile community. The adequate answer to first question, can explain why a tendency towards commercial cooperation between Indian big merchants and their European counterparts did indeed germinate.

Before we investigate the nature of prosperity as well as differentiation among various groups of Indian merchants of the 17th century, the macro-postulates of the relationship we have so far outlined between three basic functional groups of people within the Mughal Indian polity, must be captured in a precise form. The groups are : (*a*) those that derive income from direct appropriation of social surplus (that include even the servants of nobles, courtjesters and sychophants, local political bandits and such others who had to depend either on the imperial establishment or on non-imperial local establishment of coercion and its members so as to appropriate a subsistence income); (*b*) the group of productive labourers producing a surplus in its physical from (that includes villagers who rendered ancillary social or labour services to labour activity of direct producers); and (*c*) the group of merchants or traders (that includes all sundry categories to whom monetised exchange operations constituted the principal source of income). We have seen that the first group produced nothing but earned money income and spent it mainly on consumption, the second group was somehow able to retain their inflexible consumption fund (inflexibility arising from their unassailable right to have subsistence earning against their materialised labour activity – private as well as communal) out of the social production it brought into being, and the third group earned a portion of social surplus only through monetised exchange operations, not at all by direct coercion on villagers or urban dwellers.

Each of these groups contained people of dissimilar income status and intra-group occupations. For instance, the first group consists of domestic servants, powerful ministers and army chiefs etc.; the only unifying bond among them was their non-productive dependence on money income flowing from coercively appropriated surplus within the empire. Similarly, the second group includes not only the heterogenous categories of labourers but also those within a village community who, though not productive in their vocation were nonetheless associated with the supervision of village production process or its communal reproduction and earned their income only by this virtue. The third group comprised money-lenders, peddling traders, small merchants as well as big merchants who could invest in money-dealing as well as commodity-dealing businesses; the uniform characteristic of the group was earning their profit or interest-income only through unequal exchanges. Since our immediate purpose here is to show the dialectics of income-distributional relationship among the three distinctly different functional groups within the Mughal Indian polity, we abstract from intra-group local peculiarities.

For analytical convenience we make the following assumptions:

(1) The polity starts with a given money stock which is equally distributed between the first and the third groups. The money stock is assumed to be nothing but past surplus. To start with, none of these two groups hold any stock of real goods; they hold only money – the socially acknowledged command over goods that are brought into being only by the second group.

(2) The first group holds a money stock, but such money stock is not meant for investment, it is exclusively meant for consumption expenditures. The money stock lying with the third group is assumed to be only for investment expenditure. It follows that only the third group makes investible use of money.

(3) The second group has its *principal* use of money for making revenue or tribute payment to local non-imperial power establishment, if any, or to the imperial establishment of political power. Since the major bulk of consumables of the second group comes from its own produce, notwithstanding the intra-group practice of export and import activities among villages, it follows that the group *as a whole* has self-sufficiency in matters of its diverse needs. In other words, the second group is assumed to have no need for imports from either non-Mughal areas or overseas. In the eventuality of need for such imports from an alien country, the value of import is matched by its value of exportables.[1]

(4) The major bulk of consumables required by the first group is assumed to be produced by the second group and is further assumed to be supplied by the third group. It follows that the members of the first group lack a direct access to consumables in kind produced as well as possessed initially by the second group alone unless the third group negotiates the flow of consumables from the second to the first group.

(5) All goods produced and transacted against money in the Mughal economy are assumed to be the final consumer goods.

Now if P is the total production of the second group, C its inflexible consumption requirement, R its emergency provisions[2] and T as its portion of physical surplus that is fructified into cash so as to enable it to make payment of revenue or tribute to the first group (particularly to its leading members) and all are in terms of the current year's output, then we can write as follows in an one-commodity-framework.

$P = C + R + T$ (all in real terms)

or $P - C = R + T = S$, S being amount of net physical surplus produced by the second group in the current year.

Let us suppose that the second group sells at price p the T portion of S to the third group in order to secure cash. The third group makes initial investment of entire money stock lying with it for the purchase of T. Assuming that the total units of T sold by the second group is X and V is the total money value of the cash so obtained by it or alternatively total amount of money as possessed and subsequently invested by the third group, then

V = p. X = m, m being the initial money stock lying with the third group of our assumption (1)

In terms of what we assume above, V is transferred to the first group by the second group as its total of revenue and tribute obligations. V is therefore the money income of the first group that is distributed among its members as their wherewithal. But by the process V is transferred by the second group for its revenue payment purpose, its goods equivalent, i.e., X units of T (at price p) is transferred to the possession of the third group which purchases them is only merchandise wares. The X units of T (i.e.) the portion of physical surplus now form merchandise wares of the third group which must sell the same to the members of the first group necessarily at a price higher than its procurement price p. Let this higher price be designated as p'. For obvious reasons, the total money value to be obtained as proceeds out of the sale of full amount of X units of T by the third group to the first group must necessarily be higher than V or m. Let us call this increased money value of the third group's sale proceeds to be m'. Thus,

m' = p'.X, where m' is greater than the m, since p' is higher than p, X remaining the same.

m' – m = profit of the third group.

For obvious reasons the first group cannot purchase the full amount of X units even by spending its entire amount of current year's revenue income V. To do this it has to release m' - m amount of extra money from its past stock (assumption (1)). On the other hand, the third group which has earlier invested money stock m for procuring X units of T, after completing its sale transactions on X with the first group, not only gets back its invested amount m but also a money profit by the excess of m' over m. This indicates that the third group makes an addition to its present stock of money wealth by causing a proportionate decrease in the past stock of money wealth held by the first group. Such transfer of money wealth takes place in terms of our model only when the entire X units of merchandise are purchased by the first group from the third group. In this way the successive period's purchasing of entire merchantable goods by the first group from the third group leads to a gradual depletion of the accumulated money wealth of the former and a corresponding addition to the money wealth of the latter.

We can conceive an alternative situation if we assume that the third group enjoys an additional scope of selling its merchandise to the external world or that the first group restricts its consumption to what its current revenue income V permits (i.e., the first group is not willing to spend beyond its current income of V to finance its current year's consumption, whatever that may be), then it is obvious that at price p', the group cannot purchase the full amount of X, and the third group correspondingly earns profit in real terms, i.e., appropriates a part of X units that cannot be purchased by the first group owing to the fact that p'.X is higher than V. If the profit in real terms out of sale transactions of the third with the first group is π and price p' is higher than p by y times, then with its revenue income V, the first group can purchase only X/y amount of X from the third at price p'

$$\text{Then } \pi = \frac{X(Y-1)}{Y} \text{ in real terms.}$$

Thus out of the surplus transferred by the second group in the form of revenue payment to the first group, the third group can appropriate a portion of physical surplus as profit in real terms. This is what indicates surplus appropriation in real terms by the third group by unequal exchange between itself and the first group. The third group can sell its unsold portion of X which is nothing but appropriated physical surplus, to foreign merchants and secure for itself precious bullions.

However in a closed economy we find that the transactions between the first group and the third group through market lead either to a decline in the past money stock of the former or to a net leakage of actual surplus appropriated by the first group through revenue/tribute collection, to the third group.

Accordingly, the distribution in real terms of P among three groups assumes the following form :

$$P = C + R + T(1 - \pi) + \pi T$$

The first group in the second situation (i.e., where it does not spend more than what current revenue/tributary income V permits) can virtually appropriate social production worth only T(1 - π). The second group retains C+R for its subsistence as well as emergency provision and the third group appropriates πT amount of surplus in real terms.

In case the rate of growth of P is lower than the rate of growth of T, in that situation T can increase only at the expense of C + R. Since C is inflexible by our hypothesis (as developed in the Chapter III), T can effectively rise at its utmost by appropriating only R. Thus if $\delta T/\delta P$ tends to be higher than unity, that must be subject to the condition

$$\frac{\delta T}{\delta P} < \frac{\delta R}{\delta P}$$

But we have seen that any rise in T augments a corresponding increase in πT so that $\delta T/\delta P$ determines $\delta\pi T/\delta T$. If however $\delta\pi T/\delta T$ is higher than unity, i.e. higher than $\delta T/\delta P$ and at the same time $\delta R/\delta P$ is less than unity, i.e., less than $\delta T/\delta P$, the contradiction between the material interests of first and the second group, or those between the third and the first group, becomes irresistible. The contradiction between the first and the third group can, however, be temporarily shelved if the first group resorts to consumption credit in real or money terms from the third group. This is what exactly happened during the late 17th century Mughal India, but there is no scope for resolution of contradiction between the first and the second group owing to the historical fact that δP was always less than δT or even δR. This means that the rate of growth of social production (δP) was always less than the rate of growth of surplus payable as revenue and tribute (δT).

The first group is caught between the two contradictory pulls of the Mughal Indian polity, namely, low elasticity of its surplus acquisition by direct coercion and high elasticity of its surplus leakage to the third group. So it had to enter into the credit market controlled by the latter so as to make two ends meet. The third group, on its part, accumulated more money wealth necessarily at the expense of the first group and again its rate of accumulation of money wealth was necessarily higher than what was warranted by the growth rate of merchandise within the polity. This was because the third group with immense money wealth in its possession lacked effective control over social production base that, by our hypothesis,is controlled exclusively by the second group.

Since the model in its most simple and crude form as outlined above, is only of an indicative nature meant to capture the dialectics of the relationship only among the three groups, it does not portray the consequences of the above macro-trends on the decomposed strata within each individual group and is, therefore, unable to bring into focus the intra-group mechanisms. All the contradictions among the three groups arise precisely from the absence of private individual property in land.

In Chapter III we have found how the crisis brewing from an elastic growth of surplus requirements forced the imperial authority to be more prone to armed intervention against rebellious chieftains or officials as well as the communal village uprisings. The income inequality between higher and lower echelons of imperial hierarchy through the parcellisation of jagirdari rights and the proliferation of command structures in a military establishment forced it to endorse illegal claims of powerful mansabholding big jagirdars over subordinate village communities. The cumulative effect was a yawning gap between political stability and its requirement of surplus. We have seen how this gap began to produce the phenomena of financial crisis at all levels within the administrative polity of Mughals, particularly after the mid-17th century.

Despite the fact that the system of Mughal revenue bred more income inequality, even within a village community itself, particularly between large landholders and small peasants, such income inequality could not grow *ad infinitum.* This was because, as pointed out earlier, the large landholder could not materialise his unequal economic status, into infringement of subsistence income of village labouring class. Thus even though in certain regions the large landholders capitulated against small holders at the instance of powerful Mughal officials the former could not sustain it and in most cases peasants' communal uprisings had their support from village big landholders. As a whole, the self-sustaining village community of Mughal India acted as an effective deterrent to the growth of imperial acquisition of surplus from villages. Therefore, village management of social production was autonomous and was an exogenous factor of the imperial economic crisis.

Lastly, as is evident from the above model, irrespective of whether additional surplus extraction of the first group from the second group was feasible or not, the relation between the former and the third group was such that any unavoidable transaction between them necessarily involved a net transfer of surplus (either in real or money terms) from the first group to the third one. The size of social production controlled by the second group (with its inflexible subsistence consumption) did not go up *paripassu* with the growth of surplus requirement of the first group. Therefore the money accumulation by the third group at the expense of the first group invariably faced its fetter in a widenning gap between accumulation of money wealth and its intrinsic worth in real terms. In other words the rate of growth of liquid money wealth invariably engendered an inherent tendency towards outstripping the rate of growth of physical goods or merchandise. This was bound to manifest as price rise for merchandise wares.

We are certain that the merchant capital in Mughal India developed an incipient potential of investment crisis as a consequence of the widening gap between transaction demand for goods and its supply. The merchant capital could not command an effective resolution of this crisis. What it did under the circumstance, was to generate a pronounced proclivity towards investment in credit and banking business, and in speculative transactions. In Mughal India, commodity commerce slowly but steadily drifted into a circuit where it came to be completely subordinated to an expanding money dealing commerce and the latter brought within its credit network a huge mass of sundry categories of direct surplus appropriators. This drift was primarily caused by the crisis of investment outlets in a situation where money wealth of an individual could not be fructified into private property.

In Western Europe, a similar type of crisis resulting from the gap between the growth of mercantile money wealth and the narrow base of commodity production could be temporarily resolved by the emergence of three factors. Firstly, the big merchants ate up the smaller ones by fraudulent means so as to impose their monopoly over commodity movement and introduce restrictive practices on commodity production within a national economy. Secondly, the small independent merchants routed by domestic big merchants from the sphere of domestic commerce in urban centres sought to survive as speculators in real estates as in England or as money-lenders/usurors among small owners of land parcels, as in France or as owners of small manufactories, as in Holland etc. Thirdly, the business houses enjoying commercial monopoly sought to augment their exotic type of merchandise by plundering the militarily weaker nations or regions throughout the world. European state powers under feudal absolutism actively collaborated, in their fiscal interest in all foreign ventures of monopoly commercial houses.

In Mughal India, however, the wealthy merchants could not appropriate the small ones because of their indispensable need of the latter for procuring rural merchandise, for its own intra-communal credit businesses and for acquiring commercial intelligence in so vast a region. Nor could the big merchant capital of Mughal India gain so much power as to coerce the state to do away with the self-sustaining autonomy of village community. The latter owing to the absence of private property in land tended to recycle itself around its more or less stagnant albeit diversified social production base. The Indian big merchants were indeed forced to adjust with the objective parameters of the economy where a village with stagnant production base was as much an independent sellers' market to the merchant as was the stagnant Indian economy to the external world. The difference was, however, that while an Indian village as sellers' market did not possess unlimited hunger for money wealth, Indian export economy dominated by substantial merchants had boundless thirst for precious metals.

This does not mean that money wealth accumulation by Indian big merchants did not cause differentiation among members of the mercantile community. Unlike village land, the mercantile money wealth was merchant's private means of acquiring further money wealth. Since the private acquisition of money wealth by a merchant, in the Mughal Indian context, did not transform itself into its control over the means of production or productive labour power, income differentiation among Indian merchants caused no erosion of communal interdependence among small, medium and big merchants themselves. However, it is necessary to point out that the problem of investment outlets did not affect equally all the sections of a community of merchants in Mughal India. Those for whom money wealth accumulation was more than what was warranted by their available spheres of investment, had to face the difficulty of survival as accumulation of additional money wealth did not promise an augmentation of merchandise from villages or no sizable return from money-lending or usurious operations. Therefore, they could survive only as intra-local commodity traders in rural areas or as *pykars* or agents of affluent urban merchants having inter-local or international commercial network. This was the primary form of differentiation among merchants, namely, between the rural and urban merchants; the former capitulating to the latter in matters of command over local merchandise wares or local mercantile wealth.

For those merchants who could appropriate unrivalled privileges of building up a clientele network among officials, nobles and others in the civil or military administration, investment crisis at least for the time did not loom large. Two categories of urban money merchants emerged. The first category was the numerous shroffs and moneychangers in coastal port towns, centres of entrepot trade or among local trade towns. Their clients were mostly small urban traders, shopkeepers, rural traders requiring money-changing or sundry alien traders who required conversion of bullions into Mughal silver rupees for purchasing wares in the trade centres. The second category was the influential commodity merchants in administrative or cantonment towns. The latter minted money wealth by credit and banking businesses among Mughal officials. These merchants were virtually money merchants having more profit from money trade than commodity trade. The second category of money merchants could mint more money wealth for themselves than the first category. Their proximity to officialdom made them dominant not only in the sphere of commodity trade but also in the sphere of overall money trade. From the ranks of this second category of money merchants there emerged the so-called merchant princes who were not only creditors, and bankers of high-ranking imperial officers, but were also mortgagers of a revenue-catchment area. Therefore, this section of affluent big merchants dealing with substantial amount of empire's commodity or money trade had its rise in the wake of another differentiation among urban merchants themselves in Mughal India.

Tapan Raychaudhuri finds the following categories of merchants in Mughal India. At the lowest level of the mercantile hierarchy were the *Banjaras*, specialising in specific trade items such as cloth, salt, rise, pulses, etc., along with small merchants catering to the needs of a proximate small town.[3] In this connection we may refer to an observation of K.N. Chaudhury, 'the peasants [themselves] . . . acted as trader carting his produce to the local market and town'. Chaudhury, however, readily admits that this peasant-trader phenomenon in India must be an exception to the general picture of peddling traders or small merchants belonging to local trading castes that mostly acted either as *dalals* (brokers) of big town merchants or as independent small traders.[4] However, according to Raychaudhuri, this lowest category of merchants was numerically the most dominant one and it was of subsistence-earning type.

The next category was less numerous but with relatively higher mercantile income – the town-living merchants. These merchants 'with their own and borrowed capital' were engaged in inter-local trade (unlike *banjaras* and small merchants engaged in 'intra-local' trade) and employed their own agents and sometimes had 'a dealer network' for procurement of merchandise. The apex level mercantile operations between regions of Mughal India was vested in a still smaller number of very rich traders who owned emporia in large entrepot centres of trade on land routes such as Ahmedabad, Ajmer, Delhi, Multan, Kandahar, etc. or in those on river routes (e.g., Agra, Benaras, Patna, Kasimbazar, Hooghly, Dacca, etc.) or on coastal routes (e.g., Chittagong, Balasore, Chicacole, etc.) on the east coast and (Thatta, Cambay, Ghogo, Surat, etc.) on the west coast.

Ray Chaudhuri's categorisation merely shows the scale of trade negotiated by each category. It does not convey any insight into the dynamics of individual or communal relationship if any, among the merchant categories or among merchants within a category. His reference to the autobiography of Jain merchant Banarasidas or his discreet reference to social base of traders merely suggests that a community network on caste or ethnic basis might be functioning among small or big merchants. He does not investigate into whether or not there existed a hierarchical or functional interdependence among members of a regional community of merchants or any kind of interdependence among various regional merchant communities in general. Only casually does he observe that the merchants of Mughal India were divided among specialised functional groups. This means that although a merchant middleman might have earned both commission from brokerage and profit from small trade on his personal account, the functioning of the broker was itself a highly specialised one. The same is obviously true about those who were engaged both in reaping profit from *dadni* business and the business of a shroff, although their specialisation lay in either of the two.

Since we have defined merchants as those who appropriate social surplus only by a kind of unequal exchange (mediated by money) we can conceive of many functional categories of merchants in Mughal India. It was, however, possible that given an opportunity, a merchant belonging to a specific functional category, might occasionally indulge in functions belonging strictly to other categories, but such overlapping activities were natural among merchants. In general, a shroff was engaged mainly in money trade, but an opportunity to make profit from commodity trade or to supplant his activity as a shroff induced him to make occasional or premeditated forays into other functional categories of minting money wealth. The same is true in the case of a pure commodity trader who might occasionally be a broker or supplier of money credit so as to make quick profit.

The propensity towards overlapping mercantile activities that were found among all categories of merchants, does not make any type of broad categorisation superfluous. What is necessary is to identify such functional categories (not categories based simply on scale of operation under specific specialization) that helps one to locate the dynamics of commercial prosperity of the Mughal economy characterised by a more or less stagnant social production base.

The Mughal commercial prosperity lay in the high money wealth augmenting capacity of commerce. The primary functional categorisation of the Mughal Indian merchants must therefore be between the pure money merchants and the pure commodity merchants. These are, however, only analytical categories not historical ones. For in an actual historical process, one may not find the emergence of such 'pure' categories. One may discover money merchants indulging in commodity trade and commodity merchants practising money trade. But our analytical categorisation in terms of 'pure' functions can locate the process under which money dealing commerce in the Mughal period could overwhelm the commerce on goods.

At the next stage we are to locate the institutions that supplied money in Mughal India and the sources of supply of physical merchandise. Money as legal tender was supplied by mints located at the initial stage of Akbar's rule both in important administrative cities as well as in areas where copper mines were available.[4] But from 1600 onward, the Mughal mints were located more in important trade centres rather than in administrative or minting centres. Therefore, one can observe that the source of money supply was metal bullion.[5] On the other hand, the villages were always the sources of supply of physical merchandise. On the basis of this locational difference between sources of money supply and those of supply of goods we can make a subcategory, among Mughal merchants that operated in rural and urban areas dealing either with pure money trade or commodity trade.

For obvious reasons, a rural money trade had to be of subsistence type; a rural money trader had to buy money in towns at a price lower than the price at which it could be sold in the rural areas. Moreover, the village community or the individual households in a village had demand for money mainly for the purpose of revenue payment and subsidiarily for purchasing imports from other villages. In any case, village demand for liquid cash was not enough to help a rural money merchant to impose a high degree of unequal exchange on a villager or his community. Therefore, in the rural areas money trade could operate only as a close surrogate of commodity trade, an Indian village being the exclusive source of merchandise. In other words, pure money business was not a lucrative proposition for rural investors. On the other hand the inelastic demand for cash on the part of a village, was circumscribed by the size of disposable surplus that could be used as exchangable merchandise ware. In this sense money trade in a rural area could not gain autonomy unless the money trader was linked up either with his own miniscule commodity trade or with urban commodity merchants who required purchasing money trader's stock of physical wares at a high price or on commission basis. A rural money trader's business, therefore, could function in a rural area as *dadan* business or the business of a rural surrogate of an urban commercial enterprise dealing with commodity transaction.

But the rural commodity trade of *banjaras* or of pedlars or small merchants could gain an instantaneous autonomy of its own functioning provided it could fetch a subsistence profit for itself. They were the most numerous throughout the Mughal period because the marketing of their wares had much lesser problem of uncertainty compared to that of an urban merchant's problem of procuring provisions. The village demand for imports in Mughal India, though stationary, was diversified enough to keep them always in trade. Therefore, the story that with the growth of urban commerce, the pedling trade or trade of small merchants disappeared, seems to be a myth. The village demand for and supply of wares were too close to them so that the possibility of their disappearance is as remote as the unreality of the conception of a Mughal Indian village neither exporting nor importing consumables. It was, however, the humble amount of profit that prevented a rural merchant from undertaking massive investments or scales of operations and forced him to be confined to a locality.

The differential advantage enjoyed by an urban centre enhanced with its size. The small urban-centres were numerous and as *Ain* suggests, headquarters of revenue circles. Stephen P. Blake estimates that each of about 534 small urban centres collected revenue from 60 villages paying revenue on 51,000 bighas of measured land.[6] Since one-third of the total revenue collected by a revenue circle headquarter was retained by itself under the law for defraying the wages and salaries of those connected with local revenue administration, the merchants of such urban centre had the privilege of entering into unequal exchange transaction as sellers of merchandise with such town people that spent about one-third of revenue money as their income. This suggests that the scale of operations of an average merchant belonging to such towns or urban centres was much bigger than his counterpart operating in a rural marketing circle that could embrace much less than 60 villages.[7] The Mughal urban centres operating as headquarters of more than one revenue circle and discharging other imperial functions were bigger. The merchants of the larger urban centres had better opportunities of making profit from higher volume of unequal exchange activities with numerous people anxious to transform their salaries, wages, money gifts and rewards into consumables. In a Mughal urban centre there existed small merchants, shopkeepers, pawn brokers, usurers, etc as well as big commodity merchants, owners of emporia, bankers, affluent shroffs and speculators, all having their respective spheres of operations.

What is important to note is that compared to a typical rural merchant even a small urban merchant could enjoy a band of heterogeneous urban clients who allowed him to make more money profit from his transactions. A small shroff could make his profit from transaction with small shopkeepers or commodity merchants anxious to replenish his stock of wares. A bigger shroff could lend money to a relatively well-off urban commodity merchant or to a ranking imperial official when exigencies demanded. A small commodity merchant in the urban centre was always assured of profit in a predominantly buyers' market. A substantial commodity merchant could always use his money wealth for servicing his commercial network among various regions. The richest merchants could extend their profitable operations to various administrative towns, to the important centres of inter-regional or entrepot trade and augment their required money supply by converting imported bullions into standard silver rupees.

Probably with the growth of inland commerce in the post-Akbar period, the earlier differentiation between urban and rural commerce, was reinforced by a new differentiation among members belonging to the rank of urban merchants themselves. One positive outcome of the differentiation was the growth of immense money power of a relatively few urban merchants in each sizable urban centre. It is plausible that the growth of money power of big merchants caused the rise of their banking businesses that substantially curtailed the sphere of mercantile activities of independent small money merchants as well as commodity merchants like small shroffs and shopkeepers who in the changed situation themselves became customers of big banking activities in a metropolitan urban centre. It is in this context that the hypothesis advanced by Ovington and Streensgaard, that by the mid-17th century pedling trade and the activity of small merchants disappeared as a consequence of mutuality between the growth of European commodity commerce in India and the prosperity of Indian big merchants, must be examined.[8] The travelogue of Tavernier, that preceded that of Ovington, apart from appreciating the unimaginable efficiency and extensiveness of Indian big merchants' credit network, had seemingly advanced a new hypothesis that the activity of such merchants declined as a consequence of their oppression by the Mughal officials.[9]

In fact, all such European accounts of Mughal commerce fail to locate the dialectical interactions within the Mughal revenue system, the rise of new trade centres that inhered two types of differentiation within Mughal commerce (namely the differentiation between urban and rural commerce and that between urban money trade and commodity trade) and the village sphere of social production base.

As we have stated earlier, it was the incipient contradiction between the village production base and the imperial requirements that acted as an exogenous factor of rising intensity of the Mughal inland commerce that had its prime endogenous basis in inter-village exports and imports. It again fostered in a situation of absence of property rights and in the midst of a series of contradiction between the relative inelasticity in the aggregate expansion of social production base and the relative elasticity in the growth of imperial surplus requirement, as well as that between direct surplus appropriation and surplus acquisition by unequal exchange. Such contradiction is caused, in a situation of free minting facilities to bullionholding merchants, differentiation between urban and rural commerce and at the next stage between the commerce in money and the commerce in physical merchandise. The result was that an immense money wealth could be acquired by a few big merchants in important urban centres that could bring under its mercantile hegemony both small commodity trade and money trade.

The positive outcome of the second set of contradictions was the growth of pure money wealth that was not matched by a corresponding growth of physical merchandise. The negative outcome of the widening gap between surplus requirement and the actual surplus that it could acquire was the financial crisis in the state sector as a whole.

While in the 17th century the contradiction between the absolute growth of imperial surplus requirement and the relative inelasticity of growth of revenue reinforced the contradiction between direct coercive mode of surplus appropriation and the urban mercantile mode of surplus appropriation by unequal exchange, the unforeseen growth of commercial money wealth of urban big merchants produced a unique phenomenon of 'crisis of mercantile investment'. The 17th century mercantile response to this crisis was twofold. The first was, as we noted earlier, an immense growth of credit business or banking business in urban areas bringing within its network not only the wealthy members of the Mughal nobility but also the sundry categories of money or commodity merchants of humble size. This brought into being the dominance of money trade over commodity trade throughout the empire. The effect was the dominance of traders' money over all other money.

The mid-17th century price rise, particularly in urban centres, is only apparently a manifestation of this dominance of wares in kind over silver money. But the reality is somewhat different. The price rise shows the dominance of merchant money over the money possessed by the urban non-merchant people belonging to the state sector. Irfan Habib, on the basis of information on prices of the time, shows that the essential items in the consumption basket of an urban dweller, e.g., food-grains, ghee, wheat, flour, gram, sugar, etc. registered a threefold price rise in course of the 17th century.[10]

On the basis of estimates furnished by Aziza Hasan, Habib observes that since between 1591 and 1700, the total silver rupees in circulation went up three times, the price rise showing adverse terms of exchange between a silver rupee and a unit of transacted merchandise wares can be attributed simply to the rise in silver rupee supply.[11] This innocuous explanation of the 17th century price rise is valid under two presuppositions : first, the silver rupee throughout the century had no use other than as a medium of exchange; second, the trade-offs either between the state sector and merchants or between the primary suppliers of merchandise wares and merchants remained static between 1600 and 1700.

Had silver rupee functioned only as medium of exchange, Mughal India could not have witnessed during the 17th century such growth in banking and credit businesses. On the other hand, far from remaining stoic, the economic relations between the state sector, merchants and primary suppliers of merchandise underwent significant change. The financial crisis in the state sector during the century is well known. In our view, the price rise, i.e., the adversity in terms of exchange of a silver rupee in its exchange relation to a unit of urban consumer good was, on the one hand, the cumulative consequence of a growing competition among urban holders, both mercantile and non-mercantile, of silver money for village wares (in such competition, merchants were necessarily infinitely stronger), and on the other hand the phenomenal rise in the aggregate urban effective demand for consumables. This was bound to happen in a situation where the urban supply of liquid cash made a phenomenal rise with no matching increase in the supply of consumables from villages. The result was that the velocity of silver rupee per unit of transacted goods went up phenomenally during the 17th century and the rise in the urban velocity of money along with the lower velocity of goods could not sustain itself without a price rise.

The most palpable evidence of 'goods famine' among urban big merchants that wielded a tremendous money power during that period was attested to by many historians. Asin Das Gupta writing on the Surat merchants of early 18th century, observes that Indian merchants' fortune was vitiated by the chronic uncertainty about procurement of merchandise wares.[12] S. Choudhuri referred in more details to the procurement difficulties of merchants operating in the most busy centres of commerce in the late 17th century Bengal.[13]

Again it was the problem of procuring physical merchandise that acted as a check against differentiation among merchants, that prevented the wealthy merchants from driving out small subsistence merchants from the sphere of commerce. In both coastal or inland centres of entrepot trade in late 17th or early 18th century India we find simultaneous operation of independent small merchants with humble capital and extremely wealthy merchants with huge capital, their own agents and *pykars*. This suggests that differentiation among Indian merchants could not run its full course – unlike what happened in West Europe – due to the absence of a historical scope in Mughal India that could transform mercantile money wealth as individual property into its real substance, i.e., the private property in land or labour. This also explains why, notwithstanding, the differentiation within its rank, the merchants belonging to a locality, or to an ethnic or racial community could sustain its intra-communal bondage of mutual cooperation and unity. This intra-communal unity and resilience became conspicous only when the alien company of merchants after seizing political power acted as levellers of unequal money powers of indigenous merchants.

But before that, throughout the 17th and the first half of the 18th century, the in-built investment crisis within the indigenous commercial money wealth sought to use the incoming European commodity trade as its ready instruments of resolution of the crisis. If the better part of the 17th century enabled the indigenous big merchants find investment among urban nobles and officials as the readily available means of staving off the crisis, the first half of the 18th century enabled them to discover new areas of lucrative credit investment of its money capital among the European buyers of Indian merchandise.[14] This is the story about how the money wealth augmenting nature of Indian commercial prosperity could stave off, *albeit* temporarily, its inbred investment crisis during the 17th and the first half of the 18th century.

Notes

1 By civilian imports and exports of villages we mean only those which are required only for consumption purposes.

2 The second group's provision for emergency is prompted in order to cover the risk of future uncertainties such as famines and sudden invasions.

3 Tapan Ray Chaudhuri, 'Inland Trade' [Mughal India], *Cambridge Economic History of India*, Vol. I, *op.cit.* , pp. 326-29.

4 K.N. Chaudhury, '*The Trading World and the East India Company 1660-1760.* Cambridge Univ. Press, 1981, pp. 95-97.

5 During the first three decades of Akbar's rule, copper *dam* was the leading medium of exchange and it is said, *Ain* estimated all the value of transactions in terms of copper *dam* till 1595. But the beginning of the 17th century witnessed silver *rupee* as the most widely used currency. Cf. John S. Deyell, 'Akbar's Currency System and Monetary Integration' in J.F. Richards (ed.), *The Imperial Monetary System of Mughal India*, *op. cit.*, pp.13-63.

6 Stephen P. Blake, *op. cit.*, Table 14, p.125.

7 Even if we assume a possibility that a rural merchant could indeed operate in more than 60 villages, the fact was that the total amount of disposable income to be spent on imported consumables, by more than 60 villages could not exceed the amount possessed by an unproductive town having money income to be fructified into merchandise wares.

8 Cf. J. Ovington, *A Voyaqe to Surat in the Year 1669*, Ed. H.C. Ramlinson (London, 1929), *passim.* N. Streensgaard, *Carracks, Caravans and Companies : The Structural Crisis in the European Asian Trade in the Early Seventeenth Century* (Copenhagen, 1972), pp.28-30.

9 J. Baptiste Tavernier, *Tavernier's Travels in India, 1640-67* (Calcutta, 1905), *passim.*

10 Cf. Irfan Habib, 'Monetary System and Prices', *Cambridge Economic History of India*, Vol. I, *op. cit.*, pp. 372-76.

11 *Ibid.*, pp. 160-61.

12 Asin Das Gupta, *Indian Merchants and the Decline of Surat c. 1700-1750*, (weisbaden, 1979), p.26.

13 Cf. S. Choudhury, *Trade and Commercial Organisation of Bengal, 1650-1720*, (Calcutta, 1975).

14 The decline of Surat or Hooghly as centres of international commerce dominated by Indian merchants of diverse origin was caused less by the superior arms of foreign merchants or the quality of imported merchandise, more by mutual quarrels and conflicts among big Indian port merchants on the one hand and by mutual cooperation among substantial money wealth of Indian investor and the chronic credit needs of sundry European merchants on the other.

4.4: Mughal Village and Commercial Prosperity

We have no hard evidence on the basis of which one can capture the relations between a Mughal Indian village and an urban commercial entrepreneur of substantial money power. But we have argued why the nature of commercial prosperity in Mughal India could have its basis in nothing apart from accumulation of money wealth by big merchants engaged in urban and/or foreign commerce. Indeed one cannot marshall evidence to the effect that such commercial prosperity in Mughal India was based on a higher increase in the absolute size of supply of the physical merchandise. The question is why the source of primary supply of physical merchandise i.e., Indian village economy remained by and large insulated from the commercial prosperity of urban merchants of Mughal India? The primary answer may be found in parallelism between the rationale of a Mughal Indian commercial activity and that of the village-level productive activity of the time. The basic rationale of activity of a commercial enterprise of the Mughal period was to maximise its earning of money wealth by any possible means, while the rationale of productive activity of a village body including that of its non-labouring stratum was to ensure, at least, subsistence consumption or if an opportunity arose to raise the level of village consumption. The latter's liquidity need was subordinated to its rationale of productive activity. Despite such mutually exclusive rationale of commercial and productive activity, there existed a sphere of interdependence between a village community and the money power of a commercial enterprise to the extent the former required commuting a part of its produce into cash for revenue payment and purchase of imports and the latter required buying of physical merchandise wares from the former.

But this interdependence between a village community and a commercial enterprise in Mughal period was circumscribed by three important limits. Firstly, the total amount of surplus that a village would want to commute into cash or amount of income or wages a village would want to transform into food and other necessities available in the rural market, had no reason to increase unless there was an absolute expansion in the size of village production[1] (whether such expansion was due to increase in population, improved artifices, or innovation, or simply by raising total cultivable acreages are not important). We have argued why the expansion in the size of village production could at best be nominal and sporadic, it could never be considerable.

Secondly, the absence of property right in land and inflexible communal right of labouring population to subsistence consumption acted as a fetter to the growth of a symbiotic relationship between a commercial endeavour and a village process of production. It may, however, be argued that in a setting of stationary level of production, there might be an increased sale of village surplus to merchants. This is because, as we have indeed observed earlier, the Mughal revenue system tended to foster a fresh impetus to income inequality between elitist big land-holders employing hired labourers and the small holding peasants employing their own labour. But we have also observed that the growth of such intra-communal income inequality could not rise *ad infinitum* and had its barrier in working labourers' social right to subsistence consumption. Indeed to a village elite, his landholding was merely his means of procuring consumption and was not his property, i.e., not his appropriation of the material condition of labour in a village production process. Therefore the scope for acquiring greater amount of village goods as merchandise by a merchant in a situation of unequal distribution of produce is severely limited as much by the inelasticity of social production base as by the inflexibility of consumption requirement of the working people of the community.

Thirdly, in a setting of nearly stagnant production base in villages, the competition among individual money powers of either local merchants or of commercial enterprises belonging to urban areas for procuring merchandise from villages was more intense than the competition among villagers or village communities themselves for purchasing cash by their portions of disposable physical surplus, or for buying needed wares by their remaining portions of surplus in hand from merchants. The elasticity of mercantile demand for village wares was much lower than the elasticity of village demand for merchantable wares, money or imported goods.

The limits to interdependence between a village community and merchants of Mughal India highlight two things: first, the terms of exchange between a village community (or its peasants and artisans) and the merchants were not likely to go against the former; and the second is that the production for immediate consumption rather than for market was to be the dominant tendency in the pattern of social production of the Mughal period.[2] This means that an increased imperial claim (in value terms) from villages could be shifted by the latter by demanding higher prices of surplus goods they sold to merchants, and that villages preferred to produce more of such crops belonging to their individual production profile that fetched higher money value from sale. The second trend among villages towards substitution of production of low-priced crops by the high priced ones cannot be interpreted in terms of production for market as in terms of village anxiety to collect needed cash for revenue payment or for buying necessary imports for consumption. One has to remember in this connection that the phenomenon of production for market is *necessarily* guided by the *profit motive* of the person who organises/cultivates/manufactures produce. It cannot be guided either by a requirement for revenue payment or by the need for consumption of bare necessities.

During the entire course of Mughal Indian history, although there was no spectacular increase either in population[3] or total agricultural production, there was no doubt diversification of cropping pattern or artisan production. This is attested to by many historians including Irfan Habib.[4] If production is stagnant how can there arise diversification of cropping pattern and in the pattern of production in artisan goods? Does such diversifications in any way indicate a rising tendency in Mughal economy towards production for the market?

In our view, diversification of crops produced by villages cannot necessarily imply production for market unless we assume that villagers, in general, sold their entire produce for cash and purchased substantial amount of consumables from the market on account of the existence of a rural cash nexus. Since total production moved around the level of stagnation, any increase in diversification of crops was feasible under two alternative situations. First, owing to increased imperial revenue claim in value terms or to some other reason, the villagers might decide to raise a high-priced new crop by partial or total replacement of the old one. A second situation might arise when a community of villagers might plant such crops or produce such artisan goods that could fetch high prices simply because external effectual demand for them was relatively inelastic.

Exactly how much would be produced by a village for external market was as much determined by its corporate cash requirement as by the amount of surplus of low-priced use values it could forsake for the purpose. In other words, the production pattern pursued by the villagers of a community had to strike a balance between the requirements of their own consumable crop production and those of pure money-yielding crop production. If the size of total village production under a Mughal polity is supposed to be inelastic (as most of medieval historians including Irfan Habib hypothesise) it must have provided a limited scope for village production exclusively for a market in urban centre. This must be true particularly in a situation where in the absence of transactions on private property in land or labour a rural *use of money would neither be productive nor be investment-oriented.* To validate the theory that Mughal village economy produced increasingly for markets, it is necessary to show either that the villagers needed wealth for purposes other than consumption and/or revenue payment, or that villagers themselves consumed more by cash purchase of their necessities than from their own produce. No historian of Mughal India could show conclusive evidence in support of either one of the above two possibilities. It is likely that Mughal money in a village was used either to meet external cash obligations of any type or to be used exclusively for a consumptive purpose. No evidence is there to show that money in a Mughal Indian village had its use even as unproductive investment fund by which it could earn surplus by arresting the material condition of the peasant or artisan. It is true that village usurers or money-lenders possessed unproductive investment fund of their own, but the rationale of activity of a rural usurer or money-lender in a Mughal Indian village was used to acquire a subsistence amount of his consumption fund out of the physical surplus. It could function more as wage against its service rather than as *profit* from investment.[5]

Land, at no stage, figured as a purchasable item and the cultivating labour was entitled only to land he himself cultivated or was only temporarily attached to a land held by a non-cultivating village elite during the period of cultivation and harvest.[6] Money possessed by anybody in a village could be used only as an instrument of present or future consumption needs of the possessor, so it could not be used as an instrument of appropriating the condition of labour.

It is undoubtedly true that the commercial prosperity of urban big merchants and the rising foreign demand for Indian artisan wares brought in their wake an extent of specialized differentiation among Mughal Indian villages between villages producing horticultural or artisan goods for urban or overseas markets and those that raised only subsistence crops and goods for villagers' use. Many cotton or silk weavers' villages sprang up during the 17th-18th centuries in and around Hooghly, Satgaon, Dacca, in Bengal and around Cambay, Surat, Masilipatnam, or around Ahmedabad, Patna, Agra, Cossim-bazar along the inland trade routes. This type of urban-demand or foreign-demand might have led to differentiation among Mughal Indian villages. But such differentiations apart from being few and far between in a sea of other average type villages could not generate by itself an unbound thirst for money wealth even among the villages producing only artisan or horticultural wares. In most cases, the purely artisan or horticultural villages had their cash dependence on merchants for disposal of their goods. While it was a merchant who earned profit from the sale of goods in urban or overseas markets, the village craftsmen or horticulturist garden labour earned wages so as to enable them to purchase subsistence. Therefore, in the stationary setting of food or other subsistence crop production, the growth of artisan or horticultural goods prompted by widening of *exogenous* demand for them was limited by the absence of expansion of agricultural wage-goods.

Only when a village community was required to import goods from other villages, it required money in case such imports were negotiated by a local pedling trader or a small merchant and town shopkeeper. This takes us to the relation between merchants in general, and members of a village that supplied as well as bought merchandise.

We have already observed the universal phenomenon that the inter-village exports and imports always formed the initial basis on which grew the pedling trade or the activity of small country merchants. Since the elasticity of pedlars (or small merchants') demand for village wares was determined by the scale of their operations and, therefore, had no reason to be substantially different from the income elasticity of demand for imports or village sale of exports, the terms of exchange between a village and a pedlar or small merchant provided the latter with only a subsistence level of profit.

The difference between the demand for goods by an urban buyer and by a villager, was that the former stipulated a trade-off between a buyer's supply of money and a seller's demand for money in exchange mediated by goods in kind, while the latter involved a trade-off between buyer's supply of one type of goods in exchange of seller's supply of another mediated by money in cash. In the former case a seller gained more in terms of money per unit of transacted goods while in the latter case, the seller could gain more in terms of consumable goods per unit of transacted money. But the amount of gain a merchant could muster from his transaction with an artisan or village buyer was dependent on the latter's income elasticity of demand for imported goods or money.

Since by our own reckoning a Mughal Indian village had no other use for money except for revenue payment and for other marginal use simply as an exchange medium, we cannot conceive of a situation when terms of exchange, even between a merchant (not excluding an urban big merchant) and village needing imports could turn against the latter. On the other hand, since a Mughal Indian town had no other means except the money power of its consumers for the purpose of procuring goods, the terms of exchange between an urban merchant and the urban consumers necessarily inhered, in themselves, a tendency to go against the latter.

When the Mughal inland commerce with its initial anchor on inter-village commerce made a transition to the stage when commerce between a rapidly expanding urban population or money power in towns and villages as sources of merchandise became the most pronounced characteristic, the high degree of prosperity in urban commerce and its attendant price rise had no political or economic arsenal so as to impose an adverse term of exchange on the village economy – primary supplier of merchandise. At its early stage commodity trade was itself so profitable that it attracted even the Mughal officials. Quite a few Mughal officials plundered artisan wares (rather than merchants' money wealth) to sell them to merchants at a profitable price or forced investment of their idle money wealth on regional commodity trades. Only when at the next stage the urban centres put their huge demand pressure on substantial urban merchants that the latter could gain sufficient money wealth power for commanding respect and awe from politically powerful Mughal officials.

Tapan Raychaudhuri observes this process of transition of the Mughal period's inland trade from the stage when inter-village exports and imports constituted the basic stage of commerce to the stage when urban merchants became wealthy enough to engage themselves in expanding trade even among regions with separate measurement systems, currency and taxation.[7] The real prosperity and accumulation of immense money power of merchants came, in Raychaudhuri's reckoning, in the 18th century. 'While the wealth of such merchants [he is referring to the very wealthy merchants or 'Merchant Princes'] was derived mainly from trade [he does not specify the kind of trade, whether it is trade of goods or money] inland and foreign, *links with the political authorities as financiers and tax-farmers could be an important source of their capital* [he actually means money wealth] *accumulation, especially in the eighteenth century*' (italics added).[8] While in Raychaudhuri's account, the historico-imperial stages of evolutionary development of Mughal India's inland commerce is roughly similar to ours where his account differs from ours, is in an absence of a sequential analysis of historical reasons that led to such evolutionary developments. Our account shows that a stationary village economy of the Mughal period with its pervasive pattern of production for use but functioning as a sellers' market to exogenous buyers could not undergo a change in itself although it enabled the merchants to accomplish a high rate of absorption of money wealth by a high rate of pure money return from money-dealing commerce on a given amount of physical merchandise. To put it in another way, the unique set of historical factors that caused alienation of Mughal period's commercial prosperity from the stationary character of the rural production base operated as those which did not permit the growth of commercial prosperity at the expense of village economy of Mughal India. In Mughal India mercantile money wealth of a merchant could gain accumulation not by causing impoverishment of villagers who required money and, in fact, possessed little money wealth, but by causing drainage of wealth from money-holding urban people-through execution of urban unequal exchanges.

Therefore, the nature of commercial prosperity of Mughal India was to a great extent independent of the elasticity of social production base in villages. Consequently, the former could produce neither a stimulating effect nor a corrosive or degenerating effect on the village economy. To the extent such prosperity could cause differentiation among villages between those who supplied mainly village needs and those who catered to urban or foreign markets, such degree of differentiation was itself dependent, as we have argued earlier, on the size of surplus produce meant for use for villagers engaged in exclusively producing for the urban/overseas market. Since the technique of production or the level of productivity had no compelling reason for a progressive change of itself, the scope within a Mughal Polity for rising inter-village differentiation between those producing for use and those for market was severely limited.

The Indian village economy could not undergo an abrupt change on the same ground even after the European mercantile houses began to arrive. But the indigenous mercantile money wealth found in European demand for merchandise a new sphere of investment that could fetch a higher rate of return. This European commercial demand for Indian merchandise certainly caused further differentiation among Indian big merchants so as to germinate a new breed of Indian big merchants who combined their massive money trade with higher monopolisation of inter-country flows of merchantable wares. The eighteenth century prosperity of the family of Jagat Seth in Bengal or any other mercantile house in Surat or Cambay can be placed in this context. While Jagat Seth's earlier rise to financial eminence owed much to its initial access to the Bengal treasury of the Mughal Nawabs, its ascendancy to the position of a financier of European East Indian Company was an inevitable consequence of mercantile money wealth's pursuit of more money wealth by catering to the credit or commodity needs of those foreign merchants who were ready to pay highest rate of return.

Indian village communities remained, by and large, neutral either to a 17th century collaboration between Indian big merchants and the indigenous political authorities or to subsequent collaboration between the houses of Indian wealthy merchants and foreign commercial enterprises (by which both gained more than ever before only at the expense of indigenous political powers). However, when foreign commercial houses began to reign supreme in political terms the collaboration between merchant princes of India and those of Europe gave way-to subjugation of the former by the latter. Only after this, villages began to face extortionate onslaught from European merchant rulers and their middlemen. But this is the story of the later period.

Notes

1 It is claimed by historians that the average imperial revenue rate went up from one third of village output (at the time of Akbar) to half at the time of Aurangzeb. Assuming that assessed revenue from village could be actually collected, the question arises, were not Mughal Indian villages forced to raise the level of production for retaining the amount a village itself required for self-consumption? Since Irfan Habib finds no evidence of a sizable increase in village production during the Mughal period, he is tempted to conclude that during the tumultuous days of later Mughal emperors, the increased appropriation of village surplus led to what he calls 'the Agrarian crisis of

the Mughal empire'. (Potentialities of Capitalist Development in Mughal India', see below).

One can indeed hardly deny that the Mughal taxes increased over time as well as the fact that with archaic techniques of production and a, more or less, stationary population, the social production base under Mughal had no means by which it could cause its absolute expansion of a considerable size. But if we remember that the assessed imperial claims on villages were expressed in value terms not in terms of physical quantities and that an almost uninterrupted intertemporal rise in prices of goods took place since 1670s, any hypothesis of 'Agrarian Crisis' presupposes that the rural prices of goods at which a village commuted its portion of physical surplus into cash so as to meet its external financial obligations to the merchant-importers and imperial authority, showed only a downward bias, never an upward one. Neither Irfan Habib nor any other historian marshalls a single evidence to this effect.

What, therefore, seems more plausible is that along with an upward bias in urban prices of goods, the prices of village goods also showed an upward trend. The degree of price rise must necessarily be higher in the urban centres. Therefore, an increase in taxes in value terms did not necessarily involve a proportionate increase in the portion of village surplus in physical terms to be parted with by a village. Even if we make an allowance that increased taxation involved indeed a higher appropriation of physical quantum of disposable village surplus, that does not readily prove setting of an agrarian crisis in motion during the Mughal period. In a polity where labourers could not be forced to remain attached to land controlled by the village non-labouring stratum, an agrarian crisis of the type postulated by Habib, could result in the migration of peasants, and such flight would have led to an absolute decline in the aggregate level of agricultural production in the Mughal empire. Indeed a different picture emerged, the phenomenon of flights of peasant from a village was followed by a new area of cultivation. Besides, neither Irfan Habib nor anybody else has shown that during the days of Aurangzeb or any other Mughal ruler there was *sharp decline in the absolute level of aggregate production in agriculture* owing to the introduction of new taxes or the rise in the revenue claims of later Mughal rulers.

This is why we hold that increased imperial claims of late Mughal Indian villages faced no 'agrarian crisis' of the sort that could manifest either in the form of a downward movement of the aggregate social production base in Mughal agriculture or in the usurpation of the material condition of labour by a Mughal revenue official or private individual holder of village land.

2 This view contests the formulation advanced by Irfan Habib in his 'Potentialities of Capitalistic Development in Mughal India' (mimeographed), *op.cit.* He nowhere states in categorical terms that production of market was a dominant tendency in Mughal Indian economy, but the way he marshalls the facts and figures betrays the impression that he visualises a *rising* tendency in Mughal economy towards production for market.

3 Irfan Habib, 'Population [Mughal India], and 'The System of Agricultural Production', *Cambridge Economic History of India*, Vol. I, *op.cit.*, p.167 and pp.210-20.
4 Cf. Irfan Habib,'Agrarian Relations and Land Revenue', *Cambridge Economic History of India*, Vol. I, *op. cit*,, pp. 147-48. While an individual villager could hold land not as his property but as instrument of his *communal means of subsistence*, such holding could not enforce labour services from others, in case he was incapable of (or barred by his caste status from) giving labour services. Only the state or local village authority could exercise control over acquired land not, however, for its *profit* but for its revenue payment or consumption requirements.
5 Mughal Indian village households were never developed as a market for urban mercantile credit. Irfan Habib finds that a village (rather than its individual household) as 'a legal person' contracted credit from an external moneylender, 'the loan [could be] repaid out of village pool', *Agrarian System of Mughal India*, *op. cit.*, p.127.
6 Cf. Irfan Habib, 'The System of Agricultural Production, *Cambridge Economic History of India*, *op. cit.*, Section on 'Agricultural Labour'.
7 Tapan Raychaudhury, 'Inland Trade [Mughal India]', *Cambridge Economic History of India*, Vol. I, *op. cit.*, p. 339.
8 *Ibid.*, p. 341.

4.5: A Different Paradigm of Development in Non-Mughal Areas: Disjuncture Between Prosperous External Commerce and Weak Inland Commerce

South Indian inland commerce of the period was as distinct from Mughal Indian commerce, as Mediterranean commerce was from that of North Europe.[1] One of the important factors was, no doubt, related to the geophysical location of South India. An equally important factor was the differential configuration of relationships among state systems, social formations and local commercial enterprises between North and South India. In the preceding chapter (section 3.7. and 3.8) we have outlined the differential trait of evolution of south Indian village societies. However, notwithstanding such locational and other differences, there might have existed an extent of functional interdependence among all coastal centres of overseas entrepot trade. We would like to stress here that while the nature of state system, village communities and merchants – their mutual interactions – invariably beget a regional or sub-regional paradigm of development in commerce, it is not necessary to hold that such regional paradigms were completely insulated from possible interactional influence on each other.

In this section we like to emphasise more the differential attributes of commercial developments that took place in the non-Mughal South, rather than the aspects of similarity and mutual interactions between the Mughal and non-Mughal paradigm of commercial development. This is because trade in its primary form arises from uneven development within a natural agricultural economy of a macro-region with its specific eco-types and physical environs. Even when trade develops into commerce the latter cannot free itself completely from direct or remote tutelage under local natural economy with its physical attributes.

The differential pattern of development of both inland commerce and overseas external commerce in South India owes its genesis to the differential natural-geophysical attributes of the region. It is now widely acknowledged that commerce in the peninsular coast commanded an unrivalled height of treasure-accumulation since 2nd century B.C. 'Chinese records identify Kanci (Conjeevaram of Chingleput district) . . . Kaveripatnam . . . Thanjavur, Pondicherry, Masulipatam' which were important entrepots on the east coast engaged in trade with regions of southeast Asia, and the 'Malabar coast was the primary calling place for Graeco-Roman traders' of ancient Europe.[2] But what remains unnoticed is that the external commerce of early South India did not possess a major hinterland in the peninsula itself. Its hinterland, at that phase, covered a sizable part of North and Central India. This is particularly evident from the story of the evolution of peninsular commerce. With the development of commerce in Northern India the commerce of South India had to shift its hinterland to the peninsula itself.

Developmental stages of martime commerce in the southern peninsula, as discerned by Burton Stein, did not correspond with those of inland commerce within it. Moreover, the decisive determinants of each were mutually disjunctive in course of the successive historical stages till the advent of political annexation of the peninsula by the English East India Company. The overseas commerce of South India had, according to Stein, two phases of development. The first phase started from the 2nd century B.C., if not earlier, and came up to the 13th-14th centuries; and the second phase, starts from the decline of the Cholas and the simultaneous appearance of Arab Muslims in maritime commerce of the region and ends with north European armed supremacy all along the coast lines of the peninsula.

In the first phase, the maritime commerce of peninsular India was, however, frequently interspersed with predatory overseas expedition of the Cholas or of the earlier Pandya kings even to faraway islands which later on came to be known as 'Indonesian archipelago'. In the second phase external plunder ceased to be the feature of South India's maritime commerce; South Indian ports by that time became important entrepot centres.

But Stein's account of the development of regional inland commerce follows a different periodisation coinciding largely with socio-political changes in the interior. In his view, the first phase of inland commerce in South India was as usual dominated by itinerant or pedling traders who were, however, not free from caste constraints. These pedling traders belonged to the low right and left hand castes of artisan-cum-traders. Although these traders had their supra-local associations for the production of merchandise as well as mutual commercial support, they had to function within the limits and norms set by the local *nadus* under the brahmanic governance of a local *nattar* authority. This phase came to an end by the political changes of the 11th century in the wake of construction of temple-towns as a new mode of acquiring political power by the local brahmanic magnates.

The consequent increase in the freedom of operation among artisans and traders took place in spite of the lingering dominance of brahmans in the Chola as well as post-Chola political structure. The temple-towns, surrounded by rural agrarian societies were ostensibly meant for popularising the spread of temple-cults and for consolidating the power of the local *nattar* magnates. But such temple-centred urbanisation in the core region of the South worked paradoxically as an eventual catalyst for dissolution of the *nadu* organisational set-up and the *nattar* brahmanic command structure that governed local rural societies.[3] The growth of innumerable urban centres developing around temples had a liberating effect, particularly on the lowly castes of rural artisans who could earlier transact goods only with roving pedling traders. Now people belonging to the local artisan castes could sell their wares directly to a new merchant class arising in the temple-towns.

During the earlier phases of this development, the new commercial centres arising in some temple-towns were governed by the members of *nattar* brahmanic gentry and less by the people of trading-cum-artisan castes. But with the decline of Cholas and the subsequent rise of more temple-towns during the Vijayanagar imperial rule a further intensification of commerce took place in temple-towns.[4] A new development at this stage was the emergence of multi-ethnic inland merchants who could engage in trade between temple centres and adjacent villages, if not always between temple-towns and ports.

But the extent of commerce that could be promoted by such massive rise in the number of temple towns, was not spectacular. An average temple-town was not large (the great city of Vijayanagar on Tungabhadra was an exception), and was inhabited mainly by a small population consisting of temple priests, servants, a few merchants and artisans. The temple-towns could, however, attract a steady flow of pilgrims and devotees throughout the year, who constituted the major floating community of urban consumers of rural peasant produce and artisan wares. Because of their small size, temple-towns could not produce a sizable impact on the demand for merchandise in the region. In this connection we are to note a striking difference between an average Mughal town which was much larger and a small temple-town.

It is not merely the size that differentiated a Mughal town from its non-Mughal counterpart in the south, more crucial was perhaps the difference between the surplus appropriating power of the respective regional groups of town-dwellers. The richer segment of urban population in a Mughal town was directly or indirectly associated with Mughal machinery of surplus appropriation so as to constitute an ever expanding buyers' market for village wares. In contrast, a peninsular temple-town had as its richest segment in the temple priests, who however did not enjoy a steady flow of income round the year. In other words, the urban income of a Mughal town was augmented by regular appropriation of surplus from rural areas, but the income of the South Indian urban residents was made up of 'gifts' (voluntary or obligatory) from rural devotees.[5] Therefore, a temple-town in the South could not constitute a steady buyers' market for village merchandise. In this sense, the South Indian temple-town could never generate, like a Mughal town, an expanding monetised demand for local merchandise.

The main basis on which the inland commerce of the peninsular south stood was local exchange among villages and those between villages and nearby temple-towns. On the other hand, since the South Indian villages were under the governance of local societies, the inter-village differentiation among village crop productions and artisan manufactures could not make much headway in the course of the Vijayanagar or post-Vijayanagar period, and neither could there arise an objective situation for a rising frequency of urban 'tatonement' for village wares.

The dominance of brahman and of a rising group of low-caste sat sudra elites over local agrarian societies tended to inhibit the scope for either product differentiation in the rural areas or more inter-village exchanges in a locality. Whatever little inland trade that could take place was done by either brahman or sat-sudra merchants. An important component of South Indian inland commerce was the exchange between regions producing paddy and coarse varieties of artisan manufactures and those having inhospitable land tract specialising in dry crops, animal husbandry and cattle breeding.

One can locate two factors that inhibited substantial development of inland commerce in South India. The first was the absence of a powerful imperial state that could appropriate for itself a major income from agriculture and the second was the consequence of the first, namely, the insularity of South Indian agriculture from its overseas and inland commerce. The most important factor was, however, the absence of a powerful and centralised imperial state. The nature of the state system as it was developed in South India virtually precluded any need for either a plunderous or comprehensively designed land revenue system.

A local ruling establishment which initially grew up from a power-based extension of societies under dominant caste groups (belonging to local brahmans or Telugu *Nayaka*), could in the later stage establish an empire only by forming a confederate command structure over fellow local establishments of other rulers. This kind of empire-building, based virtually on confederacy, might have required occasional wars, but the pervading culture system of brahmanism constituted the basic source of power of a South Indian imperial ruler up to the 16th century. That was why for a consolidation of a confederate imperial power (whatever its caste or ethnic basis) construction of temple-towns was a necessity. The ritual obedience of local village societies to temple deities could easily be invoked for the politico-religious purpose of brahmanic hegemony by the local or supra-local political powers who founded such temple deities. Since such politico-religious obedience had its manifestation in stipualated gifts to temples patronised by rulers, all sections of society had to make 'gifts' to both temples as well as the rulers.[6] Again among local rulers the most powerful one was able to unite other rulers in order to establish a supra-local empire. The ostensible basis of an imperial power was its capacity to undertake overseas plunder to acquire additional means of procuring treasure. This again explains the phenomenon of overseas war expeditions of the Cholas and Pandyas. One of the possible reasons as to why these expeditions declined during the Vijayanagar reign was the emergence of Arab powers on the high seas. The Arabs could now combine trade with plunder.

Inability to procure booty from overseas expeditions forced the Vijayanagar overlordship to collect revenue from villages and to the conversion of *brahmadeya* villages into temple towns. Since Vijayanagar overlordship had to mediate its collection of revenue through subordinate local rulers, it is presumed that the amount of revenue that ultimately reached the Vijayanagar imperial treasury was not high enough to enable it to raise a professional army. That was again the reason why the regional rulers of localities had to supply provisions and soldiers in case an imperial war campaign had to be launched against a rebel local potentate. During the post-Vijayanagar period, there was, however, nothing to prevent the emergence of what Burton Stein calls 'segmentary states' of Deccani Sultanates and of local *Nayaka* rulers.

Under the segmentary states a king's or Sultanate's demand for revenue was more regular, and quite a few of them could develop local systems of revenue collection from agriculture. But the collection of land revenue could not assume the rigour and comprehensiveness that characterised the contemporary Mughal system. On the other hand, what is found is that a segmentary state, particularly under the *Nayaka* rulers, was more anxious to build anicuts for irrigation and supply credit to peasants not so much to augment revenue potential, as to use them as cushion against the precariousness of a required balance between village society's need for subsistence and state of agricultural cultivation. Indeed Telugu *Nayakas* were reportedly responsible for extension of cultivation in arid regions of Karnataka or in the outlying areas bordering the Tamil plains. But in spite of such extension of cultivation and the presence of state patronage in the construction of well and dam irrigations, there took place no differentiation in crop production in South Indian agriculture of Tamil plains and other arid or semi-arid regions.

If there were forty-one varieties of crops raised by Mughal village communities, the principal crops raised by South Indian villages were as few as ten or twelve, e.g., paddy, millets (Cholam, ragi, etc.) and pulses among consumable crops, and peppers, oil seeds (sesame, flax, groundnut, etc.) betel leaves and cotton among cash-yielding crops. The profile of South Indian crop pattern underwent little or no change during the entire pre-British period. The absence of progressive diversification of crop production in South Indian agriculture can be explained as much by an absence of diversity in urban demand for exotic varieties of crops as by the stubbornness of brahmanic social formations in villages that necessarily clipped the direct producers' choice of crops to be raised from land. While Mughal tax on crops under *kankut* or *zabt* system was at least half (in case of important crops more than half) of gross produce per unit of an area,[7] in South India 'the rate of tax [imposed by the Vijayanagar or even a post-Vijayanagar state power] was hardly higher than a quarter of the gross produce' till the end of the 16th century or even later.[8] The archetypal production pattern in South Indian agriculture, however, contrasts sharply with wide spread development of artisan wares there. Not that, compared to Mughal India, artisan production in south India was more diversified but it is widely acknowledged that unlike Mughal India, artisan wares formed the principal staple of inland commerce in the southern peninsula.

The other factor that inhibited the growth of inland commerce in South India was the insulation of its agriculture from inland or overseas commerce. The fact that artisan wares constituted the basic staple of inland commerce, was a factor that itself tended to arrest the growth of inland commerce. It is because the extent of growth in artisan production is itself predetermined by the extent of surplus food available from agriculture for the subsistence of artisans. Therefore, the state of agricultural production in South India determined not only the objective scope for development in artisan production, but also the degree of extension of southern commerce as a whole. In Mughal India the objective scope for the extension of commerce was provided not merely by the demand for artisan wares but also by the demand from merchants engaged in inter-local trade on raw materials as well as agricultural output. In South India, trade hardly crossed the limit of intra-local spheres.

According to Aleav, numerically the most dominant South Indian artisan communities were weavers and oil-pressers. Since the artisan occupations of weaving and oil-pressing had to depend on agricultural production for their raw materials, the local agricultural cropping pattern and the size of foodgrain output circumscribed the productive viability of these occupations.

When artisans worked under so-called jajmani system, surplus artisan products could not flow beyond the level of intra-local commerce among villagers. This was because the intra-village exchanges between an artisan and a landholder or peasant-producer acted as a limit beyond which the growth of artisan goods under a jajmani system could hardly register an advance. When the artisans came to be settled in temple-towns they could produce for the floating population of pilgrims, priests, their servants and for local ruler's establishment. Even in such situations an artisan labour could hardly be independent of prosperity and depression in levels of living among producers of agricultural crops in surrounding villages from where devotees visited there temple-towns. Only those town artisans who could combine their role as manufacturers with their role as merchants could become what Stein calls, 'trader-artisans'. But the life of a merchant-manufacturer who operated from temple-towns was necessarily vitiated by the problem of importing consumable crops either from surrounding rural areas or from outside. Only when they could amass huge money profit, could they buy imported foodgrains. But the trader-artisans could rarely accrue to themselves so much money profit as to constitute a growing buyers' market for agricultural crops.

The growth of their money profit had, moreover, its constraint in their general inability to sell directly to the coastal merchants. The coastal merchants procured their wares only through their agents whenever they needed anything from temple towns. Therefore the South Indian trader-artisans of temple towns had to be content with only a subsistence level of profit. Apart from the fact that the coastal merchants–foreign or indigenous – had their own closely knit mode of procuring merchandise from distant or local regions, the wealthier section among port merchants had their own artisan villages around the ports. Furthermore, as long as the mercantile activity of a town merchant could not be alienated from his activity as an artisan, he could not tie himself freely with external commerce nor could he identify his interest with those of indigenous port merchants or alien Muslim and/or Portuguese traders. Consequently South Indian external commerce along the coasts developed a virtual disjunction from the inland 'artisan traders'.

The traditional disjuncture between the state of inland commerce and of the prosperous maritime commerce could not be eroded by the rise of temple-towns and their artisan-traders. If the development of external commerce in Mughal ports and centres of entrepot trade could force the peninsular port commerce to be inward-looking in matters of procuring merchandise for its business, such a trend was buffeted to an extent by the rise of artisan villages around the port-towns of South India.

Indeed the inland commerce of the southern temple-towns either under the Cholas and Vijayanagar overlordship or later under various pre-Mughal Sultanates could never acquire the scale and autonomy that Mughal India's inland commerce had. The essential dynamics of inland commerce in the South were rarely derived from the dynamics of either inter-local commerce or overseas commerce. So overwhelming was the segregation of South Indian inland commerce from its coastal commerce, mainly directed at inter-Asiatic or Indo-European markets, that Simon Digby compares the ports of South India with Von Leur's 'city states' of Indonesian port towns.[9]

The centres of inland commerce in South India were either commercially insulated from each other or insulated from region's coastal commerce and acted as the factor that caused decentralisation of its monetary system creating in its wake various standards of gold currency (*pagoda*) or its fractions, gold *fanams* or copper *cash*. Unlike the foreign merchants of Mughal India, the Dutch or English merchants at Pulicat or Cochin had their own standard of *pagodas* or *fanams* minted at their own mints. There is no reason to believe that indigenous wealthy port merchants did not have their own standard of gold *pagodas*.

This suggests that the centres of inland commerce in South India were reduced to dispensable satellites of her coastal commerce. It is possible to observe that to the extent Bengal's or Gujarat's merchandise could supplant the business of Coromandel coastal commerce, the latter could reinforce the autonomy of South Indian shores from its interior.

The relative autonomy of South Indian coastal ports derived its strength and weakness from two different sources. Its strength lay in the growing cosmopolitan character and its weakness lay in the huge accumulation of gold bullion by indigenous port merchants. If the cosmopolitan character of South Indian port-towns provided the latter with rich foreign merchant–buyers of Indian merchandise, its weakness arose from regional absence of a flourishing inland commerce that could feed as investment outlets of accumulated trading profit of indigenous wealthy merchants. Unlike what happened in Mughal India, the wealthy merchants of southern port-towns could never secure a sizable sphere of credit investment among local kings, nobles and other categories of direct surplus appropriators in South India or even among the localised small merchants operating in each town centre. The frequent changes in inland political regimes or maritime powers in the eastern and western seas and the lack of community network among the indigenous South Indian coastal and inland merchants, contributed to a weakness of mercantile money wealth accumulated by South Indian port merchants.[10]

We can therefore visualize different paradigms of development of money wealth accumulation among indigenous wealthy merchants between the Mughal and the non-Mughal South. In the former, although external export or entrepot activities accounted for a part of money wealth accumulation, its major component came from the inland commerce, especially between towns and villages, i.e., from the transfer of surplus by way of unequal exchange from the direct or indirect beneficiaries of imperial surplus appropriation in money terms in urban centres to the big merchants of the region. This pre-dominantly inward-looking character of mercantile accumulation process in the Mughal India contrasts with the outward looking character of mercantile money wealth accumulation in South India.

The prevailing disjuncture between the humble inland commerce and the lucrative coastal commerce in South India was the consequence of the absence of imperial mode of surplus acquisition and of the growth of urban markets on the one hand and greater exposure of trading coast to external merchants on the other. While the secular message that both such paradigms of mercantile process of accumulation conveyed was the same, namely, a widening gap between degree of procurement of physical or real merchandise ware and that of money wealth accumulation by wealthy merchants; in the short run there were some significant differences in the behaviour of wealthy merchants of the Mughal and the non-Mughal areas. In the first place the Mughal merchants enjoyed greater durability of their accumulation process on account of a continuous feedback from inland commerce, but in the South, the mercantile prosperity was more of an enclaved type and could not gain feedback either from expanding transactions on urban consumption goods or from expanding commerce in money. Moreover, South Indian mercantile prosperity, by its very nature, failed to develop a communal or economic mechanism once a foreign merchant withdrew. In contrast, the big merchants of the Mughal region, were not so dependent on the foreign merchants for their wherewithal, and could sustain a much longer battle of survival against adversities.

But South Indian commerce was creditable in that it promoted communal solidarity among artisan labour which did not happen in Mughal areas. South Indian artisans developed a community network among themselves because the money wealth of South Indian merchants could ensure its growth only by appropriating the artisan goods. Therefore they either had to force artisans under their direct governance into an exploitative credit nexus, or they had to share prosperity with them. Under both situations, South Indian artisans had to build their community guilds to settle their terms of exchange with wealthy shore merchants. But in Mughal India, there did not develop such interdependence between artisans and the prosperity of bigger merchants.

The specifics of the objective situation in Mughal Indian economy did not, on the one hand, require the artisans to be united as a communal identity against the money power of big merchants or political power of the state, and did not require the merchants to be solely dependent on procuring physical merchandise for minting their money wealth. As soon as the foreign buyers disappeared from the peninsular shores, or the humble inland commerce failed to feed the required supply of merchandise goods, the prosperity of South Indian shore commerce tended to collapse like a house of cards.

Now from some of the historical accounts of coastal commerce of South India, let us confirm our observation on the paradigm of commercial prosperity of the shore merchants and the communal resilience of local artisans.

Digby shows that commerce and commercial settlements in South Indian port-towns were essentially of an enclaved-type. This led him to characterise South Indian coastal centres of commerce as a kind of mercantile 'city-states'. In his account, 'groups of Muslim settlers followed other settlers of western Asian origin, Jews, Christians and Zoroastrians in the port cities. Such cosmopolitan settlements of immigrant merchants, he claims were prompted by the importance the latter gained as a consequence of the pattern of 'Far Eastern oceanic trade . . . in which the main entrepot of transshipment of trade goods between China and Islamic Near East were in south India' till the first half of the 19th century.[10]

From where did such port-towns procure their merchandise? No definite answer is available but a rough comparison of goods exported from Surat or Cambay with those from Masulipatnam or Pulicat, or Calicut or Cochin, we can gain the impression that while the Mughal ports exported both agricultural and artisan wares, the South Indian ports either exported mainly coarse or fine varieties of cotton textiles. In all probability, the hinterland of the South Indian centres of oceanic trade was not large. Even if one does not admit this, it is not unlikely that the export trade on textiles had to concentrate on artisan wares supplied by villages that had sprung up near the port-towns. Alaev reports, 'practically all the artisan settlements along the Coromandel coast were under the control of one trader or another. In the seventeenth century, the biggest of them [Coromandel traders] was Kasi Viranna who had *in his hands all the coast from Madras to Aramgaon except Pulicat*. Weavers' settlements of this region were known as the *Viranna Villages*. They were divided into eighteen districts each under five of his servants'.[11] Malabar coast exported more fine cotton cloth than pepper and teakwood and imported more bullions than war horses. Along the east coast, procurement of export merchandise by oceanic traders came from prominent artisan villages as attested to by Alaev, however, nothing much is known about the source of export merchandise along the west coast. Assuming that some of the export merchandise of South Indian coastal ports came from a Mughal area, one can hardly deny that a lion's share of export merchandise came from the local artisan centres of production. This was a possibility because in the Malabar coast, it was not a professional merchant but the local Travancore king who was the main export-import trader[12] and a Travancore king must have procured merchandise not from far-flung areas but from his own kingdom. Robert Sewell also narrates the story of active collaboration between port merchants and rulers of earlier Vijayanagar empire in matters of procuring export merchandise from local weavers.[13]

The commodity most commonly exported along the South Indian coasts possessed a traditional bias for cotton textiles – coarse or fine– and cotton piece goods. South Indian weavers had to supply much merchandise either to port-merchants or the local sovereigns indulging in oceanic commerce. Therefore, to protect their interests, the South Indian artisans had to build up a community network. The objective situation where port merchants found support from local kings and Sultanates in matters of procuring artisan merchandise accelerated the trend towards community bondage among artisans. This contrasts sharply with the Mughal Indian situation where a state power in general maintained a studied indifference to the export merchants, the latter procured their merchandise from their individual commercial or community networks requiring no direct commercial intercourse between a village community of artisans or peasant producers and export merchants. In fact the total amount of turnover made by the export merchants of Mughal India was relatively insignificant compared to the amount of turnover of merchandise goods within the inland commercial network. While in Mughal India, the community network among merchants, aimed at protecting its interest vis-a-vis an imperial state power, appeared as a redeeming feature, in South India it was the community network not so much among merchants as among artisans that appeared as an outstanding feature.

It is perhaps because of the absence of a community bondage among the South Indian shore merchants who could amass huge wealth on the one hand and the small merchants stuck to inland commerce around temple-towns on the other that the wealthy merchants of South India disappeared into oblivion when either the Mughals, Maratha or local marauders plundered their wealth or a port lost its foreign patronage. This is evident from the fact that the commercial prosperity of merchant princes of the region tended to decline to an abysmal level by the time Dutch merchants lost their war against their English counterparts and Fort St. George became the new master of South Indian commerce. While in the Mughal regions the wealthy merchants could survive by acting as financiers of the East Indian Companies, and the humble merchants with their community organisation and resilience could wage a war of attrition against the interloping activities of the European companies, in South India, Indian big merchants were not there either to collaborate with or to offer resistance to the European companies. In contrast, South Indian artisans could continue their battle against oppressive European merchants till the middle of the 19th century.

The merchants of the non-Mughal South were therefore incapable of developing as ostensible sources of civilian money power either against the political power of local kings or against the advancing European merchants. While the susceptibility of maritime commerce of South India to quick depression can be largely explained by its lack of support from the inland commerce, the absence of growth of inland commerce itself can be explained by the absence of flow of surplus from villages to towns. This regional pattern of development gave relatively a long lease of life to local political powers in the South against the enchroaching European powers. Possibly this is the reason why the English East India Company, though arriving much earlier in Madras, Calicut or Cochin, had to clinch their victory first in Bengal and not in any port town of South India. Whatever little inland or external commerce could survive in the interior or along the South Indian coasts even after the political power of English East Indian Company was consolidated, it remained free from the commercial network of the Company. This explains the lingering prosperity of South Indian business community of Chettiars that could uninterruptedly accumulate wealth throughout the first half of the 19th century, while business communities in other regions of India had to capitulate during this period.

Notes

1. The early European commerce had its earlier sanctuary mainly in the Mediterranean regions, but in course of its development, it found its most prosperous centre in North Europe.

2. Burton Stein, 'South India : Some General Considerations', *op. cit.*, p.18. For the general historical account of commerce in peninsular India till the decline of Vijayanagar empire, we use the accounts of Burton Stein as well as those of Simon Digby in his contribution, 'The Maritime Trade of India - c.1200 - 1500', both available in *Cambridge Economic History of India*,

Vol. I, *op. cit.* Introduction, Section II and Part I, Section IV (for Stein) and Part I, Section V (for Digby.)

Burton Stein cites mainly the Indian sources, e.g., N. Sastri Iyengar, Dikshit, Subramaniam, etc., for his construction of narratives, while Digby uses more well-known Persian and European sources. There are, however, differences of framework. The former tries to compare inland and maritime commerce, but the latter lays overwhelming stress exclusively on maritime trade of entire India as the basic point of examination with special reference to the role played in it by South India.

3. Stein in course of examining the mode of development of South Indian towns develops an interesting hypothesis. The growth of the new towns in South India 'came at the expense of what had been, in the previous several centuries, the institution of *brahamadeya*, a rural settlement of considerable size and wealth established by *nattars* . . . It is scarcely surprising that *brahamadeyas* should come to form the bases of new towns since they were, from their inception, large, multi-caste settlements with artisan and merchant populations as well as agriculturists to serve the consumption needs of numerous brahman families'. Stein further states that before such *brahmadeyas* began to convert themselves as new urban centres, there was the rise of *Bhakti* ritual in *Sri Vaishnavism*. 'Popularisation of religious worship, the assimilation of folk (often female) tutelaries as consort deities, laid the basis for the emergence of large, new temple centres which either superseded the older, exclusive (often anticonic) religious activities of the *brahmadeyas*, or this development came to encompass the older forms', *op. cit.* , pp. 37-38.

4. Stein perhaps overemphasises the extent of upward mobility of the artisans-cum-merchants settled in the 13th century temple-towns. The change in status by itself did not have any accompanying economic significance. Previously a rural artisan under the *nadu* served the brahman ruling class or *nattars*. Now the artisan in the new urban centres had to serve the temple priests and their servants, and could gain in the process only a supra-local status. On the other hand, the merchants of a new urban centre gained only the wider dimension of activities and could perhaps lay the foundation of the urban character of future commerce fostered by town-based warriors of Vijayanagar era when 'the relation between local merchants of agricultural produce (i.e., the right *Velangai* castes) and those more mobile artisan traders and merchants (i.e., the left, *Idangai* castes) fought for precedence and privilege until well into the nineteenth century'.

5. Apart from the uncertainty factor, the income of the temples was spent not so much on lavish consumption, as on buying and *hoarding* precious metals. Such hoarding of urban income by temple authorities might have been actuated by latters' need for hedging against the risks involved in future uncertainty about accrual of income.

6. It is claimed that very often there were stratifications among the different temples in a temple-town. A temple serving the brahmans was different from

the one that catered to the left - and right-hand castes. But every temple claimed 'gifts' from its devotees and such gifts were demanded from all rural devotees who hardly had any scope for escaping these socio-religious obligations.

7. Cf. Irfan Habib, 'Agrarian Relations', *Cambridge Economic History of India*, Vol. I, *op. cit.*, pp. 238-40.

8. Cf. L.B. Alaev, 'Agricultural Production in South India, *Cambridge Economic History of India,* Vol.7, *op. cit.* pp. 226-28.

9. Simon Digby used the concept of Jacob Von Leur for characterising the South Indian port towns. Cf. Simon Degby, *op. cit.* Cf. J. Von Leur, *Indonesian Trade and Society* (The Hague, 1955).

10. Cf. Simon Digby, *op. cit.* Asin Das Gupta rejects such characterisation about Indian port towns *in general.* However, he admits the cosmopolitan character of resident merchants in South Indian port-towns. Cf. A. Das Gupta, 'Indian Merchants and the Indian Ocean', *Cambridge Economic History of India, op. cit.* Vol.I, Ch.XII. See note 2 above.

11. L. Alaev, 'Non-Agricultural Production in South India, *op. cit.*, vol. I, p.320. The italicised parts are extracts quoted by Alaev from other historical sources.

12. Cf. Ashin Das Gupta, *Malabar in Asian Trade 1740-1800* (Cambridge, 1967).

13. Robert Sewell, *A Forgotten Empire* : *Vijoynagar* (London, 1900; Reprint Delhi, 1962), pp.307, 381-84.

5

Epilogue

The catalysts that governed the stasis in Indian economy during the phase preceding the rule under mercantilist colonialism of English East India Company, grew out of the historical absence of any appropriation of the material condition of labour within her base of social production. However, the forces of change had their significant manifestation in structural changes undergone by the basic appropriation process of the village surplus flowing out from the stagnant social production base. In our view this phase went through three evolutionary stages of structural developments in the surplus appropriation process.

I

The first stage consisted of two interrelated aspects of structural development. The primary one was the rise of a surplus-producing village community. The secondary one was the rise of state power, which would not have been possible had there been no prior rise of a primary state formation or local kingship institution. The emergence of primary state formation in ancient India was the direct consequence of the intra-communal articulation of social dominance of the non-labouring stratum over the labouring population. If we assume (and such assumption is legitimate even today) that the non-labouring stratum could effectively use its supra-village lineage or ethnic affinities for feeding its intra-communal social power over the labouring population, one can safely hypothesise that primary state formations arose out of the successful supra-village endeavours on the part of the relatively more powerful members of an intra-communal non-labouring stratum towards subsumption of more social power for this stratum. In this sense, the propensity of a non-labouring stratum towards increasing its social power was instrumental in the rise of local kingship institutions. It was again the state of perpetual conflict among local primary state powers over each other's territory and wealth that caused the rise of a secondary state power in ancient India.

It may be argued that if social coercion was the basis of formation of a village community, a social resistance, or at least non-cooperation, of the labouring population against the social dominance of the non-labouring people would have been pronounced. Yet, we know from Kosambi that the formation of a surplus-producing village community by Aryans with their superior technique of cultivation increased agricultural production and indoctrinated the labouring population about the superiority of brahmans and kshatriyas. Through this indoctrination the latter could procure voluntary prestations and gifts from village labourers.

In our view, Kosambi's reasoning overemphasises the superior technique of production (indicating their use of iron-nailed plough) and does not emphasise the fact that before the formation of surplus-producing village communities both Aryans and non-Aryans practised rotational cultivation. The settled cultivation began when Aryans settled in the fertile regions of the Gangetic basin. Hence it was not the Aryan iron-nailed plough, but the Aryan requirement of settled cultivation that forcibly procured non-Aryan *dasas*. This becomes the crucial explanatory variable of the emergence of village community formations.

The phenomenon of a village community formation signalled the growth of settled agriculture with consequential increase in surplus to be enjoyed by conquering non-labouring Aryans. The *dasas* in the new situation lost nothing except their social status of the pre-Aryan period. Their new inferior social status did not take away their sovereign right to subsist by labour activity. Since the natural geographical endowment of the newly settled regions did not make the material condition of any manual labour to be subjugated by superior social status of the Aryan upper castes, the formation of surplus-producing, stratified village community, could not demolish the subsistence requirement of non-Aryan labouring people. Nonetheless this development could not *ipso facto* remove the social domination-resistance syndrome within a settled village community of Aryan variant. On the other hand, the communal process of a settled cultivation assuming the form of a village community formation had necessarily to be based on a unity between its two mutually opposing social interests: the social security of subsistence for the labouring population and the social security of assured surplus appropriation by the non-labouring stratum of a community which had earlier suffered from uncertainty due to their pastoral nature of settlements.

The self-sustaining unity of a village community manifested the labourers' acquiescence in the non-labourers' claim of prestation or gifts. But this did not indicate its ritual basis. The coercive power of a particular social group, promotes a ritualistic belief in the superiority of status of that group. But when this coercive power faced predicament due to exogenous reasons, the myth around their ritualistic superiority was exploded by the people belonging to the socially inferior stratum. Again, if the amount of surplus appropriated by the non-labouring group tends to expand whatever the reason-so as to cause decline in the subsistence level of the labouring population, the myth of social superiority of the non-labouring people was readily replaced by rebellion against coercion. Both these eventualities arose in the Indian context more than once during the period of the Delhi Sultanates and the Mughal period. This indicates that the social syndrome of domination-resistance within an Indian village community had always centred around a coercive basis.

The coercive basis of village communal unity could never assume economic articulation in the form of appropriation of the material condition of labour by the intra-communal non-labouring stratum due to natural geographical factors. The surplus entitlement of the non-labouring stratum had to concede inflexible communal right of the labouring stratum to its subsistence against labour service. As a consequence, an absolute increase in wealth and power of an individual belonging to the non-labouring stratum could rarely be materialised in early Indian history at the expense of the labouring population, but at the cost of wealth and power of other individuals of non labouring stratum itself or groups within or outside the community. This explains the rise of mutually hostile local kingship institutions or primary state formations from the rank of powerful members of non-labouring strata.

The perpetual state of conflict among local primary state formations occasioned on the one hand the objective need for a village communal unity against external intervention and caused the rise of a secondary state power lorded over by an imperial monarch.

But secondary state power in ancient India had to live with an in-built instability of its own. Its revenue collection always fell far short of its need. This was partly because royal collection had to make concession to local kings or its own officials, and partly because of its compulsion to grant revenue-free land to brahmans and others who possessed the power of extending cultivation and/or founding new villages in virgin land. This gap between imperial need and what could actually be appropriated was instrumental in intensifying state-sponsored settled cultivations by sudra peasants and the liberal patronage to brahman or kshatriya initiative to extend cultivation.

The inescapable need of an imperial monarch for extending his revenue catchment area paradoxically strengthened the local magnates to the point that it germinated a centrifugal tendency among the latter. This necessitated frequent wars against local magnates. Related to the extent to which agricultural settlement was expanded and/or new autonomous village settlements developed, there was no proportionate increase in the imperial ability to control its own *paur janapada* establishments. Because of this local power magnates could reign supreme over their respective localities. Such a paradigm of development could strengthen the political power of the local potentates in the newly emerging areas of settled cultivation rather than the power of revenue collection of a secondary state power. The inevitable consequence of this pattern of development was a decline of imperial capability to manoeuvre the local oligarchs. The decay of Harsha's empire in the middle of the 7th century AD seems to be the historical outcome of this process of development.

Following the decline of Harsha's empire, no other secondary state power could emerge in North India before the rise of Delhi Sultanate during the closing years of the 13the century. The absence of a monarchical secondary state power, during this period, caused a shift of the locus of power from the urban centres to the rural areas. Historical research on this period does not throw any light on the relationship between a local oligarch and their subordinate village communities, but what can bc surmised from available historical accounts is that beneath the dominance of sub-regional or local state powers, there grew a category of big landholders, designated by some historians as *Samantas* - essentially tax gathering miniscule local kings, not landed proprietors as such. The genesis of this type of intermediate appropriators of village surplus has been traced by Kosambi from the ancient period of secondary state powers. Apart from *samantas,* there were other categories of similar intermediate groups such as, *rais, rajas, rewats,* etc.

It is likely that during this period there was a multiplication of a class of floating intermediaries who took advantage of extension of village settlements. This ensued a perpetual state of conflict among kings or intermediary surplus appropriators that in turn provided the scope for alien external raids into North India. Most of such alien aggressors were helped by alien traders familiar with the prevailing political chaos. This period, therefore, was characterised by an expansion of social production in innumerable village communities and by a widespread armed conflict among kings and their intermediaries. From the rank of external plunderers of that period there arose warring alien conquerors, the most capricious one becoming the ruler of North India.

II

The second stage in the evolution of economic structure in India began with the Delhi Sultanates. Two most notable features of this stage were, first, a growing conflict between non-labouring superior social strata and their labouring counterparts belonging to inferior castes, and second, an extent of diversification of social production base with the adoption of new techniques of artisan, agricultural and horticultural production imported from abroad.

Since the secondary state power of Delhi Sultanates did not arise out of a competitive violence among localised state powers, the major effort of a Sultan was aimed at curbing the power of local indigenous kings or intermediaries and at negotiating a direct access to village peasants so as to disallow leakage of village surplus to indigenous political groups at the supra-village level. To accomplish this the Sultanate had to appoint its own transferable revenue officials of Muslim origin.

Although this early Sultanate mission met only a limited success, the period witnessed a paradoxical sequel to this imperial aggression against indigenous potentates. This was the rise of intra-communal socio-religious movements of lower caste people among North Indian villages against the brahmanic social order. The positive impact of the 14th century socio-religious movements was the formation of new village communities, where a new non-labouring stratum arising from the rank of hitherto inferior caste people, adopted new non-brahmanic religious faith and gained ascendancy to social power. While the old brahmanic social order came under attack by these socio-religious movements, the social division of village produce between its non-labouring and labouring strata found its newer divisive social basis. This happened either because, some anti-brahmanic socio-religious movements relapsed into the neo-brahmanic fold or because in regions where a new village community made a complete break with old brahmanic social order, a fresh category of non-labouring stratum of new upper caste people came into existence by replacing the older ones.

The antagonistic relation between a state power and a village community during the period of Delhi Sultans, did not show a steady drift towards intense mutual conflict of interests. While there was an occasion or two when a massive peasant resistance took place against an arbitrary village taxation imposed by a Sultan, historical chronicles are more eloquent about loans advanced by the Sultans to distressed village peasantry.

The later Sultanates struck a compromise with indigenous kings or supra-village potentates by incorporating many of them into their officialdom. This shift in the policy in favour of indigenous local potentates might have been prompted by two factors: the absence of a comprehensive land revenue system and considerable leakage of revenue to Muslim revenue officials who were interested in enriching themselves at the cost of the royal treasury. Not that the alliance with local potentates was more rewarding, but it could help a Sultan to tame its own officials.

Delhi Sultanates continued to suffer from a chronic inadequacy of royal collections from villages. While on the one hand, it was essentially due to the absence of an efficient land revenue administration; on the other, it was due to leakage of revenue flowing from villages. Instead of seeking to improve the revenue administration the Sultans sought to plunder wealth through war campaigns and procure slaves (so as to augment royal revenue earning from internal as well as external slave trade).

Thus the objective deficiencies of the Sultan's surplus appropriation mechanism did not lead to a heightening of conflict or tension in the relation between his state power and a village community. But this overall absence of such conflict intensified the scope for accelerated social dominance and resistance among caste-stratified village communities and paved the way for prospective intra-communal socio-religious movement, initiated and conducted by low caste people against ritualised social privileges of brahmans and kshatriyas. One of the reasons of such socio-religious uprisings during the later Sultanate period was however the alien political rule.

In the ancient period, similar uprisings did not assume such widespread form. This can partly be explained by the fact that the ancient political axis among brahmanas and kshatriyas could feed their intra-communal social dominance over inferior caste people. During the Sultanate period, the political power of this social axis declined so as to provide a historical opportunity for socio-religious uprisings against the oppressive social order. An alternative hypothesis is that the decline of political mode of subsuming power among the upper caste people in the wake of alien rule, reinforced the ruthlessness of exercising social power by the brahmans and kshatriyas, and this eventually caused the rise of socio-religious movements against the brahmanic social order. Whatever the actual historical sequence of events, the rise of alien political rule is certainly an important explanatory variable of early medieval socio-religious movements in northern India. The other historical reason was the rise of Muslim civil communities with relatively more egalitarian order in and around towns and royal seats of power during the period of late Sultanates.

It is to be remembered that the rise of a Muslim civil society was, by itself, a dialectical consequence of the chronic political instability that always vitiated the tenure of a sultanate. This political instability promoted search, on the part of immigrant Muslim officials, for independent means of livelihood by employing their slave labour in the production of novel artisan wares, and new agricultural or horticultural crops. The social tyranny of the caste-stratified order that led to innumerable socio-religious movements against the brahman-kshatriya domination facilitated from another angle the scope for the rise of a Muslim civil community from the rank of converted low caste indigenous people including slaves. Slaves could buy freedom by embracing Islam.

The rise of Muslim civil society, apart from reinforcing the social conflict within a caste stratified brahmanic social order in villages, also caused a diversification of social production base through the introduction of a new category of artisan, horticultural and agricultural productions in India by new technique and new seeds imported from the Arab world. But a Muslim civil society-though more egalitarian compared to the brahmanic order was itself not free from its own variant of stratification between the non-labouring and labouring strata within it.

Thus in the second stage of structural evolution of the North Indian economy, while the period of Delhi Sultanates had to retain both unhindered material condition of labour as well as ancient Indian set of intra-communal contradiction[1], the cumulative consequence of this development went against the old brahmanic social order and in favour of social production. The operation of a strong secondary state power could sustain the corporate socio-economic unity of a village community, but the material weakness of the state revenue administration on a village community allowed the latter to be engaged in intra-communal conflicts.

The basic changes during the period, therefore, were the predominance of intra-communal contradiction between labouring and non-labouring strata, and the expansion and diversification of social production base with the rise of innumerable non-brahmanic village communities including those of Muslims.

III

The third stage in the structural evolution of the surplus appropriation process in the early phase of Indian economy began with Akbar. The earlier stages were characterised more by intra-communal social conflicts and adjustments between the labouring and non-labouring social castes, along with a linear expansion of village communities, with a growing trend towards extension as well as diversification of production base. The third stage was characterised more by the galloping contradiction between an extant village community as a corporate socio-economic entity and a Mughal state power rather than by social domination and resistance and or absolute expansion of social production base.

The third stage caused the dialectical emergence of new forces within the polity that eventually acted as the forces of negation of both state power and the hitherto unchallenged autonomy of social production base under a self-sustaining village community. While none of those forces of negation could fully run their individual courses, they nevertheless drove India to a crossroad of epochal changes. The changes that *actually* befell India in course of such negations, had undoubtedly its exogenous origin. In other words, the surging contradiction between the Mughal state power and a self-sustaining village community effected such transition of the polity that provided a scope for external intervention. The rupture of an autonomous process of endogenous developments in India in the 18th century was the consequence of this ubiquitous development, that forced by internal developments, could be shaped only by external intervention.

Since Akbar's time Indian village communities confronted for the first time a mighty statecraft with its elaborately designed bureaucracy and a vast militia. This manifested itself in the adoption of a comprehensive land revenue system and along with it a wide spectrum of royal intermediaries between a village community and the centralised power of the Mughal administration. Indeed the Mughal revenue system became instrumental in the genesis of unforeseen structural changes in the economy.

The first was the rise of protofeudal landholding rights and privileges among official and semi-official revenue collectors of the centralised administration and the second was the widespread rise of an independent class of mercantile appropriators of social surplus.

One of the main reasons that intensified the contradiction between the Mughal state power and a village community in India was its success in taming the sundry categories of old intermediary groups by the force of its administrative arms and their subsequent replacement by its own revenue officials or semi-official local intermediaries. The Mughal imperial office delegated its coercive power of surplus appropriation to jagirdars, loyal local zamindars, and others who, on the basis of assessments of village produce made by official assessors, collected imperial tax on a village community.

Theoretically, the responsibility of official assessment of village produce was made separate from that of collecting taxes, and the official power of collecting village revenue was sought to be segregated from that of armed execution of law and order. But in a vast region that the Mughal India covered, the imperial legal norms were more violated than honoured. As a consequence the Mughal revenue official or those vested with armed power virtually assumed more powers than what were warranted by the imperial norms. They could arbitrarily impose *abwabs*, cesses and various other imposts on their subordinate village communities. By this process an unforeseen category of protofeudal rights on village output and labour developed. Many powerful mansabdars could acquire with impunity a big jagir holding right although their functions as assigned by the imperial administration, did not prescribe such right. Many jagirdars could avoid being transferred provided they could establish rapport with one of the powerful members of the imperial court at Delhi. The statecraft of Mughals and its need for coercive appropriation of a massive amount of village surplus was instrumental in the growth of protofeudal private rights outside the pale of imperial norms. But no coercive power of a holder of protofeudal rights and privileges could erect itself on the basis of private proprietorship of a village land or appropriation of the material condition of labour in a village. A protofeudal power had as its basis its own armed might or the delegated armed power of the imperial establishment. Even in situations where a holder of private protofeudal right could impose his hereditary (if not always alienable) claim on subordinate villages, such hereditarity of protofeudal claim on village output could never transform itself into an usurpation of the material condition of village labour.

What could then force the perpetuation of a hiatus between the autonomy in the material condition of labour in a village communal production process and the overwhelming power of a holder of private protofeudal right on village output? One obvious answer is that the natural-geographical environment of Mughal Indian villages acted, as in previous periods, as a historical barrier to the appropriation of the material condition of village labour. It was indeed natural geographical environment that prevented earlier a socially powerful non-labouring individual within a village from appropriating the material condition of labour within the community. In Mughal India there was an additional reason that actually prevented a protofeudal holder of coercive right on village produce from assuming his ownership right on village land. The reason lies in the specific mode by which a holder of private protofeudal power could retain his position within the complex mechanism of acquisition as well as devolution of power. Since the Mughal administrative bureaucracy was hierarchically structured with the mutually conflicting as well as competitive levels, a chronic instability in the tenure of a Mughal official was its endemic feature. The power of a Mughal official, that never grew up from below, could hardly gain even a semblance of stability, unless the official could perpetually engage himself in a race for further acquisition of power to rise in the hierarchy.

The fierce competition, and hence conflicts, either among Mughal officials belonging to various hierarchical levels or among those at the same level explains why a holder of protofeudal right on village output had to keep himself more busy in countering actual or possible manoeuvres from his rivals, superiors or subordinates, rather than concentrating on acquiring personal proprietary holdings in subordinate villages. Even in case a noble could acquire a big holding of his own he could hardly consolidate his position on it. He had constantly to be in conflict with a mightier noble or with a recalcitrant village zamindar or with the imperial power itself. Therefore the basic requirement of even a relative political stability in the tenure of a

Mughal noble was not for his acquisition of village land or labour but for his continuous and successful endeavour towards accumulating more liquid wealth and greater armed power. This particular trait of perpetuating oneself within a power caucus of the Mughal empire inexorably caused concentration of wealth and power among few at the top-level hierarchy in the imperial administration leaving a majority among revenue officials disgruntled and rebellious and relatively poorer in terms of wealth and power.

Indeed, centralised administration was dependent on the few big nobles for its revenue and war needs. Therefore, the centrifugal tendency against the locus of the centralised power became sharper. This developing centrifugalist trend within the Mughal bureaucracy that itself stemmed from the very working of the highly centralised administration of an emperor, became one of the important factors that eventually paved the way for political disfunctioning of the Mughal imperial power itself

While the Mughal imperial mode of acquisition and devolution of power only weakened its political edifice, the growth of multi-level protofeudal private rights on a village cultivated land and active labour force came into perpetual conflict apart from among themselves, with functionally autonomous village communities. But at no stage could this conflict be permanently resolved in favour of either a particular group of protofeudal holders of private rights on village land and labour or in favour of autonomous village communities. As a consequence, the protofeudal landholding right of jagirdars that appeared as a negation of the pre emptive right of a village community on its land and labour, could not run its full course, and therefore could not usher the flowering of feudal private property right in land as it happened in post-Charlemagne societies of West Europe. The private surplus entitlement of a holder of protofeudal right on village cultivated land of the Mughal epoch could never transcend its tributary character so as to be transformed into a full-fledged ground rent.

But in the non-Mughal areas of South India, no such kindred category of protofeudal supra-village right or intra-village non-labouring individual right on village output or labour could indeed surface. This was mainly due to the absence of a strong centralised power, and a comprehensive land revenue administration. However, the very absence of a coercively organised centralised state power in the non-Mughal South, led to transformation of the ancient intra-communal social contradiction into a new mode of community based *collective* economic exploitation of the toiling masses by the non-labouring strata. Whatever type of supra-local imperial power grew in the non-Mughal South up to the 15th century, they were not based on an *independent* mechanism of acquiring coercive political power or that of appropriating village surplus.

The last of such empires, Vijaynagar, had a system of organising an independent militia known as 'Nayaka' and a system of revenue collection, so as to maintain the imperial order. But the Vijaynagar empire at no stage could acquire such an extent of independent coercive power of its own that could enable its imperial system either to negate aspirations of local brahamanic powers or to ride roughshod over local Nayaka rulers. Functioning more as an imperial power of a confederate character, the Vijaynagar imperial rule was characterised by its policy of courting local brahmanic powers dominating peninsular India's village communities and that of patronising the extension of the brahmanic cultural system through construction of temple towns (as the earlier confederate empire of Cholas or Pandyas did).

The fall of Vijaynagar empire signalled the decline of supra-local political hegemony of brahmanas as the most powerful social group and the rise of political power of non-brahmanic elites in the form of emerging small states.[2] But this decline in the political supremacy of brahmanas could paradoxically reinforce the consolidation of social power of brahmanas at the village level even under the umbrella of a smaller non-brahmanic state powers. The rise of what we may call social protofeudalism manned by brahmanas as the most powerful social group within a southern village community, is in this sense a historical consequence of the absence of a strong centralised power in the subregion. Under social protofeudalism, non-labouring social appropriation of village surplus yielded by productive labour came to be based on unhindered coercion exercised by brahmanas as the dominant social group. The social coercion used by brahmanic communal order did not seek appropriation of the material condition of labour. For social coercion of brahmanic order was a convenient instrument so as not to warrant decommunalisation of private surplus appropriating right of an omnipotent communal elite.

The proverbial sovereignty of a South Indian village community was virtually the unfettered freedom of village level brhamanic or neo-brahmanic elites to exploit the village level labouring population. The specific natural-geographical environment in the Peninsular South, apart from ensuring the absence of coercive power of a centralised state, also acted as one of the barriers to the retention of autonomy of the peasant's subsistence right in that region.

Neither in Mughal India under a strong centralised power nor in the non-Mughal south under brahmanic social protofeudalism, could there at any stage arise the objective preconditions for flowering of a secular feudal mode of production. However only the Mughal India came to witness a series of far reaching structural changes. But why did such differential course of development between Mughal and non-Mughal India take place? The answer leads us to trace another facet of structural development, i.e., the emergence of mercantilist appropriation of social surplus as an institution and its different nature between the two macro regions.

IV

In retrospect, we find that two categories of people beyond or within a village community that could accumulate wealth. The first was the non labouring members within or outside a village community who could *directly appropriate surplus* either by armed coercive power or by socially devised means, and the other was that of wealthy merchants *appropriating social surplus through unequal exchanges*. Since only in Mughal India, due to the existence of a centralised state power, private accumulation of wealth by members of the nobility could expand either at the expense of other categories of ordinary nobles or at the expense of village landholders (rather than by the pauperisation of village labour),[3] private accumulation of wealth by the powerful members of the Mughal nobility was initially the most dominant feature. In contrast in South India, the absence of a strong centralised power, could enable a socio-feudatory elite to establish its absolute power mainly at the expense of the labouring population. But in both cases, namely, in the case of powerful Mughal noble or in the case of a socio-feudatory elite in South India (in short, in the case of those who accumulated wealth by direct coercion), wealth could not multiply itself unless its sole augmenting factor, namely, the power of the accumulator, could be multiplied. In contrast the private accumulation of wealth by a merchant (in other words, accumulations of wealth through exchange mechanism) could multiply itself provided he could make further investment of his wealth on the procurement and sale of merchandise.

It is true that any supra-village mechanism of mercantile appropriation of wealth or social surplus owes its genesis to a prior supra-village mechanism of the direct coercive means of acquiring surplus in money terms. While the former is dependent for its genesis on the *apriori* growth of the latter, both historically appear as rival pro-processes of appropriation of village surplus. Particularly in the Mughal Indian context, two most powerful supra-village surplus-appropriating powers, namely, powerful Mughal nobles and wealthy merchants, forced both to be in mutual cooperation at the initial stages and in mutual conflict at the later stages of development. This cooperation-conflict syndrome had its genesis from two facets of the Mughal polity, the differential patterns of end use of wealth by them and the incapacity, on the part of the both, to control or augment the social production base.

Since the end use of money wealth of the Mughal nobility was either expensive aggrandisement of power or lavish consumption expenditure, more accumulation of wealth by it invariably created a growing hunger for provisions that could be supplied only by the merchants. On the other hand, more accumulation of wealth by a successful merchant accentuated his hunger for money wealth that could be acquired by only further profitable investment. Thus, while the money wealth of a Mughal noble had necessarily to be fructified into merchantable wares the money wealth of a merchant had the dominant objective of fructifying itself into a greater money wealth. But a noble, while transforming his money wealth into merchantable wares, had to sacrifice a portion of its real worth to the merchant as latter's profit. This profit was nothing but the transfer - executed through the mechanism of unequal exchange - a portion of social surplus from the possession of a consumptionist noble to a merchant supplying provisions.

In a setting of stagnant production base and no spectacular rise in the volume of village physical surplus, the merchants could meet the growing demand for provisions only by raising the prices of the same. In this way the increase in the mercantile share of social surplus in money was correspondingly related to a decrease in the share of the supra-village nobility in terms of real goods or in money terms.

The growing financial difficulty of Mughal nobles during the 17th century can be explained by three factors operating concurrently. They are: (*a*) relative inelasticity of village production base and high elasticity of urban money supply (*b*) growing difficulty of procuring provisions by the merchants, and a consequent rising trend in prices of consumables in urban markets; (*c*) the terms of exchange turning more and more in favour of big merchants and against those who procured their livelihood and grandeur exclusively from the mechanism of direct and coercive appropriation of surplus. Since neither the great Mughal nobles nor the wealthy merchants acquired the capacity to change in their favour the sphere of social production base in villages, the situation in the 17th century reinforced mutual conflicts among all categories of Mughal nobles and sharper wealth differentiation among merchants.

In the non-Mughal South India, the growth of commercial endeavour of merchants did not have its genesis from the centralised state usurpation of surplus by direct coercive means. The spectacle of prosperity among South coastal merchants was not necessarily connected with the acquired wealth of a state power or its powerful agents. The socio-feudatory oligarchs of South Indian village communities themselves tried to acquire money wealth by taking recourse to humble intra-local trade that could produce a feedback effect neither on the size of inland commerce, nor on South Indian coastal commerce.

The growth of small temple-towns in South India that eventually caused the rise of a class of non-brahmanic merchant-artisans could not produce sizable expansive effect on the peninsular inland commerce. The South Indian prosperity of mercantile accumulation was concentrated only in enclaved centres of entrepot trade along its coasts and it was, in general, insulated from the state of commerce in the interior. In the coastal areas of South India, the mercantile accumulation had its main commodity base in craft production of artisan villages that sprang up near the coastal centres of trade. But the ebb and flow of South Indian coastal commerce and its accumulated wealth, having only a tenuous interconnection with the state of its inland commerce, was regulated by the depression and prosperity of overseas trade. As a consequence, in South India, there could take place no rise of a stable mercantile process of surplus appropriation which could cause a structural change in stagnant mechanism of socio-feudatory exploitation of village labouring population.[4]

Since only in the Mughal Indian economy, an autonomous process of mercantile accumulation of money wealth emerged by the 17th century, a substantial structural change in the mechanism of supra-village distribution of social surplus became more and more prominent. In the non-Mughal South, a similar degree of structural change could not take place. As a result Mughal India is found to be the subsequent theatre of momentous historical changes.

The basic feature of this change lies in self-augmenting character of mercantile appropriation of money wealth, not necessarily at the expense of village labour but invariably at the expense of all other modes of surplus appropriation. The significance of this structural change is that for the first time in Indian history a veritable class of private surplus appropriators from among merchants emerged who, with or without internal scope for further acquisition of surplus in money form, became at the same time ready to spare no means for attaining their objective.

This was because, under the Indian variant of evolution of social formation till the Mughal period, the surplus appropriation in its mercantile form could acquire at least a subsidiary attribute of private property (the fundamental one being the appropriation of the material conditions of labour). Only in mercantile form, could private appropriation of surplus multiply itself through investment. This could happen in spite of the fact that mercantile surplus could never be directly invested in acquiring real estate or in agricultural production managed by a village community. Consequently, by the 17th century a mercantile investment of money wealth in Mughal India found out its quick-yielding returns in various types of banking, insurance (money-changing, mortgaging, commission agency, money-lending, credit financing, etc.) and usurious activities.

The relative inflexibility of social production base of the Mughal Indian economy contrasting sharply with mercantile prowess in minting more money wealth eventually led to the domination of money dealing commerce over commerce in real goods. But this overwhelming growth of money dealing commerce of the Indian merchants could not continue *ad infinitum*. Its logic of enrichment had to force it to be in conflict not merely with the rival forms of direct surplus appropriation by political lords, but also against a centripetalist village management of the social production base. In Mughal India, none of the above possibilities could mature due to the specific constellation of the unforeseen historical developments.

What actually happened is that the paradoxical character of over-accumulation of mercantile money wealth during the late Mughal period in spite of swallowing and subjugating - by monetary means - all forms of direct surplus appropriation, failed to avoid an accelerated trend towards depression from a crisis of investment outlet. This was exclusively due to the general inelasticity of the village social production and of commodity production in particular.[5]

While the process of over-accumulation of mercantile money wealth among Indian big merchants outstripped the process of its accumulation of physical social surplus (that could flow out from the social production base of the 17th century Mughal India), the former sought to feed itself through sundry categories of money dealing commerce of the contemporary period. This trend instead of whetting its hunger for investment outlet, reinforced the same. This was because a rapid and widespread extension of money dealing commerce tended to augment more investible money capital.

Had private property in land, or labour and/or, at least, a widespread dissolution of village autonomy occurred in India, the resultant expansion of social production base or commercialisation of its inputs, would have appeared as the possible spheres of investment outlet for the enormous amount of mercantile money capital of indigenous origin. Since this did not happen, the dominant segment of the Indian mercantile money capital had no other option but to develop within itself a mercenary character. This drove Indian wealthy merchants to forge economic alliance, for the sake of higher returns from investment, with any credit-hungry West European commercial enterprise that started to operate from the 18th century commercial towns and entrepot centres of trade in India. But this development caused conflicts between wealthy merchants of India and the various categories of smaller political establishment of indigenous origin that came into being in the wake of the decline of the centralised power of the Mughals. The two simultaneous developments stated above, the growing alliance between Indian big merchants and West European traders or their companies, and a progressive decline in the erstwhile collaborationist mutualism[6] between indigenous political powers of the 17th century and the prosperous money merchants of India, constituted the economic premise of the loss of political independence of India.

The cumulative growth of this premise had weakened the economic base of indigenous political powers of 18th century India. This was fostered by the specific nature of development undergone by the Indian merchant capital. The political premise of this had however its genesis in the centrifugal trend we mention earlier. A growing contradiction between the protofeudal local powers and village communities made direct surplus appropriation a contentious issue during the first half of the 18th century.

In fact, the centrifugal political trend grew during the Mughal period itself. Indeed the growth of political centrifugalism was inescapable in a situation where political power of an imperial state power developed its total dependence on its protofeudal intermediaries who were vested with power to make coercive and direct appropriation of surplus from subordinate centres of social production. After the decline of the centralised power of the Mughals, the erstwhile provincial Mughal governors sought to build, through exercise of armed power, their respective territories of lordship. The erstwhile territory of Mughal empire was reduced, by the first half of the 18th century, to an area comprising Delhi and a part of the Agra Suba. The other regions of the empire were divided into provincial principalities headed partly by powerful Mughal officials and partly by political lords of obscure origin who could assume power in the wake of ethnic uprising of Rajputs, Jats, Sikhs, Afgans, Marathas etc.

Bengal, Awadh and Hyderabad in the Mughal area and Mysore in the South (Mysore had witnessed a very short spell of Mughal rule immediately before its decline) came into being as virtually independent principalities governed by erstwhile Mughal nobles, who could establish their political lordship by the force of arms. Simultaneously there emerged a parallel paradigm of political developments in the form of the rise in sovereign local political power of smaller kings of various ethnic origin (i.e., not from the rank of Mughal officials). The first category of rulers acknowledged a formal obeisance of the Mughal throne in Delhi, which the latter did not. But this in itself, carries no historical significance. What is more significant is the historical cause that led to such ethnic uprisings and to the formation of semi-independent principalities by powerful Mughal nobles particularly at the stage when the centralised coercive power of the Mughal imperial state declined. The decisive historical cause for these political developments is the gathering momentum of old contradiction between the Mughal centralised power and village communities.

This happened because of the enormous growth of mercantile appropriation of social surplus at the expense of surplus appropriation by direct and coercive means in a setting of inelasticity of principal social production base manned exclusively by the village communities. A continuous rise of the mid-17th century price levels, particularly in urban centres of the Mughal India, showed how the terms of exchange between wealthy urban merchants and the other urban dwellers (who were mostly direct and indirect beneficiaries of direct surplus appropriation process) went in favour of the former and against the latter. While the phenomena of urban price rise and accumulation of wealth by merchants caused sharper income inequalities among individual members of the multi-level imperial bureaucracy, the development itself intensified conflicts and rebellions among members of the Mughal establishment, and caused a series of expansion of administrative wings of the empire and its militia. The plunder of small merchants by local Mughal governors and the widespread imposition of various taxes and cesses on the subordinate village communities by the protofeudal political lords during Shahjahan and Auranzeb's reign reflected the predicament to which a direct and coercive surplus appropriation process was subjected. The frequency of various categories of peasant uprisings during that period was the cumulative consequence of a heightened contradiction between village communities and the growing imperial requirement for more surplus so as to feed expanding officialdom and militia.

It was extremely difficult for a village community to withstand this onslaught on its self-sustaining existence and reproduction. Many historians contend that during the last years of the Mughal empire, the additional tax burden fell on the village labouring population. But such hypothesis, not based on a set of specific historical evidences, cannot explain why the pauperisation of village labour failed eventually to cause an appropriation of the material condition of labour either by an aggressor political lord or, at least by a village big landholder in the late 17th century.

Our hypothesis is that since the self-sustaining autonomy of a village community could continue to reproduce only on the basis of an absence of appropriation of the material condition of labour in villages, it is quite likely that, an imperial agent could coerce a village community into parting with greater amount of village surplus, only at the expense of the dominant non-labouring elites, and not at the cost of the subsistence requirement of its labouring population.[7]

This must be the reason why most of the *peasant* uprisings of the 17th and 18th centuries were led by the non-labouring stratum of a village community. This also explains why almost all the *ethnic* uprisings of the late 17th or early 18th century were led not by the labouring peasants or artisans themselves but by non-labouring elites. This also explains why particularly the latter type of uprisings, without restricting its orgy of violence against the local Mughal agent, extended to coercive subjugation of other ethnic communities. For instance, the Jat or Afghan uprisings caused dismemberment of big Rajput landholders. A similar trend is found under sovereign Sikh, Maratha or Rajput kingdoms of the 18th century.[8] In most cases these ethnic kingdoms imposed heavier levies on subordinate village communities by introducing, if necessary, revenue farming practices and plundered small local merchants for forcible acquisition of wealth.

The semi-independent principalities administered by virtually sovereign princes of the Mughal period (Haider Ali of Mysore was an exception) similarly tried to impose additonal cesses on secondary zamindars in their respective territories. In case the secondary zamindars were not ready to acquiesce in such additional claims from the Nawabs, they were forcibly ejected and replaced by the newer ones.[9]

Thus the decline of the Mughal centralised power and its substitution by a centrifugalist trend of Mughal political lords and the establishment of sovereign kingdoms stemmed from the constraints that vitiated the direct and coercive surplus appropriation process in a background of growing mercantile accumulation. It is true that as a consequence of the constraints faced by the coercive mode of surplus appropriation, the various categories of state powers in the 18th century raised the levy from their respective village communities. But no such development could cause disruption of the social production processes in villages. From this it appears that the political turmoil and subsequent changes caused *only* a transfer of direct surplus appropriating power within a village community or at the supra-village level from one set of non-labouring elite to another.[10]

There is disagreement among historians regarding whether the mercantile mechanism of surplus appropriation was a victim or a beneficiary of this phase of political turmoil. The British chroniclers highlight the plunder of merchants by sovereign Jat kings, Mughal governors and Maratha marauders. A completely opposite view is that the growing fiscal crisis of indigenous political lords of the period provided the money merchants and bankers the scope for investment in revenue farming in all regions.[11] While one may cite instances of plunder of small merchants by Mughal officials, Jat kings or the Maratha Peshwas, this certainly was not the general picture, and actually reflected, more than anything else, the general crisis in which the coercive mechanism of surplus appropriation from villages was entangled. On the other hand, in the 18th century political milieu of India, even in the most commercially ebullient regions like Bengal, Agra or Gujarat a wealthy merchant-banker was unlikely to make a hazardous investment on revenue-farming that could fetch only an uncertain return. It is true that revenue farming developed in some outlying regions like the Peshwa dominated Rajasthan, Maharashtra and in other politically sovereign kingdoms, but such farming was undertaken only by powerful local elites and was never prompted by a mercantile expectation of high return. Even in regions where such local elites required guarantors from money-merchants or bankers for securing revenue farming assignments from the state, it cannot be claimed that the revenue contractors themselves were merchant-bankers. Therefore, only to the extent a mercantile investment of money wealth on various categories of armed or unarmed political conflicts of the period could help a wealthy merchant or banker to reap financial benefit, can one hypothesise that wealthy merchants benefited from the politically unstable situation of the 18th century.

In general, the mercantile process of acquiring money wealth through unequal exchange particularly in a setting of political turmoil, had to follow an independent path of its extension, consolidation and fortification. Since the tenure of an indigenous political power was uncertain and there was a wild hunger among West European commercial powers for Indian money and merchandise, collaboration between Indian big merchants and their European counterparts became the most spectacular development in the 18th century.

The pattern of structural change in India during the 17th and 18th centuries, namely, the over-accumulation of mercantile money capital and the weakening of the hitherto independent process of coercive and direct mode of acquiring social surplus, contrasts sharply with the changes taking place in private property-oriented societies of West Europe.

Under the pre-modern social formations in general, the structural change in the modes of surplus appropriation took place as a consequence of interactions between surplus appropriation through exchange mechanism and through direct and coercive usurpation. The extant material conditions of labour in the social production base did not by itself exercise much influence on structural change. In West Europe, any structural change in the process of appropriation of social surplus was occasioned not merely by interactions among rival processes of appropriation but by a change in power relations among the surplus appropriating classes. Due to this change, powerful merchant houses of West Europe during the period of mercantilism, were able to use the national political powers in order to invoke the support of feudal aristocrats. But with much greater wealth power, the Indian money merchant of the late 17th century could not acquire political power which could reduce the extant state powers to be his accomplice, and nor could he develop an entrenched interest within a village community. Consequently, the acquisition of money wealth by substantial merchants drove them to a crisis of investment outlet.

This crisis induced indigenous merchant capital to develop a mercenary character. Given the complex of actual historical developments, endogenous as well as exogenous, it would be entirely arbitrary to ignore the alternative historical possibility that could marshall its rationale of development from within. The autonomous processes of development characterised by the inbuilt weaknesses of indigenous political powers and the built-in over-accumulation of mercantile money wealth and its growing investment hunger, drove India to a historical crossroad where the objective potential of a conflict between the self-sustaining village autonomy in matters of social production and the autonomy of the mercantile process of money accumulation had been gaining momentum. The resolution of this conflict lay in the dominance of merchant capital over the material condition of labour. Unfortunately for India, this resolution found its distorted manifestation under the dominance of a European merchant capital.

To put it in a somewhat simplistic way, had there been no external commercial intervention, the autonomous process of over- accumulation of mercantile money capital would have little stimulus for attaining its unfettered mercenary character. On the contrary, this process would have been forced to undermine (with or without the help of a surrogate political power) the self-sustaining autonomy of village production process in the given situation of weakening political overlordships and to release production forces by converting private money capital of merchants into the private property relations in land.

This *graphic* outline of an alternative historical possibility of autonomous change does not ignore the role of coercive power in bringing about the phenomenon of private property in the sense of appropriation of the material condition of labour. In any case,this historical possibility of an autonomous change was forestalled by the politico-commercial intervention of the European trading companies in general, and the English East India Company in particular.

The historical task of demolishing the self-sustaining character of the Indian village community and thereupon imposing state appropriation of the material condition of labour on villages could eventually be vested with the mercantilist colonial power of the English East India Company. It accomplished the task for securing its mercantile prosperity and political stability.

Notes

1. The term contradiction connotes conflict potentiality.
2. Unlike in North India, in South India brahmanas constituted the only social group that used its supra-local caste affiliation not only for political purposes but also for extending the socio-cultural domination of brahmanic cult over village communities. In contrast to Mughal India, there were no other non-brahmanic social castes or ethnic groups in the sub-region which could acquire a comparable degree of dominance on the basis of a supra-local affiliation.
3. In this connection we are to remember our reasoning as to why despite its pomp and splendour, the Mughal nobility could hardly earn more wealth at the expense of village labouring population. The latter's inflexible right to subsistence was the necessary condition of social reproduction in a village. Therefore, the scope for a Mughal noble to further augment his wealth depended either on the relative pauperisation of his fellow nobles or the appropriation of the wealth of big landholder within the village community through various devious means (e.g., by coercive dismembering of a big landholder from his community by a big jagirdar or by confiscating accumulated wealth of a supposedly rebel big landholder in a village, etc.)
4. Not that social exploitation of village labour was absent in Mughal India, but unlike South India the social exploitation of labouring population in North India could not usurp or disrupt the subsistence right of labour. This was because in Mughal India or even in the India under the Delhi Sultanates, functioning of an alien state power as a coercive appropriator of village surplus, acted paradoxically as a barrier to eventual transformation of social power of an indigenous non-labouring stratum into an unrivalled politico-economic power of itself so as to subjugate autonomous economic power of the labouring population in villages.

While the self-sustaining autonomy of a Mughal Indian village community had its basis on the subsistence autonomy of village labouring population, the autonomy of a village community in non-Mughal India was based on an unhindered autonomy of both social as well as economic exploitation of village labour by its socio-feudatory oligarchs. Since neither in Mughal Indian villages nor in their counterparts in non-Mughal South India, acquisition of surplus in the form of money wealth by the non-labouring supra-village or intra-village strata had use of such wealth other than transforming it into consumables, such form of wealth accumulation was necessarily delimited by the inelasticity of the social production base. The absence of a strong inland commerce in South India did not cause any spectacular rise in mercantile form of money wealth accumulation and forestalled the possibility of structural change in the modes of surplus appropriation.
5. This situation contrasts sharply with the mercantilist period of Europe where the narrowness of commodity production base led to a growth of monopolistic trend among merchant houses with the active collaboration of a state power. The basis of such monopolistic growth among European merchants was fostered

by the take over of small merchants by the bigger ones who formed a monopoly and also by monopoly merchant-inspired restrictive practices on producing firms so as to monopolise sources of commodity supply. Mughal India being a sellers' market to the outside world, the chronic insecurity of mercantile sales that vitiated the competitive behaviour of European merchant and promoted the trend towards monopoly, was largely absent among Indian merchants. Only in matters of procuring provisions Indian merchants faced a sort of competition, but since none of them had any control over the source of supply, i.e., a village community, a monopolistic trend could not develop among Indian merchants. A small merchant could always procure at least some mercantile wares from his locality. A big merchant with greater money power possessed the advantage of procuring a bigger amount of provisions from different localities through the credit mechanism.

6. As we have pointed out earlier, the collaboration between the substantial merchants and individual protofeudal political powers of the Mughal imperial order had two phases of development. In the first phase, loyal merchants were helped by the political lords with liquid credit because that would ensure the overlord's interest earnings, tax earnings and,the most important, the required supply of provisions. But in the second phase, characterised by expanding Mughal establishment and financial crisis among the Mughal officials, it was the wealthy merchant who had to supply credit and provisions to the political lords. Nonetheless this relationship between the two most important categories of wealth accumulators underscored the mutuality of immediate convenience and such mutuality eventually strengthened mercantile money accumulation at the expense of the wealth power of the political lords.

7. From our hypothesis we can arrive at an interesting conclusion: While at the earlier phase of the Mughal rule, the imperial land revenue mechanism helped the non-labouring segment to derive greater economic benefit (hence caused greater income inequality within a village), at its later phase of growing imperial fiscal crisis and subsequent increase in tax burden on village, it was the non-labouring elite of a village community (thus causing greater economic equality within a village) that became the easy target for imperial surplus acquisition by coercive means.

8. Eric Stokes by.citing the account of Richard Temple tells us about how a sovereign Jat established his command over conquered villages inhabited predominantly by alien ethnic groups. Stokes observed: 'the Lal family [that] built up Barah raj south of Jamuna in the Allahabad district' . . . first got 'the village landholder into their financial grip by loans' and stood 'as revenue security and firmly resorted to forcible eviction. On a much more extensive scale the self-made Bhuinhar rajas of Benares constructed within their territory a personal enclave of Family Domain . . . The same historical process secured in the building up of Tenwa Jat raj of Mursan in the Aligarh district, as also in the more ancient Chauhan raj of Mainipuri. Eric stokes 'Agrarian Relations' (Northern and Central India) *Cambridge Economic History of India*,

Vol. II, *op. cit.*, p.40.

9. In Bengal, this trend started from the reign of Alibardi Khan and attained its most notorious form during the reign of Murshid Culi Khan. In Bengal the target group of attack was the secondary zamindars. In Awadh the talukdars of the Nawab sought to demolish the entrenched interest of village zamindars and replace them by a band of *birtias* (revenue collectors) from the rank of powerful brahman household of villages. N.K. Sinha, *Economic History of Bengal* (Calcutta, 1956), Vol. II, pp.1-20. Charles Stewart, *The History of Bengal from the first Mohammedan invasion until the virtual conquest of the Country by English in A.D. 1757* (Calcutta, 1903), pp.420-21. Asiya Siddiqi *Agrarian Change in a North Indian State :Uttar Pradesh 1819-1833* (Oxford, 1973), p.8,46,47.

10. K.K. Trivedi notes that according to the account supplied by *Ain-i-Akbari*, 75 per cent of supra-village zamindars in the middle or upper Doab regions belonged to various Rajput clans and that there were very few Brahman, Gujar or Jat zamindars. But by the early British period, settlement officers found that the majority of village zamindars in that region belonged to Gujar, Jat and Brahman castes. Cf. 'Changes in Caste Composition of the Zamindar Class in Western Uttar Pradesh: 1595 - Circa 1900', *The Indian Historical Review*, Vol. II, No. I, 1975, pp. 47-67.

11. N.A. Siddiqi is the most notable Indian historian holding this view. In his *Land Revenue Administration with Mughals*, 1700-1754, (Asia, 1970), he finds that the jagirholders or old zamindars in the wake of fiscal crisis resorted to revenue farming as early as the seventeenth century. In the 18th century, the Mughal jagirdars and/or zamindars, because of their inability to collect revenue from villages began to incur debts from local money merchants and bankers who acquired revenue farming right in exchange. He holds that 'this practice gave rise to a class of bankers and speculators who invested their money in the business of revenue farming and they [i.e., bankers and speculators] emerged as a class of intermediaries distinct from hereditary zamindars' (pp. 97-98).

It is true that during the 17th century, the various Mughal lords contracted debt from money merchants not only to meet their obligation to superiors , but also to meet their own ends. That the growing debt bondage of hereditary zamindars to speculators and bankers was the only reason for the emergence of a new class of zamindars from the ranks of merchant-bankers, seems to be an oversimplification. In fact, *isaradars* of the Mughal period rarely came from the ranks of merchants. Again *isaradars* themselves were not exactly revenue farmers. The preconditions of revenue farming are (a) a general absence of revenue assessment and collection by the local imperial establishment, and (b) the coercive or persuasive power of a revenue farmer is to be evidently higher than that of a jagirdar or zamindar. It is difficult even to imagine how a merchant-banker of the 17th century Mughal India or of a politically turbulent 18th century could satisfy the above preconditions in order to be a revenue farmer *per se*.

Select Bibliography

A. Journal Articles

Brenner, R., 1976 'Agrarian Class Structure and Economic Development in Pre-industrial Europe'.*Past and Present* No.70.

Brown, A.R.E., 1974. 'The Tyranny of a Construct: Feudalism and Historians of Medieval Europe'. *The American Historical Review*. Vol.79, No.4.

Divekar, H., 1980. 'Emergence of Indigenous Business Class in Maharashtra in the 18th Century'. Proceedings *of International Seminar on trade and urbanisation Western India during Sixteenth to the Nineteenth Century*.University of Baroda.

Fukazawa, H., 1972. 'Rural Servants in the 18th Century Maharastrian village-demiurgic of *Jajmani* System?', *Hitshobashi Journal of Economics*. February.

Habib, Irfan, 1964. 'Usury in Medieval India : *Comparative Studies in Society and History VI*. The Hague.

——,1971. 'Potentialities of Capitalistic Development in the Economy of Mughal India', *Enquiry* (*New Series*). Vol.3, No.3.

——,1978. 'Economic History of Delhi Sultanates - An Essay in Interpretation', *Indian Historical Review*. Vol.IV. No.2

Habib, Mohamed, 1964. 'Chengiz Khan and the Mougals', *Enquiry*. Vol. 1, No. 1.

Jha, D.N., 1979. 'Early Indian Feudalism : A Historiographical Critique', Presidential address, Section I, *Proceedings of the Indian History Congress*.

Joshi, P.C., 1943. 'Coins Current in the Kingdom of Golkonda', *Journal of Numismatic Society of India V*.

Kosminsky, E.A., 1935. 'Services and Money Rents in the Thirteenth Century'. *Economic History Review V*.

Kulkarni, G.T., 'Banking in the Eighteenth Century : A Case Study of a Pune Banker' *Artha Vijnan XV*.

Majumder,Arun, 1991. 'Structural Evolution of Indian Economy : the Pre-colonial Specifics', *Visva-Bharati Quarterly (New Series)*, Vol.I, No.3.

Moosvi, Shireen,1978. 'The Zamindars' Share in the Peasant Surplus in the Mughal Province', *Indian Economic and Social History Review XV*.

Mukhia, H., 1979. 'Was there Feudalism in Indian History?' Presidential address, Section II. *Proceedings of the Indian History Congress*.

Rudra, A., 1981. 'Against Feudalism', *Economic and Political Weekly* Vol.XVI, No.52.

Shoji, Ito, 1966. 'A Note on the Business Combine in India - with special reference to Nattukotai Chettiars'. *The Developing Economics*. April

Trivedi, K.K., 1975. 'Changes in Caste Composition of Zamindar Class in Western Uttarpradesh 1595 - Circa 1900', *Indian Historical Review*, Vol.II, No.1.

B. Books and Articles from Collections

Alayev, L.B., 1982. 'Agricultural Production'(South India) in Tapan Raychaudhuri & Irfan Habib (Ed.), *Cambridge Economic History of India* (referred hereunder as CEHI) Vol.I.

Alexandrowics,C.H., 1967. *An Introduction to the History of the Law of Nations in the East Indies*. Oxford.

Ali M. Athar, 1966. *Moghul Nobility under Aurangzeb*, Bombay. reprinted, 1970.

Anderson Perry, 1974. *The Lineages of the Absolutist State*, Verso, London.

——,1978. *Passages from Antiquity to Feudalism*. Verso, London.

Aristotle, 1950. *Politics*, English Trans. H. Rachham, Harvard University Press & W. Heimann Ltd., London.

Baden-Powell,B.H., 1982. *Land System in British India*, in three volumes Oxford, Clarendon Press.

——,1913. *Land Revenue and Tenure in British India*. Second Ed. Oxford, Clarendon Press.

——,1986. *Indian Village Community*, London.

Bhadra Gautam, 1981. *Mughal Junge Krishak Bidroha* (Peasant Revolts during Mughal times), (Bengali) Calcutta, Subarnarekha.

——,1983. 'Two Frontier Uprisings in Mughal India' in R. Guha (Ed.), *Subaltern Studies* Vol.II, Oxford University Press, Delhi.

Bhattacharya, N.N., 1976. *Bharatiya Dharmer Itihas* (History of Indian Religions) (Bengali 1384 B.S.), Calcutta.

Blake, S.P., 1987. 'Structure of Monetary Exchange in North India' in J.F. Richards (Ed.), *The Imperial Monetary System of Mughal India.*

Bloch Marc., 1965. *Feudal Society.* English Trans. L.A. Marryon in two volumes. London.

Bullough, D., 1965. *The Age of Charlemagne*, London.

Chandra, S., 1959. *Parties and Politics at the Mughal Court 1704-40.* Aligarh.

——,1979. 'Shivaji and Maratha Landed Elements' in R.S. Sharma (Ed.), *Indian Society: Historical Probings.*

Chatterjee, A., 1967. *Bengal in the Reign of Aurangzeb.* Calcutta.

Cheyette, F., (ed.), 1968. *Lordship and Community in Medieval Europe*, Newyork.

Childe Gordon, 1935. *New Light on the Most Ancient East.* Second Edn., 1952. London.

Chopra, P.N., 1963. *Some Aspects of Social Life during the Mughal Ages*, Jaipur.

Chaudhury, B., 1975. *Trade and Commercial Organisation of Bengal* 1650-1720, Calcutta.

Chaudhury, K.N., 1981. *The Trading World and the East India Company 1660-1760.* Cambridge University Press.

——, 1982. 'European Trade with India' in *CEHI.* Vol.I.

Cipolla, C.M., 1973. *The Fontana Economic History of Europe : The Emergence of Industrial Societies.* Glasgow, Collins/Fontana.

——,1974, *The Fontana Economic History of Europe : The Sixteenth and Seventeenth Centuries*, Glasgow, Fontana.

Cohn, B.S., 1969. 'Structural Change in Indian Rural Society 1596-1885' in R.E. Frykenberg (Ed.), *Land Control and Social Structure in Indian History.*

Coulburn, R., 1956. *Feudalism in History.* Princeton.

Das Gupta Asin, 1967. *Malabar in Asian Trade 1740-1800*, Cambridge University Press.

——, 1979. *Indian Merchants and the Decline of Surat C.1700-1750.* Weisbaden, Frans Steiner, Verleg.

Deyell, John S., 1987. 'Akbar's Currency System and Monetary Integration' in J.F. Richards (Ed.), *The Imperial Monetary System of Mughal India.*

Dharma Kumar and Tapan Raychaudhuri *et al.*, 1982. (*CEHI*) Vol.II. Cambridge University Press, reprinted Orient Longmans, 1984.

Digby Simon., 1982. 'The Maritime Trade of India - C.1200-1500 in *CEHI*, Vol.I

Dodwell, H.H., 1929. *Cambridge History of India Vol.5. British India 1497-1858.* Cambridge.

Dopsch, A., 1937. *The Economics and Social Foundations of European Civilization.* Trans. E.Patizelt, London.

Dutta, K.K., 1961. *Survey of India's Social Life and Economic Conditions in the Eighteenth Century, 1707-1813,* Calcutta.

Engels, F., 1878. *Anti-Duhring* reprinted, Moscow 1947.

Feinstein, C.H.,(Ed.), 1967. *Socialism, Capitalism and Economic Growth : Essays Presened to Maurice Dobb*, Cambridge University Press.

Frykenberg, R.E.,(Ed.), 1969. *Land Control and Social Structure in Indian History*, London.

Fukazawa, H., 1971. 'State and Caste System (Jati) in the Eighteenth Century Maratha Kingdom' in M.R. Sinha (Ed.), *Integration in India*, Bombay.

——, 1982. 'Maharastra and the Decan : A Note', in *CEHI*, Vol.I.

Furber, H., 1951. *John Company at Work.* Cambridge Mass, Harvard University Press.

——, 1976. *Rival Empires of Trade in the Orient (1600-1800).* University of Minnesota, Minneapolis.

Green, D.H., 1965. The *Carolingian Lord.* Cambridge University Press.

Habakkuk, H.J., and Postan,M.M., 1965. *The Cambridge Economic History of Europe*, Vol.I-IV, Cambridge University Press.

Hasan S., Nurul, 1969. 'Zamindars under the Mughals' in R.E. Frykenberg (Ed.), *Land Control and Social Structure in Indian History.*

—, 1973. *Thoughts on Agrarian Relations in Mughal India.* PPH, Delhi.

Habib, Irfan, 1962. *Agrarian System of Mughal India*, Asia, Bombay.

——, 1974. 'Pre-British Land Settlements' in R.S. Sharma (Ed.), *Indian Society : Historical Probings.*

——, 1982. 'The State and Economy' in *CEHI*, Vol.I.

——, 1982. 'Agrarian Relations and Land Revenue' in *CEHI* Vol.I.

——, 1982. 'The System of Agrarian Production' in *CEHI* Vol.I.

——, 1982. Monetary System and Prices in *CEHI* Vol.I.

——, 1987. 'A System of Trimetallism in the Age of the price Revolution' in J.F. Richards (Ed.), *The Imperial Monetary System of Mughal India.*

Habib. M., 1974. *Politics & Society during the Early Medieval Period* PPH, Bombay.

Hegel, G.W.F., 1978. *The Philosophy of History* (English Translation) London, Oxford University, Edn. 1942.

Hindess B. and Hirst P.Q., 1975. *Pre-capitalist Modes of Production* Routledge & Kegan Paul, London.

Hilton R.H., 1967. 'Some Problems of Urban Property in the Middle Ages' in C.H. Feinstein (Ed.), *Socialism, Capitalism and Economic Growth : Essays Presented to Maurice Dobb.*

——, 1976. *The Transition from Feudalism to Capitalism*, New Left Book, London.

Hobsbawm, E., Ed., 1964. *K. Marx: Pre-capitalist Economic Formations.* Lawrence & Wishart, London.

Jaiswal, S., 1974. Studics in thc 'Social Structure of Early Tamils' in R.S. Sharma (Ed.), *Indian Society : Historical Probings.*

Jones, R., 1831. *An Essay on the Distribution of Wealth and the Sources of Taxation.* London.

Kosambi, D.D., 1975. *The Culture and Civilization of Ancient India in Historical Outline*, Vikas, New Delhi.

——, 1975. *An Introduction to the Study of Indian History.* Second Revised Edn. Bombay.

Kumar Ravinder., 1968. *Western India in the Nineteenth Century : A Study in Social History*, London.

Leach Edmund, *et al.*, 1985. Feudalism, Comparative Studies, Sydney.

Leur J. Von, 1955. *Indonesian Trade and Society.* The Hague.

Ling Trevor, 1968. *A History of Religions - East and West* Macmillan, London.

Marx, K., 1853. 'The British Rule in India', Newyork Daily Tribune, 25 June, reprinted in K. Marx and F. Englels, *On Colonialism*, Moscow, Foreign Language Publishing House, n.d.

——, 1859. *A Contribution to the Critique of Political Economy*, Moscow, Progress Publishers, 1970.

Moreland,W.H., 1910. *India at the Death of Akbar*, London.

——, 1929. *Agrarian System of Moslem India.* Allahabad.

——, 1943. *From Akbar to Aurangzeb*, London.

Naqvi, H.H., 1971. *Urbanisation and Urban Centres Under the Great Mughals*, Simla.

Ovington,J., 1929. *A Voyage to Surat in the Year 1689* (Ed.) H.G.

Rawlinson.

Piggot, S., 1950. *Prehistoric India*, London.

Plekhanov, G.V., 1974. *Fundamental Problems of Marxism*. Progressive Publishers, Moscow.

Polanyi K., Arsenberg C.M. and Pearson H.W.,1957., *Trade and Market in Early Empires*, Glencoe, Illinois, The Free Press.

Prakash, Om, 1987. 'Foreign Merchants and Indian Mints' in J.F. Richards (Ed.), *The Imperial Monetary System of Mughal India*.

Prasad, B., 1968. Ideas in History, London.

Ray, H.C., 1973. *Dynastic History of Northern India : Early Medieval Period*, in two volumes, Second Edition, Delhi.

Raychaudhuri Tapan, 1982. 'The Mughal Empire' in *CEHI*, Vol.I.

——, 1982. 'Inland Trade' in *CEHI*, Vol.I.

——, 1984. *'The State and Economy under Mughal Empire'* in *CEHI*, Vol.I.

Raychaudhuri, Tapan and Habib Irfan,(Ed.), 1982. *Cambridge Economic History of India*, Vol.I. Cambridge University Press, London, reprinted Orient Longman, 1984.

Richards, J.F., 1975. *Mughal Administration in Golconda*. Oxford University Press, Bombay.

——, (Ed.) 1987. *The Imperial Monetary System of Mughal India*. Oxford University Press, Delhi.

S.Krishnaswami Aiyangar, 1921 *South India and the Muhammadan Invaders*. Oxford.

Sastri, K.A. Nilkanta, 1958. *A History of South India*, Second Edition, Madras.

Sen, Surendranath, 1925. *Administrative System of the Marathas*. Second Edition, Calcutta.

Sewell, R., 1900. *A Forgotten Empire: Vijoynagar*. London, reprinted Delhi, 1962.

Sharma, R.S., 1965. *Indian Feudalism* C.300-1200, Calcutta.

——, (Ed.) 1974. *Indian Society : Historical Probings*, New Delhi.

Siddiqi Asiya, 1973. *Agrarian Change in a North Indian State : Uttar Pradesh 1819-1833*, Oxford University Press, London.

Siddiqui, N.A., 1970. *Land Revenue Administration under Mughals (1700-1754)*, Asia.

Sinha, N.K., 1956. *Economic History of Bengal*, in three volumes, Firma K.L., Calcutta.

Sinha, M.R.,(Ed.), 1971. *Integration in India*, Bombay.

Smith Adam, 1776. *The Wealth of Nations*. Edited by E. Cannan and reprinted by Methuen, London, in two volumes in 1950.

Stein Burton, 1980. *Peasant, State and Society in Medieval South India*, New Delhi.

——, 1982. 'South India : Some General Considerations, in *CEHI*, Vol.I.

Stewart Charles, 1903. *The History of Bengal from the First Mohammedan Invasion until the Virtual Conquest of the Country by English in A.D, 1857,* Calcutta.

Stokes Eric, 1982. 'Agrarian Relations' (Northern and Central India) in *CEHI* Vol.II. Cambridge University Press, reprinted Orient Longman, 1984

Streensgaard, N., 1972. *Carracks, Caravans and Companies : The Structural Crisis in the European Asian Trade in the Early Seventeenth Century,* Copenhagen.

Tavernier, J.B., 1905. *Tavernier's Travels in India*, Calcutta.

Thapar, R., 1984. *From Lineage to State*, Oxford University Press Bombay.

Thompson, E.A., 1969. *The Goths in Spain*. Oxford University Press, London.

Thurston, E., 1909. *Castes and Tribes of Southern India*, in 7 volumes, Goverment Press, Madras.

Twichet, 1962. *Land Tenure and the Social Order in Tang and Sung China*, London.

Yasin, M., 1958. *A Social History of Islamic India 1665-1748*, Lucknow.

Index